JOURNAL FOR THE STUDY OF THE OLD TESTAMENT
SUPPLEMENT SERIES
109

Editors
David J.A. Clines
Philip R. Davies

THE SOCIAL WORLD OF
BIBLICAL ANTIQUITY SERIES
9

General Editor
James W. Flanagan

Almond Press
Sheffield

SCRIBES AND SCHOOLS IN MONARCHIC JUDAH

A Socio-Archeological Approach

DAVID W. JAMIESON-DRAKE

The Almond Press · 1991

I dedicate this to my wife Vicky,
who kept me in touch with our children
and kept them loved
while I burned the midnight oil.

Published by JSOT Press
JSOT Press is an imprint of
Sheffield Academic Press Ltd
The University of Sheffield
343 Fulwood Road
Sheffield S10 3BP
England

Typeset by Sheffield Academic Press
and
Printed on acid-free paper in Great Britain
by Billing & Sons Ltd
Worcester

British Library Cataloguing in Publication Data

Jamieson-Drake, David W.
    Scribes and schools in monarchic Judah. - (The social
    world of biblical antiquity ; 0265-1408, 9).
    1. Palestine, history, B.C. 1225–B.C. 63
    I. Title   II. Series
    993

    ISSN 0265-1408
    ISSN 0309-0787
    ISBN 1-85075-275-3

CONTENTS

List of Charts

ACKNOWLEDGMENTS

Special thanks are due to several of my colleagues, with whom it has been my privilege to work, study and share ideas.

Allen Zagarell provided guidance, especially in the formative stages of this work. Roland Murphy and James Crenshaw kindly offered their reactions to aspects of this study as well.

I especially wish to thank Professor David Clines, whose queries enabled me to clarify and correct a great many points. His assiduous efforts in this regard have greatly enhanced the final quality of the work. I remain extremely grateful for his scholarly expertise and for the patient good cheer of him and his staff.

PREFACE

The question of scribes and scribal schools serves a dual function in the present study. It is addressed as a significant problem in its own right, but it also functions as an occasion to map out a strategy of approach to such problems generally. Like many other studies, the present one attempts to relate the evidence from textual studies to that obtained through study of archeological remains. However, this study departs from the procedures usually followed in integrating textual and archeological data in that the archeologically based investigation is given precedence, so that the written evidence is allowed to speak within an archeologically established context. This reversal of the usual mode of examining the relationship between the written and the archeological evidence mandates a refocusing of the discussion and reframing of questions.

The question of the existence of scribes and scribal schools in ancient Israel has been debated primarily by those interested in biblical 'wisdom' literature. The terms adopted for this debate have, naturally, been defined to serve the needs of the approaches that use them: historical, literary-critical, literary-comparative, and the like. In placing the question of scribes and scribal schools in monarchic Judah in a socio-archeological context, the question itself has been reformulated to a certain degree, and the terms utilized in the discussion have had to be redefined. For instance, 'scribes' are viewed in this study as 'professional administrators', the focus changing from the mere fact of their literary skills to the broader question of the function of those skills within the society.

The shift in perspective from literary context to sociological context will be explained in Chapter 1. There, the question of scribes and schools will first be raised in the context in which it has previously been debated, that is, the literary context. A rationale for approaching this question from a different perspective, namely a socio-archeological one, is given. The issues will then be redefined in sociological terms, in order to bring a new body of evidence, namely archeological, to bear on them. In the latter half of Chapter 1 the methodology employed in the rest of the study will be presented in detail.

The second through the fourth chapters present the archeological data in three categories: settlement (Chapter 2), public works (Chapter 3), and luxury items (Chapter 4). The way in which each of these sets of data informs the discussion of scribes and schools is covered in the concluding 'synthesis' of the later discussions; the public works data constitute a powerful tool for investigating management of labor and materials; and the luxury items data provide the most direct insight into the presence of administrative control systems.

For each of the three chapters in which data are discussed, an appendix ('A' of the settlement data, 'B' for the public works, and 'C' for the luxury items) giving tables, charts, and maps is provided. The approach used here draws upon archeological data from a great variety of sources. In order to distinguish meaningful patterns from 'noise' in the vast quantities of data from the excavation reports and surveys, it has proved essential to portray the data visually and statistically. Ashton-Tate's *dBASE III+* was used for most of the database management; Borland's *Quattro* was used for the spreadsheets, charts and line graphs; and STSC's *Statgraphics* was used for statistical analysis, maps, double-log graphs, and some database manipulation.

The final chapter (Chapter 5) consists of three parts. In the first, a final synthesis of the archeological data integrates the analysis from all three kinds of data into an archeological based picture of the development of administrative control systems in Judah during the Iron II period. In the second part, the textual-historical discussion in which the question of scribes and schools was initially raised will be re-evaluated. The archeologically based model achieved in Chapters 2, 3, and 4 serves as a basis for the re-evaluation. In the third part, directions for further research are suggested. This concluding section affords an opportunity to restate the methodological goals, which transcend the particular question of scribes and schools studied here, and to suggest directions in which the discussion of scribes and schools—and other discussions as well—might profitably move.

Chapter 1

INTRODUCTION

The Question of Schools in Monarchic Judah

The broad question of the presence or absence of schools in ancient Israel may be analyzed as two related, yet distinct, questions: (1) the presence and character of schools to train professional scribes for administrative service to the state, and (2) institutions which promoted literacy of the general populace. R.J. Williams (1962) and A. Lemaire (1981, 1985) have made a case for both, with a chronological progression from schools for professional scribes to schools for the general populace.

Williams makes the case as follows:

> The report of Wen-amon, an Egyptian official who was sent to Byblos ca. 1100 B.C., mentions that five hundred papyrus scrolls were delivered to the Syrian ruler in partial payment for a load of timber. This gives some indication of the extent to which writing was practiced there. The OT references to writing in the time of Moses (Exod. 17:14; 24:4; 39:14, 30; Deut. 27:3; 31:24; cf. Josh. 18:4-9) are thus not to be regarded as anachronisms. An episode from the time of Gideon, in the twelfth or eleventh century, bears witness to the knowledge of writing on the part of a young man from a small town who was captured at random (Judg. 8:14). As in Egypt and Mesopotamia, those who were able to write were usually government officials, as in the case of David's 'scribe' (RSV 'secretary') Seraiah (II Sam. 8:17). We must assume the existence of scribal schools as in the neighboring nations. The products of such schools would be known as 'ready scribes' (Ps. 45:1). Isaiah could read and write in the eighth century, although this was not true of all (Isa. 29:12). By the late seventh century, however, a certain degree of literacy was presupposed (Deut. 6:9; 24:1) (Williams 1962: 914-15).

Williams assumes the presence of schools for scribes linked to the crown by David's time. By the seventh century literacy is assumed for the general populace.

Lemaire adduces archeological evidence in addition to biblical texts (among them some of those cited by Williams) in support of his portrayal of the development of schools in Israel, with results which closely parallel those of Williams. The results of his 'Essai de synthèse sur les écoles de l'Époque royale' may be summarized as follows:

1. 13th–10th centuries: Israelites assimilate cultural heritage from 'Canaanite' schools at Aphek, Gezer, Megiddo, Shechem, Lachish and Jerusalem.
2. 10th–9th centuries: David–Solomon: created royal schools to educate and indoctrinate, 'probably inspired by the Egyptian model' (p. 47). After the monarchy divided, the northern kingdom had to create such schools at successive capitals: Shechem, Tirzah and Samaria; also less important schools were established in capitals of Solomonic prefectures = ancient Canaanite capitals.
3. 8th century and later: the development of writing and the spread of schools to fortresses like Arad, Kadesh-Barnea and Kuntillet Ajrud, even to most villages.

Like Williams, Lemaire posits a development from schools dedicated to producing state administrators early in the monarchy to general literacy late in the monarchy, such that by the seventh century 'chaque chef de famille sache lire et écrire' (Lemaire's inference from Deut. 6.6-9 and the widespread distribution of inscribed seals and jar handles in that period).

In addition to the direct evidence from literary and archeological sources, Lemaire draws upon analogies to Egypt and Mesopotamia throughout his presentation. This reliance is implicit, for example, in the following introductory remarks:

> En poursuivant cette recherche, nous serons amenés, à la lumière des institutions parallèles des autres pays du Proche-Orient ancien, à étudier le problème plus général des conditions concrètes de la transmission de la culture écrite dans l'ancien Israël, de la fonction primitive des textes bibliques et de la for-

mation de la 'Bible', c'est-à-dire d'un recueil officiel de textes canoniques (Lemaire 1981: 5).

Lemaire's dependence on drawing analogies from other ancient Near Eastern societies to Israel is explicitly reiterated on pp. 46, 54, and 61.

Later, Lemaire claims a general consensus concerning schools on the basis of such parallels:

> En fait, surtout après la découverte de textes scolaires en Egypte, en Mésopotamie et Ougarit, la plupart des exégètes admettent l'existence d'écoles à l'époque royale israélite et proposent de comprendre certains textes bibliques en référence à l'enseignement donné dans ces écoles (Lemaire 1981: 35).

Lemaire's remarks on this point are not baseless. Both von Rad (1972: 31) and Hermisson (1968: 188, 192), two of the most respected scholars in the broader area of 'wisdom' studies, in which the question of scribalism has been most commonly raised, regarded the presence of schools for scribes in monarchic Israel as indubitable. A. Demsky (1977), commenting upon an abecedary from Izbet Sartah, follows Galling (1933) and Reviv (1969) in identifying the *na'ar* of Judg. 8.14 as a Canaanite official and does not construe this verse as evidence for general literacy as Williams had. However, he goes on to say:

> Accepting this conclusion, tribal leaders such as Gideon recognized the usefulness of the alphabetic script, a medium that was employed in the Canaanite city-states. Learning from the Canaanites, the Israelites developed their own scribal schools for administrative purposes. It is then quite plausible that the scribes at Izbet Sartah were part of that tribal administration (Demsky 1977: 24).

We shall return to a discussion of the sociological assumptions implicit in the kind of reconstruction illustrated here by Demsky at a later point.

According to Lemaire, three kinds of evidence converge on the conclusion that schools existed during the monarchic period: epigraphic materials, biblical texts, and analogies drawn to other ancient Near Eastern societies:

> En effet, une fois admise l'existence de ces écoles comme la conséquence logique de l'interprétation d'un certain nombre de

données épigraphiques paléo-hébraïques (cf. supra) et de notre
connaissance actuelle des systèmes scolaires dans le Proche-
Orient ancien, alors tous ces textes deviennent plus cohérents et
plus concrets, reflétant divers aspects du fonctionnement de ces
écoles, comme nous allons essayer de le montrer tout à l'heure
(Lemaire 1981: 41).

Lemaire is to be credited for drawing upon different, largely
independent sources of information to support his views. He
makes the strongest case possible, given his approach to the
data he uses, on the basis of these sets of evidence. However,
certain aspects of his approach have met with objections from
other scholars. F. Golka (1983) has raised some questions
about both the methodology and the results of investigations
into the issue of the presence and character of schools in
monarchic Israel in response to the work of Lemaire. One
concern Golka raises addresses the strategy of making comparisons between monarchic Israel and other ancient Near
Eastern cultures:

> Es zeichnet sich bei Dürr nun die Methode der Beweisführung
> ab, die für die weitere Forschung charakteristisch werden
> sollte: Man stützt sich auf die ägyptischen und mesopotami-
> schen Parallelen (Analogieschluss)... Diese Methode beruht
> jedoch auf einem Trugschluss hinsichtlich der Vergleichbar-
> keit der ägyptischen und israelitischen Institutionen (Golka
> 1983: 262, 264).

Golka also disagrees with Lemaire's use of biblical texts in
support of the thesis that schools existed in monarchic Israel.
He notes that many of the biblical references adduced by
Lemaire in support of this thesis are oblique, and others are
dated to a period later than the monarchy by many scholars.
Golka's conclusion is that the case for schools in monarchic
Israel is 'gebaut auf Sand'. Others also (e.g. Dürr 1933;
Gerstenberger 1965: 130, 140) had argued that schools were
late institutions and that evidence for them in monarchic
times was lacking.

Crenshaw (1984) has emphasized that the evidence upon
which this discussion is based may fairly be characterized as
extremely tenuous. All agree on this point at least: the biblical
and epigraphic evidence for schools is quite minimal and
sketchy, and subject to varying interpretations. Lemaire and

others rely upon different kinds of data in support of this thesis partly because no one kind of data, epigraphic, biblical or analogical, provides sufficient support in its own right.

However, it should also be noted that critical methodological observations such as those set forth by Golka do not prove the converse of the hypotheses about schools. The main writing media in different regions of Palestine during the monarchic period were almost certainly perishable sheepskin or papyrus scrolls, so the minimal epigraphic remains do not constitute evidence for an absence of scribalism or general literacy. Also, the biblical accounts do not record in any detailed, systematic fashion the training of other artisans beside scribes, so that we cannot draw negative conclusions from the absence of extensive references to scribes in this case either. Golka is right to point out the tenuous quality of the positive arguments made on the basis of these data, but he may overstate the negative case to be made from the absence of data. Both sides are conducting *argumenta e silentio* until additional data or an improved approach can be brought to bear on the question.

The strategy of combining textual (biblical and epigraphic) data and reasoning from cross-cultural analogy suggests the possibility of a different source of new data which may be brought to bear on this question. The textual data are not likely to increase quickly, for reasons mentioned earlier; but it is possible that archeological data exist which have not been fully exploited in their applications to the problem of schools in monarchic Israel. Archeological approaches can, in the first place, help provide a meaningful and pertinent sociological context for each of the three kinds of data utilized in the debate hitherto: epigraphic, textual, and analogical. When the data are as sketchy and incomplete as they are in this case, they can all too easily be interpreted in a number of different ways with little control over the results and little means of checking the various interpretations. It will be helpful to review some of the work which has shown the manner in which archeological approaches might supplement and clarify interpretations of each of the three kinds of data used in the debate thus far (textual, epigraphic, and analogical).

Possibilities for Contributions of
Archeological Research to the Discussion

In what follows the potential for archeological contributions to an understanding of each of the three kinds of data mentioned above, textual, epigraphic, and analogical, will be assessed. These assessments will begin to provide rationales for the methodology to be set forth in the next chapter and utilized in succeeding ones.

The textual data
It is highly desirable in investigations such as this to bring all available textual evidence to bear on the problems in order to complement the witness borne by the archeological sources. This, indeed, is the general approach outlined by Lemaire. Certain kinds of epigraphic remains, e.g. abecedaries, are treated as artifacts indicative of a social function—education in a school setting. The textual evidence, in this case citations from passages in various biblical texts, is drawn upon to corroborate the interpretation of the epigraphic materials. Ideally, researchers should be able to corroborate and extend the conclusions drawn on the basis of one kind of data by considering the other. However, one often wishes the attempt were made with more sensitivity to the very problematic nature of the relationship between these two kinds of data.

In the first place, the two kinds of data we are considering here, textual and archeological, are well known to be characterized by biases peculiar to each. In the case of the textual data, it is axiomatic for historians to regard ancient documents as a product of a literate elite. Clarke puts the matter thus:

> The colouring of historical documentation arises from the inevitable filter effect of the individual author as a literate member of an elite literary subculture writing from the point of view and with the prejudices of his set, about selected matters of interest to that set (Clarke 1977: 394-95).

Frick (1986: 13) expresses the same conviction. The perspectives of a relatively narrow segment of preindustrial societies, it is maintained, are implicit in both what is written and what is not written, and even to an extent what is selected for preservation by successive generations. The evidence from literary data must, therefore, be handled with care if the investigation which utilizes it is not to reflect in its results the same set of biases inherent in the literary data upon which it is based.

Archeological data are subject to their own forms of skewing. Adams has argued persuasively that the collection of archeological data in Mesopotamia has been biased toward excavation of larger sites, and suggests regional surveying as a corrective measure:

> Reference to the documentary sources reminds us that the availability of massive numbers of texts completely transforms the character and potentialities of the ancient record. Authorities may differ on the relative potential contributions of archaeological and historical approaches to the subject matter of the fully historical portions of this book, but there is no doubt that heretofore the archaeological contribution has been strictly secondary and ancillary. Work has been focused primarily on large-scale, relatively uncontrolled excavations of public buildings and tombs and has largely eschewed the quantitatively based, interdisciplinary theorems of investigation pioneered by the prehistorians to whom no information from texts is available... the dominant strategies of study—the avenues of investigation followed, the priorities, the questions asked—are still very largely those geared toward narrowly corroborating and supplementing texts as well as maximizing the chances for further textual recovery. The irony is that in the long run such strategies are precisely the wrong ones with which to complement and extend the textual testimony most effectively (Adams 1981: 62-63).

Adams' criticism that larger sites are the primary target of most archeologists' attention would be difficult to contest. However, the reasons Adams gives for this bias must be focused somewhat differently if one is to apply his criticism to archeology in Palestine. It is certainly the case that the possibility of finding ancient texts has always been and continues to be an exciting one for archeologists in Palestine as elsewhere. However, the focus on larger sites is probably due to a need to survive professionally in a world which generally requires an artifactual return on its excavation investments. In addition, a near-dearth of ancient libraries in Palestine may have rescued the discipline there from some of the document-seeking which has tempted excavators in Adams' area.

The citation from Adams raises the question of a further difficulty in handling textual and artifactual data quite separate from the biases peculiar to each. This is the problem of correlating information gained from these two different sources. Clarke brings this issue into quite a sharp focus:

> Archaeology is a discipline in its own right, concerned with archaeological data which it clusters in archaeological entities displaying certain archaeological processes and studied in terms of archaeological aims, concepts and procedures. We fully appreciate that these entities and processes were once historical and social entities but the nature of the archaeological record is such that there is no simple way of equating our archaeological percepta with these lost events. We must certainly try to find out the social and historical equivalents of our archaeological entities and processes but we should not delude ourselves about the simplicity of these equivalents or our success in isolating them (Clarke 1977: 11-12).

Clarke later argues that historical data may contribute to efforts to explain archeological data by increasing the archeologist's repertoire of possible explanations, but the archeological data should be as fully assessed and explained in its own right as is possible before they are subjected to comparisons with historical data (1977: 376). Only under this condition can the witness of the archeological data to ancient cultural processes take a fully independent place alongside that of the historical data.

The danger to be avoided is the utilization of the results of archeological research as mere footnotes, whether corroboratively or critically, to historical reconstructions based on texts. The safest and best approach, and the one which will be taken here, is to analyze the archeological data in an effort to develop an explanatory model. Only after this step has been taken should an attempt be made to develop a higher-level synthesis of the archeological and historical witnesses. Again, even when this higher-level synthesis is undertaken, great care must be exercised to avoid simple equation between the patterns and processes revealed by archeological study and those revealed by historical study. By thus maintaining the independence of archeological investigation from study of ancient texts, the analytical repertoire of the student of ancient societies can be expanded as many have desired. Again, Clarke provides succinct expression to this qualified hope:

> ... archaeological data and its [sic] entities are not so much less accurate or less informative than historical data and entities, as differently focused. Artefacts provide different information and bias as behavioural documents to those provided by written documents. The difficulty of equating archaeological and historical entities resides in this difference; no simple or exact equivalence is possible but correlation does exist within limits (Clarke 1977: 404).

The evidence of written records can be made to function within a synthetic framework which is archeologically based, as I hope to show. Normally, the reverse occurs: historical materials are given the priority in establishing the terms of the discussion, and archeological evidence is interpreted within this—to a degree—alien context. Neither procedure is perfect, but each can contribute a valuable perspective on the past if they are permitted to complement one another.

The epigraphic remains
Epigraphic remains are often among the most valuable of historical documents, despite their comparative brevity in most cases. An upper limit for their date of promulgation can often be independently checked by reference to the archeological context, and they are freer of the kinds of variations that invariably creep into documents which are recopied and transmitted over a period of generations or centuries. In addition to their qualities as historical documents, they are archeological artifacts, and potentially can yield more information to the researcher than that provided by the texts inscribed on them.

Lemaire (1981), Mettinger (1971) and others have employed the epigraphic data in both of these aspects: as historical documents and as archeological artifacts. However, it is possible that in some cases insufficient attention has been given to the necessity of providing objective controls to the interpretation of the epigraphic remains. A brief example will illustrate this point.

In his discussion on p. 30, Lemaire (1981) suggests that a scatter of inscribed *pithos* fragments on the floor of a room indicates the presence of a school there. At this point in our discussion we are primarily interested in the manner in which the data were handled rather than the actual validity of the argument. It must first be noted on a general level that there are many other possible explanations for those *pithoi* than that they are school texts. We want to know which explanation is the most likely on the merits of the data. If we wished to test the hypothesis that this scatter of sherds was due to the presence of a school, we would need to enumerate the alternative possibilities, establish the criteria by which we would choose between them and the school hypothesis, and then see which criteria fit best with the data in this case.

Another way of describing criteria such as those suggested in the preceding example is to call them 'predictions': each explanation for this particular data set can be used to predict a corresponding set of conditions under which we would expect to find the data set in question. This procedure involves little more than exercising one's creativity and imagination to outline the expected ramifications of a model or set of hypotheses, and then looking to see which set of conditions best fit the data. To continue the previous example, we would need first to define 'schools' so as to enable us to establish criteria for their presence. Crenshaw suggests such a definition: professional, paid educators; literacy as part of the curriculum; education takes place at a specific location outside the home (1984: 602). In the case of the sherd scatter we would, in addition to the inscribed materials themselves, like to see evidence at the same site of other full-time non-agriculturalists, indicating that the community at that site was capable of sustaining non-food-producing adults. An analysis of the size and complexity of that site's economy would provide circumstantial evidence that it might have been able to devote some of its energies to the institutionalized propagation of literacy. Analysis of the layout of the site, and the distribution of other types of artifacts within the site, might help to determine whether the room in which the sherds were found was a classroom or was devoted to industrial or commercial uses.

The method used in this study will be outlined in detail in the next chapter. Our goal here is merely to raise the possibility that artifactual evidence may be able to speak more clearly to issues such as the presence or absence of schools if such evidence is permitted to speak within the context of an archeologically (as opposed to textually) established explanatory framework. The recent focus of anthropological archeologists on 'explanatory models' (see below) is an expression of a desire on their part to move their discussions onto a footing similar to that of other scientific disciplines. The return on an investment in theory-building through hypothesis testing is greater control and objectivity in evaluating archeological data, which is our goal here.

Golka suggests a move in this direction in the question of schools by proposing a different explanation of the epigraphic and textual data:

> Da das Amt der Schreiber in den Familien erblich war, bedurfte es keiner Schulen zur Ausbildung: Elihoreph und Ahia, die Schreiber Salomos (1 Kön. iv 3), waren Söhne des Schischa, der dieses Amt unter David innehatte... In keinem Fall kann er [Lemaire] jedoch den Beweis erbringen, daß diese Funde einer Schule, und nicht dem Privatunterricht nach dem Famulussystem entstammen. Wäre all diese Material an einem Ort, besonders in Jerusalem, gefunden worden, sähe die Beweislage schon ganz anders aus (Golka 1983: 263, and n. 19).

Golka's alternative model, education in the home of biological children, 'apprentices' who were called *bānîm* ('children'), or both, distinguishes the question of schools, as defined by Crenshaw, from that of the promulgation of literacy generally, which apparently could take place outside of schools. Golka also suggests a criterion for determining the circumstances under which a school model would be preferred to his home-education model: concentration of epigraphic finds in one locale. I do not feel that even Golka has gone nearly far enough in a the direction of a systematic analysis on this point, but he is certainly correct in pointing out the basic problem. More such criteria could and should be suggested, and the case for preferring one model or the other thereby strengthened.

What is lacking here is an objective theoretical context or framework within which to interpret the data. The present level of the discussion is more subjective than it need be because not enough work has gone into making the models predictive, and no attempt has been made to ground the models in their larger systemic environments. The cybernetic or systems approach which is now being refined within anthropological archeology (see below) allows the researcher to move in the direction of creating a systematic theoretical framework within which to interpret individual artifactual data types, of which epigraphic data are an example, in a more objective manner.

Cross-cultural analogy

The concern expressed by Golka about the advisability of drawing parallels from societies which are better known via textual or historical evidence, such as Egypt and Mesopotamia, to temporally and/or geographically adjacent societies such as Israel, is confirmed in several ways by the basic assumptions of anthropological archeological approaches.

We have already seen some of limitations of textual data in discussions of historical societies and institutions. Cross-cultural analogies, insofar as they draw on textual materials for their basis (which is often the case) are subject to the same criticisms as were outlined above. Just as important, however, is the further complication that the relationship between supposedly parallel institutions in cultures at a distance from one another in time or space is highly complex, and is often the object of study as a technical question in its own right; and appropriately so. To jump ahead somewhat, the Israelite state of c. 1000 to 600 BCE is a non-pristine or secondary state, i.e. it arose at least to a degree out of a pre-existing sociopolitical context of Canaanite urban centers which were themselves subject to the influence and control of even larger foreign states, namely Egypt and Mesopotamia. Mendenhall (1975) has suggested that upon capturing Jebusite Jerusalem David incorporated the professional Canaanite bureaucracy into the nascent Israelite state; Mettinger (1971) characterized the Solomonic bureaucracy as being of Egyptian derivation in all its essential aspects. Demsky (1977), Lemaire (1981) and Williams (1962) all seem to regard the Canaanite urban bureaucracy as the means by which Israel incorporated urban institutions into itself upon its emergence as a national state.

Price, however, has warned that in many cases one cannot assume that institutions in a primary state transfer naturally to secondary states spawned or influenced by them in the course of their development.

> Processes of change, whatever their ultimate origin, necessarily work upon, and through, the selective pressures of local eco- systems and the mode of production of the populations occupy- ing them. Thus there is a strong implication that institutions per se are not exportable (Price 1978: 182).

The independent technological and economic development of the highland Israelite social system and the Canaanite, then Philistine, lowland social systems occurred at least in part because of the differential selective pressures placed on those systems by the hill-country and coastal-plain ecologies of that region. Institutions geared to adapt an economy and social system to the local ecosystem may be maladaptive under dif- ferent ecological pressures. As Price puts it, institutions cannot be passed on from one society to another like 'family silver' (1978: 163).

If there is a real possibility that the relation of a secondary state to its larger cultural context is not simply 'genetic', as Price puts it, then the validity of parallels posited between such a secondary state and its neighbors or precursors must be established and defined, not merely assumed. This is not to say that cross-cultural analogies have no place in a critical exam- ination of a particular society's institutions. On the contrary, cross-cultural analogies can play a fruitful role in such inves- tigations in two ways.

First, such parallels, even if not critically established, can aid the investigator in imagining further alternative explanations for the data at hand. It is not necessary for the parallel to be true or accurate at all in this case, since the validity of any hypothesis will depend on the success with which it predicts the behavior of the data, not its subjective appeal. The source of a hypothesis has nothing to do with its ultimate success as part of an experimentally validated theory. In fact, the annals of science are full of peculiar sources for such inspirations, from

Newton's apple to Einstein's use of a 19th-century mathematical game, for which even its inventor saw no practical use, as a basis for his theory of relativity. This is part of the creative dimension of scientific research.

Second, cross-cultural parallels can suggest the possibility of a direct or indirect relationship between institutions in different societies. This possibility must at times be technically discussed in an attempt to estimate the likelihood of actual influence in one direction or both. This is especially the case with smaller, non-pristine societies which arise on the borders of larger cultures and under strong political, economic or cultural influence from them.

A systems approach is helpful in developing the theoretical framework on which to base an analysis of institutions similar in appearance or function in different cultures. Any institution will be embedded in a larger societal setting. Variations in the structure or function of an institution will be reflected by changes in key, related variables within that same system (Clarke 1978: 75; instead of 'variables' he calls them 'attributes'). This fact enables us to predict the effects of changes within the particular institution on the larger system of which it is a part. Thus, even when we cannot compare institutions directly because of insufficient attestation for one culture, we are not reduced to merely supplying the missing parameters from another culture. Instead, we can focus our attention on key variables relating to the institution or institutions in question, and monitor the behavior of these under varying conditions. Such a contextual analysis would enable us to make affirmative claims about the institutions in question.

In the case of school systems in ancient Israel, we wish to assess the strength of parallels between Egyptian and Mesopotamian models, for which we have more extensive data, and Israel, for which direct evidence is in scarce supply. First, we would need to define 'schools' in terms of the existing models, in this case Egyptian and Mesopotamian. Then we would select a set of variables which we would expect with a high degree of confidence to be linked to an educational system in the different societies. Such a set of associated variables would include evidence for the presence of an elite class which could act as sponsors of full-time professionals, aspects of the degree of complexity of the urbanization of the different societies, measures of centrality of control of means of production, and the like. The configuration of relations between these variables can be predicted on the basis of a set of different models for educational systems. A school system might be one model, an apprentice–master model might be another, family education a third; varying combinations of these should produce further models. Each model should then be used to project an appropriate configuration of the variables decided upon at the outset. Finally, the actual configuration of these related variables will enable the investigator to assess the ability of different models to explain the data at hand.

Again, this approach is a basic tool in scientific research. It enables the researcher to reason from what is directly perceivable to what is not by analyzing patterns in what can be seen and refining models which explain the patterns until their predictive ability is perfected. Clarke describes this process using the 'Black Box' analogy:

> The problem of the Black Box arises in theoretical and practical terms when the investigator is faced with a complex system, completely concealed but for an input terminal and an output terminal. The only information available about the system within the box must come from observing the changing relationships between varying values at the input and output terminals. Consequently the investigation of Black Box systems depends upon the tabulation of as many varied input states and sequences of states as is possible together with a record of the corresponding output states. The investigator will primarily look for any evidence for constraint in the variety of states and for regularities in states or frequencies of states, such regularities as we can often observe in archaeological and anthropological data (Clarke 1978: 59).

The situation for archeologists is dissimilar from that of some other scientific disciplines in that the input terminal cannot be deliberately manipulated experimentally in order to facilitate the process of checking models. However, other disciplines do exist which operate successfully under this 'disadvantage', such as astrophysics, geophysics and oceanography. Theoretical development has not been limited by an inability to 'experiment' in the traditional sense in the case of these other disciplines, nor should it in archeological research.

The desirability of placing questions such as the one addressed here in a larger sociological framework has been argued quite persuasively by Mendenhall (1962, 1971), followed by Gottwald (1979) and others. Mendenhall first applied the theoretical sociological framework developed by M. Fried (e.g. 1967) to the question of the manner of Israelite settlement in highland Palestine during the 12th and 11th centuries BCE. Certain aspects of his results, and the extensive amplification of the same by Gottwald, will interest us at a later point. Here we need only note that, while his conclusions have been debated by many and rejected on at least some issues, and have been much modified even by those who largely agreed with him, Mendenhall succeeded in forcing all subsequent scholarship to come to terms with his methodology and its ramifications for the settlement question.

Summary

So far we have seen that the discussion of schools in monarchic Israel has had to operate under somewhat difficult conditions due to a dearth of evidence which can be handled in a direct manner. The epigraphic and textual data are both minimal and open to widely varying interpretations. Likewise, the discussion of analogies to other cultures was seen to contribute little in a substantive way to the discussion, at least as formulated in the discussion heretofore.

The suggestion was made above that archeological data working within a sociological framework could provide a systematic context within which to assess the various models of literacy and schools in monarchic Israel. The general outlines suggested here must now be fleshed out in a description of and rationale for the specific methodology to be employed in the present study. To this task we now turn.

Methodology

I propose to approach the question of writing in monarchic Israel via analysis of data gathered through archeological excavations and surveys. This approach will be a particular application of selected anthropological-archeological theory and techniques which have developed over a period of several decades and which continue to develop today. In order to facilitate a description of the methods used here, I will briefly summarize some of the developments in anthropological-archeological theory and technique to date. Against the backdrop of this synopsis, the rationale for the present approach will become more clear.

Theory in anthropological archeology
A basic assumption common to analyses of archeological data to which the present analysis is indebted is that social, political and economic structures in human society arise and develop in response to the need to deal collectively with the physical environment (Kohl 1981). Karl Marx formulated this perspective in terms of control of means of production as the basis for political class struggle (Price 1978: 163; Gottwald 1979: 631f.). This materialist perspective remains central even where, as in this case, the dynamic for societal change is assumed to be evolutionary rather than dialectical (cf. Price 1978). In other words, a further assumption of the present approach will be to explain social change in terms of adaptive and selective responses which enhance survivability (Price 1978: 162-64).

One emphasis deriving from the above-mentioned assumption is that ecological factors are loci for explanations of developments in social systems. This focus was worked out theoretically by van Thunen, a Danish geographer of the previous century (Chisolm 1970). Van Thunen developed a model for ideal exploitation of areal resources around an agricultural community. He showed how land use could be optimized by reducing the work needed to utilize areal resources to an absolute minimum. In developing his model van Thunen considered: distance to resources such as water, cultivated land, range land and trade routes; intensity of use of each of these resources; and frequency of use. Using these criteria he produced a map showing bands of land utilization around a single agricultural settlement. He also suggested ways in which such a model could be modified to account for variables such as land quality, multiple access routes, multiple homesteads in the same area, etc.

Van Thunen's approach provided archeologists with a model against which to check the land utilization of inhabitants of ancient sites. By analyzing changing spectra of plant and animal remains, tool kits, and available areal resources, archeologists could begin to discuss exploitation strategies of ancient cultures. These ecological factors were properly perceived as an important addition to the archeologist's repertoire of explanations for cultural change.

Van Thunen's method of producing an ideal model of land utilization by projecting the optimal use of areal resources onto a map was taken up and extended to regions and relationships between sites in the early part of this century by Cristaller (Smith 1977). Cristaller proposed an ideal configuration of sites based on the need to optimally distribute economic, political and administrative functions among networks of settlements. In Cristaller's model, societies would consist of tiers of sites of varying sizes and functions. Sites of the same tier would be equidistant so as to distribute access to their functions most evenly among the smaller sites. The largest sites would combine the most diverse set of functions, political, economic and administrative, and be centrally placed. Cristaller's model has been called Central Place Theory because of its use of the principle of centrality of function to optimize regional distributions of site location.

The potential applications of Cristaller's model to archeological investigations are quite tantalizing. Archeologists would like to be able to look at a map of ancient sites, perceive there a societal network, and predict distributions of societal functions such as trade and administration (Clarke 1977: 128; Frick 1986: 23). Clarke expresses the hope thus:

> This last point leads us conveniently into the analysis of settlement patterns and site location strategies in terms of factors such as markets, transport and administration... [such analysis] involves the archaeologist in the analysis of settlement distributions to define different types of patterns (e.g. nearest-neighbour analysis) and then the application of models (e.g. Central-place theory) in order to interpret these patterns. In this way the archaeologist can hope to relate site location to such fac-

tors as social and political hierarchies, trade and markets and resource localization. Only when we can interpret site location strategies within this broad framework, as well as in terms of specific resource constraints, will our understanding of the economic subsystem increase to a more productive level (Clarke 1978: 128).

Ziph (1949; cited in Adams 1981) has contributed a variation of Cristaller's model based on observation of modern societies. Ziph's model suggests that, rather than tiers of settlements of decreasing number and increasing geographical dispersion, what we see is a continuum of sites with no marked boundaries dividing one category of sites from another. In Ziph's model, the size of sites, as determined by population in this case, will follow a 'rank-size' rule: the largest site will be twice as large as the second largest site, three times as large as the third largest site, and so on (Ziph's principle is elucidated more fully below). Again, this is an ideal model whose value to archeologists is that variations from it can be observed and invite explanation.

The contributions of van Thunen, Cristaller and Ziph have recently begun to realize more of their potential for archeological applications. Archeologists have for some time perceived a need for theoretically sophisticated explanations of data rather than mere descriptions of them. Indeed, Binford's articles in the mid-sixties (see the bibliography) helped make 'explanation' something of a *cause célèbre* among anthropological archeologists. When the desirability of models for theory-building became clear, the value of the works of van Thunen, Cristaller, Ziph and others, which essentially propose simple, ideal systems with explicit rules for why they appear as they do, became obvious to archeologists. Cybernetics, or systems theory, which emphasizes the need to make explicit the rules governing the functioning of systems, was seen to be a helpful paradigm for bridging between archeological data, explanatory models, and ancient cultural systems (Flannery 1972; Clarke 1977).

The very important contribution of systems theory to archeological studies has been the addition of many more explanatory tools to the archeologist's kit bag. In systems theory, it is axiomatic that systems are influenced not only by their environments, but also change in response to internal forces such as continuity or inertia, feedback, equilibrium, and homeostasis, to name a few (Clarke 1978: 45ff.). Systems theory also demands an explanation of cultural change in terms of interactions between the cultural system and its environments: ecological, political, and economic. A wholistic approach to cultural explanation is thereby promulgated.

Techniques in anthropological archeology
The advances in theory in the areas of ecological exploitation and cybernetics do not fully account for developments in the ability of archeologists to pursue their research goals with greater and greater rigor. Improvements in techniques, both of data collection and data analysis, have paralleled advances in theory, sometimes deliberately but sometimes also seren-dipitously.

The advances in theory mentioned above have tended to demand more and more in the way of predictive capability from explanations proposed by archeologists for changes per-ceived in cultural processes. However, the ability to predict the behavior of archeologically based models is dependent on two factors: first, the refinement of our theoretical models dis-cussed above, and second, the precision with which we can describe the archeological realia. The ability to evaluate and test models is limited by our ability to *perceive* the ancient cul-tural systems against which we are testing those models. If we can improve the clarity with which we can describe ancient systems, we increase the explanatory capabilities of our theoretical models. Some of the advances in descriptive capa-bility for archeology have resulted from very significant im-provements in the techniques of data collection and data analysis.

The advances in data collection include, first and foremost, close stratigraphic excavation. While this methodology is not exactly a recent development, it has taken many decades to build up the corpus of data thus collected to a degree sufficient to permit its use in systematic regional studies such as the pre-sent one. Close stratigraphic excavation sharply increases the chronological resolution with which we view archeological remains. This enhanced resolution greatly improves archeologists' ability to isolate and characterize cultural shifts, and to link explanations of those cultural shifts to environmental, political, or other factors.

Other advances in data collection have perhaps had a less revolutionary impact on the descriptive abilities of archeology but are important also. Examples would include such techniques as flotation for minute floral and faunal remains, which has decisively invigorated the environmental exploitation patterns (e.g. Hole, Flannery and Neely 1964), and the application of sampling techniques to excavation and surveying (e.g. Adams 1981). More generally, the strategy of including specialists from other disciplines to advise in the field and laboratory, such as geologists, botanists, palynologists, and osteologists, has proven to be a fruitful complement to the field repertoire.

Advances in data analysis have also been remarkable in recent years and continue to be so. Archeologists have begun to apply increasingly sophisticated statistical techniques to their evaluation of their data with fruitful results. The emphasis of the systems approach on the articulation of rules or laws governing the system under investigation paved the way for many of these advances in data analysis. The formulation of 'laws' to describe cultural processes is simply the perception of patterns in various aspects of the archeological data and the articulation of those patterns in mathematical or logical form. Statistical methods are mathematical tools designed to help researchers isolate patterns in large masses of data, such as are commonly faced by archeologists.

Binford's characterization of statistics as 'merely' descriptive (1977: 5-6) unfortunately does little justice to the dependence of hypothesis formulation on precise and accurate description. Without accurate and rigorously controlled articulations of patterns in the data, hypotheses based on these data will also lack accuracy and rigor. In other words, the clarity of our hypotheses is strictly limited by the clarity with which the data can be described; data analysis and data synthesis are interdependent. Binford's criticism also fails to take proper account of the emphasis of statistics on the isolation and characterization of patterns—a particularly valuable emphasis for those attempting to formulate hypotheses. It is dangerous to separate the process of hypothesis formulation too sharply from the processes of data collection and description on which it is completely dependent. Clarke's wholistic model of data collection, analysis, hypothesis formulation and further data collection to test hypotheses (1978: 32) recovers the essential interdependence of the various aspects of archeological investigation.

The method in this study
a. *Introduction.* The analytical techniques utilized here will be developed from a specific sociological model. I will start from a model of urbanization well known in sociological and anthropological literature, exploring the model to see how it might be adapted to address the more particular questions of this study. The model will consist of a set of key societal attributes. I shall hypothesize that different configurations of those attributes correlate more or less highly with the social features we are studying, namely scribalism and schools.

The next step will be to determine a set of archeological correlates to the key societal attributes established in the development of our model. I will then analyze archeological data selected to facilitate the study of these archeological correlates. In other words, archeological data will be used to recover the actual configuration of the key societal variables of our model in a particular region and to show how the configuration of these variables changed over time.

After the archeological data have been allowed to address the questions of scribalism and schools, I will correlate the picture of these institutions developed from the archeologically based model with the picture derived from biblical, epigraphic, and cross-cultural analysis. This procedure will enable us to reinterpret the biblical, epigraphic, and cross-cultural evidence in the context of an archeologically established sociological framework. The conclusions drawn in this way will be compared to the conclusions drawn from the textually based data alone. Differences between the two sets of conclusions will be evaluated and discussed, and proposals suggested for further research into the set of questions addressed here.

b. Sociological model. Studies of the development of increasingly complex forms of human society have long occupied the attention of students of human culture. One approach to such studies has been to address the question in terms of *urbanization*. Many attempts have been made to define 'cities' in terms of key functional attributes. We have already encountered one such attempt: Central Place Theory defines central places as nodal points in one of three kinds of networks: economic, administrative, or political. The assumption of CPT is that the more complex the set of functions carried on at the central place, the higher a position in the social hierarchy occupied by that site.

G. Sjöberg (1960; cited in Frick 1981) works from functional-materialist assumptions and suggests the following list of key urban attributes (Frick calls them 'definitive urban criteria' [1981: 9]):

1. presence of full-time specialists
2. larger, denser populations
3. great art, produced by specialists
4. presence of writing and numerical notation
5. exact and predictive sciences
6. tribute or taxes paid by farmers
7. society organized on the basis of residence
8. monumental public works
9. 'foreign trade'
10. a class-structured society

(Frick 1981: 9-10).

These key attributes are directly related to control of agricultural production. Left to their own devices, agricultural workers will grow enough food to meet their own needs but no more. In this model, urbanization is defined in terms of social stratification: an elite class must be able to force the agriculturalists to grow a surplus and hand it over to the ruling elite. This surplus is then used to support not only the elite class itself, but full-time artisans and technical specialists.

For the present purposes, we should note that the phenomenon of writing is listed as a key urban attribute under Sjöberg's regime. The inclusion of writing here results from centralization of control of agricultural production. The ability to control economic transactions is limited by the amount of information which can be processed to track regional inventories and 'payments' in the form of foodstuffs taxed or extorted from the rural population. In addition, writing facilitates the transactions of long-range trade, which provides the elite with luxury items used to publicly symbolize higher status.

To Sjöberg's list of key urban attributes, Frick has added the presence of walls and/or fortifications for Palestine. This addition was suggested on the basis of a linguistic evaluation of Hebrew words often translated as 'city' in biblical literature. Frick supports this conclusion with a comparison of the archeological record to the results of his linguistic analysis.

The key attributes listed by Frick are of two kinds: societal characteristics not directly observable, and material phenomena resulting from the societal characteristics. Compare, for example, items 1 and 3 in Frick's list. It is vital to preserve this distinction. The presence of variables directly observable, by means of archeological data in our case, does not *necessarily* prove that the underlying societal characteristics are present as well. For instance, foreign trade has been documented for non-urban, relatively egalitarian societies: Redman (1978: 184) notes that 90% of Çatal Hüyük's obsidian came from a distance of 250 kilometers, and that the villagers also imported cowrie shells from the Mediterranean, 100 kilometers distant, and copper and turquoise from distances of 500 to 1,000 kilometers. The site measured thirteen hectares, and was occupied from approximately 6250 to 5400 BCE (Redman 1978: 183). Also, complex urban cultures have existed for fairly long periods without writing systems (e.g Mesoamerica).

The fact is that none of the key urban attributes is a *sine qua non* for the affirmation of a particular settlement as a city. A superior approach to the application of these attributes is set forth by Clarke (1978: 35ff. and cf. Needham 1975: 366). He suggests employing a polythetic approach to utilizing sets of attributes to classify social phenomena, of which the city is one example. Such phenomena may occur naturally along a continuum of values for each of the key attributes listed for it. If significant breaks occur in the continuum, we may say that when the number of shared attributes leaps to a new level, a new class may be defined. However, if we observe no such breaks, we must adopt a more probabilistic approach, namely, that as the number of shared attributes increases to or past some arbitrary level, it becomes increasingly likely that the phenomena in question should properly be grouped together.

Clarke's polythetic approach, applied to the phenomenon of urbanization, would call for a definition of urbanization in terms of increasing functional complexity. Key urban attributes would be prioritized in the model according to the degree to which thay reflect a concentration of functions, whether economic, political, or social. This approach is remarkably similar to the definition of urbanization articulated above via Central Place theory. Adams also identified diversity of functions as a key indicator of urbanization, though he found a high correlation between site size and social complexity, and so used one as a flag for the other (1981: 75). However, he recognized limitations to his approach as well: sites small in area according to surface survey can prove to have harbored a surprisingly broad range of social functions associated with complex social stratification upon excavation (Adams 1981: 78f.).

We must now attempt to focus our model, which was developed to describe the degree to which a culture may be characterized as urban, on the issues of scribalism and schools. We may accomplish this by posing several questions: what key attributes, discussed above, would we expect to correlate most highly with the phenomenon of writing as an instrument of administrative control? And how might these attributes help us to evaluate the issue of training of personnel skilled in the use of writing? In the first place, we would expect writing to function in a context of administrative control, whether economic, social, or political. Writing would be employed to monitor, and thereby enhance the capacity to direct, economic and social transactions at many levels. We would then expect the use of writing to correlate highly with the degree and extent of control exercised by centralized (urban) elites over agricultural producers. The greater the need for such control, the more likely the presence of full-time administrators to facilitate the exercise of control by the elite class.

Before we can use this model to evaluate schools, we must define 'schools' for the purposes of this study. Mettinger focuses on the question of schools in Israel using Egyptian models and, according to him, 'in Egypt all education was essentially scribal education' (1971: 140). Since Mettinger is not concerned with the possibility of other forms of schools, but only to show the dependence of the Israelite version on the Egyptian model, he defines Israelite schools in these terms as well (1971: 144f.) Other definitions are possible. Crenshaw (1984: 601f.) has observed a failure to define adequately what is meant by 'school'. Such a definition is needed, or else there is no basis for evaluating whether a body of evidence confirms or denies the hypothesis of a school's existence at any particular time and place. Accordingly, Crenshaw has offered a definition of 'school' that deserves attention: a school may be defined as 'professional education, which involved both reading and writing, at a specific location to which young people came and for which fees were paid to a teacher' (1984: 602).

Crenshaw's definition has several key components: (1) among the skills or subjects taught is *literacy*; (2) the learning takes place at a fixed *location* outside the *home*; and (3) fees are paid to a professional educator. Crenshaw's definition succeeds in distinguishing between a school and home education. However, it may not adequately distinguish between a school and professional tutoring (cf. Demsky 1972: 390). Crenshaw's inclusion of education in literacy as part of the curriculum enables him to keep his discussion of education in touch with the work of others who focus on the literacy aspect of training in schools (e.g. Lemaire 1981; Mettinger 1971). For the present purposes, we shall define schools as Crenshaw has done, but add a clearer emphasis on the training of professional administrators, i.e. those who functioned in positions of administrative control. Even in Mesopotamia, scribes were not merely encoders of information; they also functioned as managers of estates and businesses and as arbiters in legal disputes (Kramer 1967: 124).

The degree of administrative control and the diversity of social institutions falling under such control, then, would be expected to correlate positively with the use of writing as one instrument of that control. This follows from the inclusion of writing as a key member of a polythetic set of attributes identifying increasingly stratified societies. Such control presupposes the presence of an elite class, under whose warrants the administrative direction was exercised. It follows, further, that direct evidence of such a class, as well as evidence of other full-time non-agriculturalists whose presence also presupposes the existence of the elite class, would correlate positively with writing as a tool of that class.

The key variables we expect to correlate most highly with scribalism, then, are as follows:

1. centralized administrative control: concentration of increasingly large numbers of functions in fewer and fewer settlements
2. social stratification
3. other full-time non-agricultural specialists

Having suggested some of the key variables which, according to the model we have adapted, should correlate positively with the extent of the use of writing, we are now in a position to define archeological correlates to those variables.

c. Archeological correlates: data and data analysis. Price has approached the question of centralization of control in terms of cultural energy: the question of what institutions were utilized to concentrate work and production within societies. What she and others following Julian Steward (1955) have called 'core institutions' are those institutions central to a society's ability to concentrate energy and production (1978: 167). The clearest archeological correlates to these institutions, according to Price, are settlement patterns and public works.

> Anything made by man represents the transformation of energy into matter, energy produced by and circulated in a human community. The transformation to some extent removes that amount of energy from general circulation by 'spending' it, transmuting it into permanent material form. A pot fossilizes in this fashion a relatively minute quantity of energy; a building, proportional to its size, considerably more. The criterion of relative scale is thus the material isomorph of the capital and labor required for the energy transformation in manufacture or construction. Monumental architecture—a diagnostic of nonegali-

tarian society—is a large chunk of fossilized energy permanently removed from general circulation.

Probably the most powerful class of data to use in a sociocultural explanation is settlement pattern—the arrangement of population upon a landscape. This may be taken as the material isomorph of the entire mode of production in its broadest sense, and of the core features of social and political organization (Price 1978: 165).

In her discussion of monumental public work, Price avers that mass and scale are more directly reflective of the concentration of energy than architectural style. In the present case, however, I will also track architectural style as a clue to the presence or absence of full-time skilled artisans, which would in turn imply a means of redistribution of foodstuffs to support professionals who did not grow their own. Patterns of architectural style over a broad geographical area can be explained by propagation of popular architectural traditions, or alternatively by some central authority's deliberate campaign of public building. Such campaigns can be a form of propaganda, articulating the authority of the upper class over others within the society, and hence indicative of a tiered social sturcture (Frick 1981: 11ff.). Analysis of public works alone may or may not provide a means of choosing between these hypotheses; thus, here also, a means of cross-checking with other kinds of analysis is highly desirable. The possibilities for correlating results of such analysis with locational analysis are obvious.

The phrase 'settlement patterns' is used here as Price has done, with one exception. Since populations are not directly measurable, archeologists are limited to the study of settlement patterns in terms of the spatial distribution of sites with attention to site size. Settlement patterns of the region and period selected for this study will be evaluated through analysis of excavation and survey data. Site size (for the excavated sites only) and location (for surveyed sites as well) through time will be the variables studied. Regional political and economic boundaries can be reflected in settlement patterns. The changes through time in the patterns of settlement in a given region provide valuable insight into the changing styles of exploitation of regional resources, responses to outside threats, trading opportunities, and other kinds of internal and external pressures. These factors will enable us to assess the quality and extent of regional administrative control through time.

Site-size estimates can also be utilized in conjunction with regional agricultural productivity estimates to determine patterns of land use. In Mesopotamia, Adams (1981, e.g. p. 90, and figs. 22-24) has done this by using site-size estimates to arrive at a rough approximation of population size. Human nutritional requirements are known, and agricultural productivity for the region under study can be reconstructed by factoring in variability in soil quality, rainfall, and crop yields. The amount of arable land required by sites can be calculated, and maps showing land use radii reveal the size of the hinterland that urban centers had to control in order to sustain their populations. Again, these processes as they changed over time provide us with a window on regional control over productivity.

Settlement patterns are a logical place to begin the study, since they provide a locational framework with which one can correlate results of other kinds of studies. The goal is to provide a spatial and temporal frame of reference for the explanatory model, as well as to begin to articulate features and parameters of the model; settlement patterns will therefore be the first type of data analyzed in this study (Chapter 2).

Settlement pattern studies have been applied to many regions and periods, with a resulting helpful refinement of analytical techniques. Hodder (Hodder and Orton 1976) and Renfrew (1982), among others, have contributed critical cautions to the use of locational analysis. Limitations in the quality of data and a too-simple model are key obstacles to utilizing locational analysis alone as a window on social structures. These difficulties can be met by rigorous evaluation of systematic and random error in the data on the one hand, and by not relying solely on locational analysis for model articulation on the other.

To Price's set of correlates I am adding an analysis of the distribution of luxury items. The distribution of luxury items provides a valuable set of data to complement and amplify the picture derived from analysis of settlement patterns and public works. First, the distribution of luxury items in burial sites provides a measure of the absolute wealth of the site and region, and also gives insight into the degree to which the society in question was socially stratified (Clarke 1978: 429ff.; Chapman *et al.* 1981; Renfrew 1982). Second, the provenience of luxury items can show how far-flung were the trading relationships of a given site. Third, trend-surface analysis (Hodder 1977; Clarke 1978) produces a contour map of the distribution of a set of luxury items which can reveal directionality of exchange and the relative importance of sites along trade routes. Such analysis can even help distinguish between different kinds of trade and highlight market boundaries. Fourth, locally produced luxury items, whose value derived from a high degree of artistic skill in production, provide direct evidence for other full-time artisans. These factors have a direct bearing on our evaluation of the key attributes relating to the scale of administrative requirements and limitations for the region and period in question.

Again, analysis of luxury items alone can be misleading; luxury wares tend to be preserved for longer periods of time and are most likely to be retransported and even redeposited (Mazar 1966: 56-57). Also, by their very nature, they tend to be rare. The presence of an imported luxury item in a given excavation stratum may or may not indicate commercial relations with the distant site that produced the item during the period to which the stratum is dated by other remains (Hodder 1976: 18). More evidence would be required to draw such a conclusion, and best of all would be an analysis of the distribution patterns of luxury items on a regional basis, correlating with data from other kinds of analysis. Just such a procedure is our goal here.

d. Research design. In the case of each of the three kinds of data to be analyzed (settlement, public works, and luxury items) the discussion will begin with an evaluation of the quality of the data, including possible sources of error in sampling procedures, whether survey or excavation. Descriptive statistical procedures will be used to provide a survey of the data for each of five periods: Iron 1, Iron 2a, Iron 2b, Iron 2c, and Iron 3. The reason for including data from the periods which preceded and succeeded the period under direct investigation is that the societal transformations which take place moving into and out of the monarchic period are as revealing about the period as are the data from the Iron 2 period itself. The dates used for these periods in the present study are given below (§f). Graphs will be used to pictorially summarize data from hundreds of sites in a manner which is clear and relatively easy to understand. In some cases, it will be appropriate to employ somewhat more technical forms of analysis. In all statistical analyses the probability of error will be discussed and estimated. It is understood that statistical analyses are very helpful in describing large amounts of data, but they do not replace the process of hypothesis generation, testing, and model-building.

By integrating the results of the analysis of settlement patterns, public works, and luxury items, the changing requirements of the society for its administrative class in successive archeological periods can be articulated, and the question of the extent and nature of the class addressed in a fairly detailed fashion. This information, in turn, provides a valuable framework for the interpretation of the epigraphic remains and of the textual data on the distribution, role, and training of this administrative class. The distribution of epigraphic remains among sites, for instance, can be correlated with the results of the archeological analyses to help decide whether a scatter of sherds with incised characters indicates the presence of a school, or whether a different hypothesis should be preferred.

Another question, namely the degree to which Israelite administrative institutions resembled those of neighboring cultures, can also be meaningfully addressed utilizing the results of the archeological analyses. If societal needs for administrative functions in monarchic Israel were vastly different from needs of the neighboring societies, then we should be quite hesitant to draw close parallels between the ways in which analogous functions were handled in the different societies.

e. Analytical techniques. The choice of analytical techniques used in this study is based on the principle that analyses from different kinds of data which converge complexly on certain conclusions will be much more convincing in the long run than a single, slick analysis of one type of data which points clearly to a simpler conclusion. Therefore, several types of data will be utilized, and analytical techniques appropriate to each employed. The features of social structure articulated by each kind of analysis will overlap and provide a convenient means of cross-checking results. On the basis of the analysis of each kind of data—for settlement, public works and luxury items—provisional conclusions will be drawn so that each kind of data can be utilized to cross-check the others' testimony on the questions we are addressing here.

Then, finally, a *synthesizing analysis* of the different sets of results will follow in an attempt to draw together the separate threads of the previous analyses. A regional overview of the extent and nature of politically and economically tiered relationships between sites through time will be the result of the analysis. The degree to which different sites were political and/or economic centers during different periods will be assessed on the basis of the preceding analyses of settlement patterns, public works and distribution of luxury items.

The ultimate goal of the synthesizing analysis will to be direct the discussion back to the question of writing in monarchic Judah. This question will be addressed on two levels. First, on the individual site level, epigraphic and biblical evidence for specific sites will be correlated with the previous political/economic assessment of the site in the present study. This procedure will enable us to use the analyses of archeological data as a sociological context for evaluating the biblical and epigraphic evidence for writing on a site-by-site basis.

Second, on the regional level, we can assess the extent of urbanization through time by evaluating the degree of urban control over the hinterland and the degree to which sites were dependent and interdependent in a political and economic hierarchy. The greater the degree of social complexity, the greater the need for forms of long-range communications, such as writing. Our evaluation will provide us with a means of preferring certain hypotheses which have been put forward about writing over other such hypotheses.

f. Baseline parameters for the model. An important feature of systems analysis is that *changes* in the values of key variables through time are as integral to a model's explanatory power as are the static values themselves. In other words, shifts in the patterns of data from one period to the next will demand explanation from our model. The success of our model will be determined precisely by its ability to explain such shifts. This being the case, we must establish baseline values for our model, so that as we set it in motion patterned shifts in the data can find expression in the model itself.

The data presented herein are derived in every case from excavation and survey reports. The temporal classification systems used to categorize ceramic horizons in Palestine are not standardized. 'Canaanite', 'Israelite' and 'Persian' periods in one report correspond to 'Iron 1, 2, 3' in another, and so on. More insidious is the fact that Iron 1-2-3 and the subcategories (1a-b, 2a-b-c, etc.) may be nominally shared but not have the same values from one excavation report to the next. Not wishing to add yet another classification scheme to an already sufficiently confusing situation does not exempt me from establishing my own for the purposes of the study. Therefore, I have adopted the following nomenclature and values in my cataloguing of the data:

Iron 1   12th and 11th centuries BCE
Iron 2a   10th century
Iron 2b   9th and 8th centuries
Iron 2c   7th century
Iron 3   6th century and later

All dating systems in original reports and survey have been subverted to this one, even those that use the same 'Iron 1-2-3' system.

The initial period for data retrieval, the 12th–11th centuries, was chosen because it is the ceramic horizon which precedes the establishment of the Israelite state under David or Solomon, as is assumed on the basis of historical records (Alt 1967; Mettinger 1971; Demsky 1971; Flanagan 1981; Frick 1987). In order to capture the transition from non-urban to urban-based society, I elected to catalogue data beginning with the 'settlement' period. The final period for evaluation was selected on a similar basis: the Israelite state in Palestine is known from historical and archeological data to have ceased in the south in the early sixth century.

The present study is also limited geographically to the area south of map reference 1450 and west of the Jordan river. This was done for purely logistical reasons: it would have quadrupled the number of sites to be analyzed if sites in Ephraim, the Galilee and Transjordan had been included. The published data for these other areas would certainly allow extension of the model and analytical techniques into them, and I hope to do so. However, one would hope to enter on such a venture with a team of colleagues to share the work.

As the data sets to be evaluated begin with the period of the 12th–11th centuries BCE, it is necessary that the values for the key attributes of the model we have adopted be discussed in this temporal context. These values will then serve as the baseline for comparison with 'states' (correlated sets of values) of the model in the later periods under study here.

The debate surrounding Israelite settlement in Palestine has been adequately summarized by Gottwald (1979). My interest here is not in the matter most often discussed, namely the precise manner and mechanisms of settlement. Rather, I am interested in the question of scribalism and schools. We have even less direct knowledge of indigenous Israelite scribal institutions for this period, if indeed there were any, than we have for the later periods. However, we are fortunate that through the discussion of the manner of settlement a more systematic reconstruction of Israelite institutions exists for this period than for any other. We shall use the key variables enunciated above:

1. centralized administrative control: concentration of a large number of functions in single settlements
2. social stratification
3. other full-time non-agricultural specialists

Gottwald has concluded that precisely the *converse* of these variables characterized Israelite society during the 12th and 11th centuries:

> ...the conclusion is patent: as a pejorative expression of what early Israel wholeheartedly opposed and struggled to overthrow, 'Canaanite(s)' refers to a hierarchic socioeconomic and political system (or system set) peopled by kings, administrators, armies, feudal landlords and overseers, deities and priests—in short, a

system and a set of roles and functions ideologically justified
and energized by certain beliefs about gods and by cult acts reso-
lutely geared to solidify the system and to extend the system as
far as the forces of its ideas, its armed might, and its administrative apparatus could be made to reach (1981: 587).

Gottwald's expression of this dimension of Israelite society is a
highly nuanced and somewhat re-emphasized version of
Mendenhall's portrayal. Mendenhall and Gottwald share the
view that the Israelite settlement involved a rejection of the
rebellion against the urban Canaanite city-state regime and
its socioeconomic control (or attempts at control) of the rural
hinterland. Gottwald goes much further than Mendenhall in
enunciating this rejection as part of Israel's ideological self-
understanding, and in clarifying the political dimensions of
Yahwism along deliberately and self-consciously egalitarian
lines on Israel's part. He calls his book 'a sociology of the religion of liberated Israel, 1250–1050 BCE'. His example on the
religious dimension of the sociological setting resonates
strongly with the insistence of Adams (1981: 77) on the place
of religious institutions alongside the economic and political in
his explanatory model of the development of urbanism in
Mesopotamia.

Mendenhall's views have by no means prevailed in all
quarters (cf. Gottwald 1981: 736-37 n. 148). However, the
component which most interests me—namely, the argument
that Israel's settlement represents a non-urban culture's
rejection of the administrative control characteristic of the
Canaanite urban system—would seem to fairly characterize
the conquest as well as the revolt models of settlement.

Therefore, as the initial state of the key variables in the previously outlined working model for Israel I am adopting low
values: little, if any, centralized administrative control, social
stratification (of classes, as distinguished from trade specialization; cf. Flannery 1968: 403), or full-time non-agricultural
professionalism characterized Israelite society during the first
two-century period of this study. Few if any of Mendenhall or
Gottwald's strongest critics over the nature of Israelite settlement would quibble with this characterization. However, it
was and remains a testable hypothesis, and if this working

model fails to account satisfactorily for our data, it will be rejected in due course.

The ramifications of these parameters as the initial state of our model for the presence of scribes and scribal schools as an integral part of Israel's early society are clear: if there was no indigenous scribal institution, we would not expect Israelite society to have adopted one from the Canaanite urban system. Sensitivity to these issues proves its value in consideration of reconstructions such as Demsky's. The parameters of our model would not lead us to suspect that tribal leaders would appreciate and wish to adopt scribalism into the Israelite institutional repertoire. Indeed, that may not even have been possible in such an egalitarian society (cf. Gottwald 1979: 474ff., 591ff.).

g. The data to be used: a polemic. It is axiomatic among archeologists that archeology is a destructive discipline. The ethical dimension of the obligation to publish excavation data is generally understood and accepted. Financial constraints and personal mishaps are usually blamed for the present scandalous backlog of unreported or inadequately reported excavation data.

However, there is another cause: field archeologists have little real incentive or guidance in the extent and manner of their reporting of excavation results when systematic, secondary research attempting to utilize that data is so rare. Individual studies limited in scope such as the present one are the rule, and there is little sense of a comprehensive framework for the discussion of archeological-anthropological issues in Palestine.

What one would hope is that such secondary research would make clear the need for certain kinds of data to be retrieved, and for certain sites to be excavated, in order to help resolve specific issues and move the whole theoretical framework on to the next set of problems. A clearer understanding of the pressing need to *preserve* sites for future excavation and study, not only in the light of new field techniques but to answer new questions, would go hand-in-hand with such an approach.

The present study is an attempt to increase the harvest of information from the abundance of published data, and to make a contribution toward the larger goal of sociologists of ancient Israel: to construct a comprehensive sociological framework for ancient Israel.

Conclusion
Having laid out the overall research design and its rationale, given an overview of the analytical techniques to be used, adapted a sociological model and established baseline parameters for it, we can move on to the first analysis set: settlement patterns.

Chapter 2

SETTLEMENT

Introduction

Although the data to be used in this chapter on settlement
were collected partly through survey and partly through
excavation, the analytical methods used on them were developed by archeologists who based their work primarily on survey data. The approach taken in this chapter shares with such
survey-based analyses a regional outlook, but, for reasons
which will be explained below, the primary data employed
here are derived from excavation reports. Therefore, a brief
review of current methods and purposes in areal surveying
will provide a natural entrée to an explanation of our
approach to the data.

We have already seen in our general discussion of archeological theory that advances in economic theory tended to
refocus archeological analysis on a regional level. Investiga-
tors began to study the environments and microenvironments
of sites and regions in order to estimate the manner in which
inhabitants at one site or another might have exploited the
ecological resources at their disposal. Central place theory
provided a theoretical framework within which archeologists
could evaluate the relationship of sites to their sociopolitical
neighbors.

Another factor responsible for the renewed interest in site
surveying has been the appropriation by archeologists of
statistically advanced sampling techniques and computer
modelling for archeological analysis. The utilization of computers has in many scientific disciplines facilitated investigation of large data sets. Such data sets are commonly created in

the analysis of large sites, and even larger ones in investigations of entire regions.

However, survey data are also characterized by distinct limitations in their usefulness for archeological research. The weaknesses of one of the most ambitious recent efforts to use survey data to model the development of sociopolitical systems in a particular geographical region, namely that of Adams (1981), is a case in point. Since some of the analytical techniques to be employed in this study are modifications of Adams' approach, a review of the weaknesses of Adams' method will provide the backdrop for an explanation of my modifications of his approach.

Adams spent several seasons visiting and recording sites in Mesopotamia. His survey technique involved locating sites by traversing the survey area at one-kilometer intervals where possible; approximately one-quarter of the total surveyed area could be covered in this way. He attempted to evaluate his own success using this method as follows:

> Using a grid of 10-kilometer squares in uncultivated areas... a stratified systematic unaligned sample of one-kilometer squares was drawn with the aid of a random-number table. This sampling design assures a wide dispersion of locations while maintaining randomization within each larger square in order to avoid the effects of possible periodicities in the phenomena being studied. Having designated loci for restudy in the fashion shown, without reference to sites already known within these squares,... I attempted to delimit the boundaries of each of them and conduct an intensive resurvey within those boundaries (Adams 1981: 40).

Adams' resurvey indicated that he had missed as many as one-third of the sites, all small ones near larger settlements. Adams' research is noteworthy for many reasons, but for the present discussion the most important is the circumspection with which he assessed the reliability of his data. Adams admitted that his efforts were in the nature of a first foray and could certainly be improved (1981: 242-43).

Adams noted several systematic limitations that reduced the effectiveness of his research design (1981: 47ff.). First, he acknowledged that even the most intensive survey can fail to detect phases of occupation, especially earlier phases in long-inhabited sites, and can also fail to detect significant numbers of whole sites (see above, and cf. Lapp 1962: 89). Second, noting the common ancient practice of deeply excavating foundations of large buildings, he pointed out the difficulty of determining the areal extent of ancient occupational phases from the surface debris. Such debris is almost never recovered *in situ*, yet the ability to measure its dispersion over the site, i.e. its location, is critical to the success of Adams' approach (pp. 130-31).

Employment and quality of data in the present study

Two problems preclude simple adoption of Adams' approach in our region of study. First, the many surveys which have been undertaken in our area made no systematic attempt to collect the kind of data necessary for the analytical techniques I would like to apply here (see below for more details on this point). Second, and perhaps more important, even if such data did exist in the survey literature for our region, their reliability for such analyses would doubtless be as problematic here as they were in Adams' study. The highly uncertain relation between the areal extent of surface finds and areal extent of phases in a particular ancient community's existence raises serious doubts about the results of analyses performed on such data.

A rigorous evaluation of error in the data is a fundamental requirement of any statistical study. Two kinds of error are possible in statistical analyses: systematic and random. Systematic errors are also called 'biases'; they systematically tend to push the data in one direction or another. Random error is simply the limit of the data's resolution, in a sense: it is the 'plus-or-minus' part of a datum. Since random error is tied to the method of data collection, it remains the same for each datum collected. Thus, the larger the data set, the smaller the proportionate error. Another way of looking at random and systematic error is that while random error proportionately decreases as the data set becomes larger, systematic error increases in proportion to increases in size in the data set with which it is associated.

However, neither kind of error necessarily undermines the study of which it is a part. Random error determines the lower size limit of the data set to be studied; below a certain limit, the data set is small enough that the proportionate error is unacceptably large. To use a somewhat gross example, let us assume we wish to measure the size of sites. Our measurements are only accurate to within one acre. If our data set were to consist of only one site, measuring one acre, our error would be 100%, which is under most circumstances unacceptably large. If, on the other hand, our sample size is one hundred, and we are sure that there is no systematic error in our sample, then the variation about the measured site size will approximate a normal distribution. We can be much more certain of the average site size because of the large number of observations.

Systematic error is properly handled in one of three ways: the results can be modified by a corrective factor proportionate in size and opposite in effect to the bias; the data can be recollected in a modified fashion to reduce or eliminate the error; or the error can simply be announced as part of the results. In the case of either kind of error, however, the results of the analysis are of little or no use unless the extent of each kind of error can be determined with an acceptable degree of precision.

The difficulty in using data provided by surface surveys as the basis for the kinds of statistical approaches which have been applied to them is that acceptable precision in determinations of systematic and random error is seldom possible. If, as in our case, the datum one is collecting is the areal extent of surface scatters of potsherds, and one wishes to learn more about the areal extent of different phases of an ancient community, one would need to know what the relation was between the surface scatters and the original areal extent of the community under study. This relation is well known to be complicated by such factors as the tendency of later communities to redistribute earlier remains with their own building projects, erosion, earthquakes and the soil liquefaction commonly associated with them, and the like. It is likely that some of these factors introduce a systematic error. For instance, it seems logical that for sites characterized by somewhat severe topography (on the top of a hill, or crest of a ridge), later disturbances would tend to scatter earlier remains further and further down the hill.

Two methods have been used to enhance the reliability of the data sets in this study. First, the basis of the primary analysis is not survey data, but a set of excavation reports. Areal extent of occupation and phasing in a given site will be far more reliably determined in excavation than they can be in surface surveying. Adams repeatedly acknowledges this, but excavations in his area were, unfortunately for his purposes, concentrated in a few huge sites. Our excavation coverage is quite remarkable by comparison; see below. In essence, excavation reports from some 31 sites will be used instead of surface surveys to build up a regional picture. Second, survey data will only be used to supplement the regional picture built up by excavation report data. Both these steps will greatly facilitate the accuracy with which we are able to measure the amount and kind of error in the data sets with which we are dealing. Such evaluation of error, as we have seen, is essential to reliable data analyses.

The excavation reports
In this study, the data used consists of the following:

    a. site location by elevation and map reference points
    b. site size, by period

The first category of data is commonplace and needs no explanation. The second category of data, site size by period, had to be extracted from excavation reports which sometimes did not report on this kind of data per se. The method for determining site size by period when this information was not directly provided by the excavator was as follows: top plans were reviewed, and excavation areas noted. Phases containing 12th–6th century materials were located on the top plans. Phasing of encircling walls was noted and their areal extent calculated. In some cases, the entire extent of a given phase of encircling wall could not be traced; in these instances, I used the excavator's best guess as to the location of the wall in conjunction with the extent of Iron Age debris discovered through soundings in the excavated areas. If surveys or soundings outside the encircling walls or excavation areas were conducted, these data were included in the phase-by-phase analysis. In most cases, excavators provided a reasoned estimate of the areal extent of the community during each major phase. Where this was not the case, such information could be reconstructed directly from the top plans and descriptions of loci containing material dating to the period in question.

This approach is possible because a relatively large number of sites (30) have been excavated in a relatively small area (80 × 80 km). The number of excavated sites is actually higher than thirty, because only sites with materials dating to the 12th to 6th centuries BCE are included here. The survey data used in this study falls in an even smaller area, 60 × 60 km. Within this area are 22 excavated sites and 151 surveyed sites dating to the period between the 12th and 6th centuries BCE.

However, the present claims for comparatively good coverage of the major sites in the region under study should not be misconstrued as complete coverage. Hebron and Bethlehem are sites that a complete analysis should include, but, regrettably, extensive modern occupation precludes the precise location of the ancient remains. Many of the sites in our region are more heavily settled now than they were in ancient times. Nevertheless, the data which are available for the region under study are, compared to most regions in the world, remarkably and perhaps uniquely complete.

Random error in excavation report measurements is as follows. Accuracy in elevation measurements is 12.5 meters, since for some of the measurements I had to locate the site on a topographic map with 25-meter contour intervals and determine the elevation by proximity to the nearest contour line. Accuracy in map reference points is 0.5 kilometers. In most cases, the map references were given by excavators to four digit accuracy, but in some cases only three digits were given. Since we may assume that the map references were rounded to the nearest kilometer in these cases, 0.5 km is on the conservative (large) side of the estimate of random error here.

Random error in dating is 25 years for excavation reports. Excavators most often discussed phasing in terms of quarter-centuries; however, the dates for ceramic horizons on which such discussions are based are all rounded off to the nearest century. The conservative approach, therefore, is to acknowledge the accuracy of excavation reports as falling within a 25-year span on either side of the excavator's estimate (a 50-year spread). When the dates given in the original excavation report have been corrected by later evaluation or re-excavation, I have utilized the figures from the most up-to-date research (see the Bibliography of Sites).

Finally, random error in site size is due to two causes, which must be added to one another to arrive at the total random error for site size. The first is measurement error, which must be conservatively estimated at 10% for all sites. I measured the areal extent of phases of sites by counting the number of grid squares fully filled by the site. Two half squares were counted as one filled; quarter-filled squares were counted together with three-quarter-filled squares as one square, and so on; then the area for all was added together. This method of measurement seemed the easiest and most accurate for irregularly shaped sites. Adams' method of estimating site size, namely by calculating the size of the smallest rectangle which would enclose the entire ovoid shape of the site, has not been adopted here. That system of measurement was expedient in his case because the error in areal extent estimates was a much greater source of error.

The second source of error in site size is the uncertainty of boundaries of the community. Several factors influence the estimate of error here. First, I am defining the 'boundaries of the community' as the permanently settled areas; seasonal settlements in hinterland areas are not included in measurements of the area of the permanently settled site. I assumed, unless soundings outside an encircling wall indicated otherwise, that the permanent residences of a community were all to be found within the encircling wall. Exceptions to this assumption are documented in the cases of 'lower city–acropolis' complexes; fortunately, in the one or two instances of this phenomenon in the Iron Age, the excavator conducted soundings to determine the extent of the lower city. I also assumed, unless soundings inside an encircling wall indicated otherwise, that all area inside an encircling wall was utilized for architectural structures. Again, there are exceptions to this assumption, but here also the excavators have attempted to estimate the amount of space not used during the appropriate phases.

The main difficulty of this kind in estimating site size was the determination of size of large sites (in our case, let us say seven or more hectares), which had entered a phase of partial habitation with disuse or only partial use of an encircling wall. The upper limit of habitable area in such cases was much larger than for small sites which never grew beyond a certain size. In such instances, the range of error increases, and the excavators themselves usually seemed to be at a loss to estimate areal extent of occupation for that phase. I estimated areal extent of those phases, if the excavator failed to do so, by reviewing the location of soundings reporting evidence of habitation from such phases and measuring the area enclosed by all such soundings and by the highest point in the vicinity of those soundings on the site.

Error due to these uncertainties may conservatively be estimated at 25%. In the vast majority of cases, the error is certainly much less, but I have averaged in those few cases where the uncertainty is very large, approaching 50% of the total site size, to arrive at the final estimate of error from these factors. The total estimate of random error in site size estimates is thus 35%. This amount of random error is not unacceptable given our sample size of 31 sites in the period and region under study here.

Since reported finds from stratigraphically excavated sites are recovered *in situ*, the major source of systematic error characteristic of areal size data from surveyed sites is eliminated here. The result of using only excavated sites for areal size estimates by phase has been a much higher resolution in phasing, an ability to measure the random error of areal size measurements with a relatively high degree of precision, and the elimination of the major source of systematic error from the analysis.

The results of many hours of scrutinizing top plans and hunting through excavation reports are presented with a brevity disproportionate to the labor that went into cataloguing them as Table 4: Settlement Size—by Century. The locations of these sites by map reference points is pictorially displayed through time in Maps 1–7. Sites of five hectares and larger in each century are named on the map for that century.

The survey reports
The surveyed area is as limited as it is because of the high temporal resolution demanded by the analytical techniques used here. Excavation reports can distinguish several strata in a single century. Several surveys could not be used in this case because they did not distinguish subphases within Iron 2. The survey used here, *Judaea, Samaria, and the Golan Archaeological Survey 1967–1968*, edited by M. Kochavi, distinguishes Iron 2 subphases in all areas except the Golan. Occasionally, the size of the site was given, and structures noted and drawn to scale. Also, not infrequently the location on the site on which sherds from a given period were scattered is noted. However, these data were collected too unsystematically to permit their use alongside the excavation report data here. This is not meant as a criticism of the surveyors: on the contrary, the intermittent presentation of data such as site size probably represents a laudable effort to report such data only where it was reliably ascertainable.

In the case of Kochavi's survey, the information consistently provided is: site location by elevation and map reference points, and a rough estimation of the number of sherds dating to a given period: 'scattered sherds', 'large quantity', or amount not specified indicating (I assume) an average quantity. In recording these data, I have coded 'large quantity' as 10, 'scattered sherds' as 0.5, and no specification of amount as 1. For the purpose of the analyses used here, however, I have treated the codes equally as indicating presence or absence of occupation. See Table 5: Occupied Sites from the 'Israelite' Period: Judaea, Samaria and Golan Survey.

The reasons for not utilizing quantities of sherds as an indicator of extent of occupation are several. First, clearing of hilltop sites to shallow bedrock for later building foundations is frequent in Palestinian sites, and tends to invert and confuse the strata. Earlier phases can be represented to a disproportionately high degree under such circumstances; a 'large quantity of sherds' from a given period will often reflect later site redeposition rather than earlier heavy inhabitation. Second, Redman and Watson have shown that in many sites very minimal surface scatters can belie heavy occupational strata below the surface (cited in Hodder and Orton 1976: 20). Thus, the data from the Kochavi *et al.* survey has been encoded to preserve detail in what they found, but in the present analysis this greater detail has not been utilized.

Presentation and Analysis of Data

In this segment we will look at the broad sweep of changes in three aspects of human settlement in 12th- to 6th-century Judah: population, settlement size, and land use. On the basis of the results of these analyses, I will propose a model of urban development and decline in Judah during the period under discussion, which can then be compared with models similarly generated from the two other kinds of data to be utilized later: public works and luxury items.

Population

Students of ancient societies have devoted much effort in recent years toward refining a formula for translating site size into population figures (see below under 'Land use' for references). At this point, however, I propose to temporarily postpone addressing this difficult problem and approach the question of population somewhat differently.

First, rather than attempt to quantify population size at this point, I will proceed on the more solid ground of looking at population shifts. The data we will use for this analysis are site size and total number of sites (see Charts 1-3). It is possible to arrive at values for changes in population size on the basis of site-size data even when population density is not known simply by assuming that whatever the constant (population density) was, it remained stable for that region over the period in question (12th–6th centuries). We recognize that population could also increase by increasing population density rather than expansion of settlement size or creation of new settlements, as seems to have been the case at Tell Beit Mirsim during our period (Albright 1943: 1, 25). However, changes in density of settlement are rarely noted in excavation reports, and when they are they are never quantified, so it is unfortunately not possible to include such data in the quantitative portion of our analysis. Such information will be included in discussions and synthesis where it is available.

We must use these two variables (site size and number of sites) in conjunction because either parameter alone will, under certain fairly common circumstances, produce misleading or false results. If we consider just the number of sites and conclude that as the number of sites rises the population must also be increasing, we would err in our conclusions if large urban centers were simultaneously shrinking. What we would be witnessing would not be a surge in population size but a dispersion of the population from urban centers to smaller but more numerous settlements. Likewise, focusing on site size alone tells us little about regional population: if an urban center, or even all urban centers, grow in size there still may be no overall growth in population if the smaller, dispersed settlements are shrinking. We will therefore need to constantly compare the two variables in order to trace population shifts.

The average size of an excavated site (Chart 1) is arrived at by dividing the total area enclosed by sites in a given period (Chart 3: Area in Excavated Sites, and the bottom line of Table 4: Settlement Size—by Century) by the number of sites occupied in that period. By 'area of sites occupied' I mean only the sites in our sample of 31. We cannot yet speak of real total populations, since we do not know precisely what percentage of the population of all sites is comprised by our sample. In this instance, we must be content to identify trends in the data.

The figures for Chart 2 (Number of Surveyed Sites) are, similarly, to be considered a sample whose relation to the overall population of sites is not precisely known. Adams was able to estimate the real population of sites by resurveying a small part of his survey area with ten times the intensity of the original survey in order to check how many sites had been missed in the first pass. He discovered that he had missed a quarter to a third of the sites, all of them very small and all close to larger mounds (Adams 1981: 40ff.). This incident demonstrates the value of conducting surveys in a statistically sensitive and systematic fashion. However, as with the excavated site sample, the information we do have is useful for identifying trends, which is our purpose here.

One further point must be made in our use of the survey data alongside the excavation data. The temporal resolution of the survey data is lower, but, more important, it is less even than the data from excavated sites. Excavators commonly discuss phasing in relation to 'centuries' because their control over the ceramic horizons of their sites is usually close enough to allow them to speak with such precision. In fact, upper and lower limits of habitation and destruction strata were plus or minus a few decades to a half-century in the majority of excavation reports since 1960. This precision is the fruit of close stratigraphic excavation, without which the present project would be impossible. Small-scale re-excavation of large, important sites in order to pin down the phasing with greater precision has been conducted on a broad enough scale to include many sites originally excavated prior to the 1960s in the survey of excavated sites.

However, data from areal surveys simply cannot provide such high precision. Lacking stratigraphy, they are almost completely dependent on ceramic horizons and small finds for dating phases of occupation. Another problem in comparing excavation data with survey data is that the two kinds of data are scaled differently, and, in the case of the survey data, the scaling is uneven.

To illustrate, consider Chart 2: Number of Surveyed Sites in Judah. At first glance one might conclude that the number of sites had not changed significantly from Iron 1 to Iron 2b. Such is not the case, however. The Iron 1 period in this particular survey includes the 12th and 11th centuries; Iron 2a is one century only, the 10th; Iron 2b is two centuries, the 9th and 8th; Iron 2c is one century, the 7th; and Iron 3 is three centuries, the 6th through the 4th. Since we cannot (and should not) assume that sites were continuously inhabited throughout these periods, and in fact we should assume the reverse, we can expect the number of sites found over a two-century period to be much higher than the number of sites found in a later, one-century expanse of time, within the same geographical area.

Turning again to Chart 2, we should say that the number of occupied sites rose very significantly in the Iron 2a period. Ninety-one sites were found which were occupied at some point in the two-century Iron 1 period, but 97 sites were found which were occupied within the 10th century alone. Likewise, we should say that the number of surveyed sites occupied in Judah during the Iron 2b period declined, in real terms, since 95 sites were found which were occupied at some point during this two-century expanse of time, but certainly not continuously throughout it. The increase in the number of sites in the Iron 2c period is the more striking because it is an increase which is reflected in only a century-long sample. Finally, the decrease in the Iron 3 period is the most striking of all, because such a small number of sites were found with materials dating to a relatively long stretch of time (see Albright's description in *Archaeology of Palestine*, pp. 141-43, and also Jer. 4.23ff.).

Because of the uncertainty in the exact temporal extent of the ceramic horizons involved, and because the precise lengths of occupation of sites within those periods are not known, I would hesitate to place a precise weighting value proportionate to the number of centuries comprised in each ceramically determined period on the values in the survey data table. For instance, it would be possible to multiply the number of sites in two-century expanses of time by one-half, and in three-century expanses of time by one-third, as a corrective to the scaling inconsistencies noted above. However, it may also be that a greater number of sites identified as representing a two-century time span may indeed represent more than one century's occupation, whether continuous or non-continuous. For our purposes it is not necessary to place a misleadingly precise value on weighting factors which are not so precisely ascertainable.

With these considerations in mind, let us now turn to the relation between our two parameters, average site size and number of surveyed sites. Using these two parameters we have nine possibilities, outlined in the following table.

		Number of Surveyed Sites		
		Increase	*Constant*	*Decrease*
SITE SIZE	Increase	increase	small increase	large diffusion
	Constant	small concentration	no change	small diffusion
	Decrease	large concentration	small decrease	decrease

Table 1. Regional Population Shifts

Note that implicit in the table is the notion of *change*. What we are scrutinizing are the shifts in population location and/or overall size through time. The kinds of shifts detectable through our data are as follows: the regional population can increase, decrease, diffuse away from centers to smaller sites in the hinterland, concentrate in major centers, or remain more or less constant. Population shifts in Judah from the 12th to 6th centuries may be described thus:

From Iron 1 to 2a	significant population increase
Iron 2a-b	significant concentration of population in urban centers
Iron 2b-c	significant population increase
Iron 2c-3	highly significant population decline

By making a few assumptions we can go a step further and make rough estimations of the size of these shifts. I shall, for the purpose of estimation, assume that population shifts are proportionate to shifts in total site size and number. Something approaching this assumption must be made in order to calculate the population of ancient settlements, but the simple assumption is almost certainly more correct on a regional level than it would be on the single site level, because the variations in population density from site to site (by as much as a factor of ten; see Adams 1981: 350) will be at least partially smoothed over a group of sites. Also, we are trying only to place a numerical value on trends, not to calculate numbers of actual people, so we are still not subjecting the data to any specific notion of population density. We need to assume only that, for our sample over time, the net population density remained roughly constant.

The reader is referred to Charts 2 and 3. Recalling our need to weight the number-of-site data according to the approximate length of time represented by the sample collected, we may say that the population increase from Iron 1 to Iron 2a was 25% or more; from Iron 2b to 2c it was 40% or more; and the decline from Iron 2c to Iron 3 was a disastrous 70% or more. From Iron 2a to 2b we see a concentration of population in settlements, so that the population shifts which followed would have occurred primarily in those centers. Note that we are not yet speaking of these central settlements as functional central places; the degree of functional centrality for these sites will be evaluated in light of further data. These figures, again, are only rough approximations, but they do give an idea of the scale and direction of population changes which were taking place during these periods in Judah.

Cornfeld (1976: 96) asserted that there was a population explosion in the 10th century, on the basis of the number of sites newly occupied from the previous period (12th–11th centuries) to the 10th century. Our data do not bear this out, as the following chart shows.

	Iron 2a	Iron 2b	Iron 2c	Iron 3
No. of Sites newly occupied	20	0	25	15
No. of Sites abandoned	14	2	2	92

In drawing his conclusion, Cornfeld neglects to consider the number of sites abandoned in addition to the number of sites newly occupied. The data for the 8th century—Iron 2c—reflect a much more significant net increase in the number of newly occupied sites than do the data for the 10th century.

We shall not stop at this point to discuss the import of these data for our overall study. Instead, these trends in population distribution will form the backdrop for our next analyses, in which we will look at regional urbanization development in Judah and at the city–hinterland relationships through time. Later, the population trends outlined here will be drawn into the explanatory framework that is the goal of these analyses.

Settlement size
In the next analysis we shall examine the development of communities classified according to size. There is no attempt

here to claim any social, political, or economic significance for the divisions according to size. Attempts to assert site centrality on the sole basis of site-size histograms have met with considerable disapproval (Adams 1981: 76; Renfrew 1982: 3). In this study the issue of site centrality will be addressed in light of a complex of factors rather than of size alone. The site-size divisions in this case are chosen simply as the clearest format for presenting the data. The divisions are fine enough to distinguish variations in development between sites grouped fairly roughly, so that trends at one end of the spectrum may be distinguished from trends at the other. Here, as previously, we are interested not in absolute values for the classes of data so much as in the direction and scope of trends through time.

Again it must be emphasized that the data in the charts grouped by site size represent an unknown portion of the entire population of sites. The major bias in the sample is in fact here revealed: fewer large sites are missing than small. At the large end of the scale, we can be fairly sure that not many sites of such magnitude are absent from our database. On the small side of the scale, dozens of sites are missing, to judge from the survey we are using elsewhere in this study. This conclusion is supported by the results of Adams' resurvey as well (see above). Most of the sites in the survey data should be placed somewhere in the left half of the charts. Again, however, since no attempt is being made here to determine the size of sites which have not been excavated, they have not been included in the data at this point.

For this discussion two sets of charts are provided, Chart 4: Percentage Area by Site Category, and Chart 5: Area vs Rank, on double-log scales. Let us begin with the 'Percentage Area' charts, since in their case what is being portrayed is self-explanatory. In the case of the 12th-century chart, the bars corresponding to percentage area for each size category approximate the shape of a bell curve. This is misleading. Actually, as was mentioned earlier, many real values are missing from the left side of our chart, and perhaps the more so the farther left one goes; hence, the real picture should look more like a straight line descending from left to right, or perhaps even the left half of an upward-opening parabola.

The 11th-century figures show no significant variation from the 12th-century chart. A noticeable shift occurs in the 10th century, where a decided jump in the percentage of area comprised by the largest sites occurs. In the 9th century, there is again little change; the three largest categories still comprise c. 70% of the total percentage. The only difference is that the area has shifted from 8-16 ha sites to 16+ ha sites; this shift is due to the areal growth of Jerusalem and the decline in size of Gezer in this century.

When we arrive at the 8th century, another pattern has emerged. The size categories now describe an upward sweep to the right. This pattern becomes slightly more pronounced in the 7th century, and in the 6th century all large sites in our sample are abandoned.

We can summarize these trends as follows: an initial stage, which could be characterized by balance between sites of intermediate size, was followed by an increasing predominance of larger and larger sites (cf. Kempinski 1977: 147). Initially, this growth was seen in sites ranging in size from 4 to 16 ha. By the 8th century, the percentage of size in the 4–16 ha categories began to decline, and this decline continued throughout the rest of the period under examination. Meanwhile, the largest-size category increased in percentage to over 50% of the total area in excavated sites in our sample in the 7th century, then was largely abandoned along with the other large sites in the sixth century.

The only site in our sample for which the largest-size category has been claimed is Jerusalem. This site dominates our statistics from the 8th century onward, and it had a pre-eminent place even earlier. Its rise seems to have coincided with a decline in importance, in our statistics at any rate, of the larger intermediate-sized sites in Judah. This phenomenon is well-enough attested from other societies to be classified and described:

> As was initially pointed out by Ziph (1949), advanced industrial nations tend to be characterized by a 'rank-size rule' in which, if the cities of a region or country are arranged in order of size, the largest will be about twice as large as the next largest, ten times as large as the tenth largest, and so on. Plotting population against rank on double-log paper, systems of cities that follow

this rule will describe a straight line with a downward slope of forty-five degrees. The existence of a harmonic progression of this kind, termed a log-normal distribution, generally is thought to reflect a condition of regional balance dominated by neither the center nor the peripheries...

Urban 'primacy' is a feature said to obtain when the rank-size graph is concave instead of straight, or in particular when the largest city rises well above the general slope to which the lesser cities and towns conform (Adams 1981: 72-73).

A version of the plot Adams describes has been produced from our data for the 12th–6th centuries as Chart 5. Two points must be noted. First, because of limitations of the software on which the charts were reproduced, the length of the X and Y scales is not equal. Thus the angle of the line drawn between corners is not 45° in this case. However, the plot should parallel the line drawn from equally scaled (though in this case not equidistant from 0) points, which is the case in our graph. Second, the plot is not population vs rank but area vs rank. Unlike the previous analysis of population shifts, we cannot here assume a directly proportionate relationship between area and population, because here we are considering individual sites, not overall populations. While population density is a notoriously difficult variable to characterize from situation to situation, one regularity we may expect is that, as the size of the site increases, population density may increase. Larger sites tend to be more crowded (see the very informative chart cited in Adams 1981: 350).

The effect this latter point has on our plots is to create a 'bubble' above the line drawn on the diagonal between the extreme ends of the X and Y axes. If we were to correct for this bias, the smaller sites would move left and the larger sites right. Again, the smaller sites are almost certainly incorrectly ranked, since they have not been as fully excavated as the larger sites and therefore are not well represented in our sample. The visual effect would be to accentuate the concavity in the larger intermediate sites for the 9th–7th centuries, and to move Jerusalem even farther right relative to the other points plotted on the graph. This fact may point out another documented feature of primate sites, namely their relationship to the intermediate-sized sites:

> Berry (1961) has... found two major types of relationship, the one corresponding to the rank-size rule, and the other being a 'primate' relationship in which there are deficiencies of intermediate sizes so that one or two very large settlements dominate the distribution (Clarke 1977: 74).

We have already noticed a correspondence between the growth of Jerusalem and the contemporaneous decline in area in the next smaller arbitrary category of sites. The plots in Chart 5 illustrate the development of Judean settlement from a rank-sized pattern in Iron 1 through Jerusalemite urban primacy in the 8th–7th centuries followed by collapse in the 6th. We shall treat these observations as further data to be accounted for and included in our explanatory model alongside the population trend data discussed above and the land use data, to which we now turn.

Land use
Variations in the number and size of settlements, and trends in population growth/decline, can also be pictured graphically in such a way as to indicate the impact that these variables can have on land use. In order to facilitate our interpretation of such graphic representations of land use, we shall first perform a nearest-neighbor analysis. This analysis will enable us to characterize broadly the clustering or relative evenness of the settlement pattern in our region of study through time.

Nearest-neighbor analysis. Nearest-neighbor analysis tests a distribution of points on a map to determine whether they tend to cluster, are distributed randomly, or are distributed regularly. The most clustered distribution would consist of all points on a single spot; the most regular distribution would consist of all points at the vertices of equilateral triangles, i.e. equidistant from one another.

This type of analysis can aid an examination of land use as follows. Cristaller's model predicts that if all the land in a given area is optimally utilized by the sites in that area, that is, if all sites are provided with equal access to goods and services, they will be distributed evenly across the area (Hodder and Orton 1976: 56, citing Cristaller 1933: 33). If the sites are tiered according to function (goods and services provided), then sites of a given tier will be arranged in the same, regular, triangular-shaped lattice. Nearest-neighbor analysis enables the investigator to determine how closely a given distribution of sites on a map approximates the theoretically optimal distribution. Close approximation to the theoretical optimum can be interpreted in terms of a high degree of social organization, competition for goods, services, access to trade routes, and the like (Hodder and Orton 1976: 54-55).

Such analysis makes assumptions about environment which do not occur naturally in the archeological setting, e.g. a smooth geographical landscape. Sites organized linearily along rivers do not lend themselves to nearest-neighbor analysis (Zagarell 1982). In our case, the unsuitability of large tracts of land for settlement due to a dearth of reliable water sources, soil infertility and extremity of topography mean that the surveyed area, all of which is nominally available for settlement, is in all likelihood many times larger that the de facto available settlement area.

Just as difficult a feature of the archeological landscape is the problem of sites that are missing, whether through destruction or through simple oversight in the survey process (Hodder and Orton 1976: 53-54). Sampling techniques, coupled with an investigation into the causes of possible site destruction in the area to be surveyed, can overcome this obstacle. However, this type of data is not available in the present case.

We must interpret the values of the statistics we produce in light of these limitations. We can partially compensate for some factors influencing the results, but our compensations must in many cases be rough estimates, as will be seen. However, many sample disturbances can be to a large degree factored out simply by comparing changes in the statistics from one period to the next rather than focusing on the absolute values of the statistics. An increase in the statistic through time would suggest some pressure on the society under study to increasingly optimize the available geographical area, and so on. We shall certainly consider this dimension of the evidence in our interpretation.

A final factor which risks undermining the accuracy of our settlement statistics in this case is one mentioned earlier in

another context, namely the problem of variable length in the
ceramic periods used as the chronological framework for the
survey. Sites dated to ceramic horizons which cover a longer
period may have been occupied at any point within that time;
a shorter ceramic horizon systematically decreases the likelihood of site discovery for that period (see also above). In this
case it is possible to factor out this bias by considering the rate
of site occupation and abandonment during the periods in
question. The reader is invited to consider again the following
chart, utilized above in a different context:

	Iron 2a	Iron 2b	Iron 2c	Iron 3
No. of Sites newly occupied	20	0	25	15
No. of Sites abandoned	14	2	2	92

(The Iron 1 period does not appear because it was used as the
baseline.)

The rate of site settlement in the Iron 2a and 2c periods would
lead to a net increase of 6 sites per century in the 2a period and
23 in the 2c period, with 2b remaining stable. These figures, 6
for 2a and 23 for 2c, have been added to the number of surveyed sites for their respective periods so that the data for each
period will not be biased by the variable lengths of the ceramically determined chronological framework, *solely as a corrective to the statistic*. The figures are placed inside parenthe-
ses to show that they have been corrected for bias as described
above.

Having armed ourselves against these several sources of
error, we may consider the data. A catalogue of sites occupied
in the Iron 1 to Iron 3 periods south of map reference 1450 and
their nearest neighbors is given in Table 6. For each site, the
distance in kilometers to the nearest neighbor is given for each
period in which the site yielded ceramic evidence. Also, the
survey code of the nearest-neighbor site is given. Sites at less
than 400 meters distance were eliminated from consideration
as possible duplications. Missing values are due to an absence
of ceramic evidence from a site during that period.

The nearest-neighbor catalogue was produced via a computer program I wrote in Ashton-Tate's *dBASE III+* pro-
gramming code. Distances between sites were calculated by
triangulation using the map reference points given in the

Judea–Samaria–Golan survey of Kochavi *et al.* (1972). The nearest neighbor in each case was determined by calculating the distances between a site and all contemporaneous sites and encoding the closest one as the nearest neighbor. This process was repeated for all sites in all periods in which there was ceramic evidence for occupation. The program required approximately six hours to run. The map reference points are given to the nearest 100 meters (a tenth of a kilometer) in that survey, so that is given as the precision of our data and the nearest-neighbor calculations as well. A copy of this *dBASE III+* progam is provided in Table 7. The average distance between sites (r in Table 3) should be compared with Kochavi's own calculation: 'the average distance between sites of the Israelite period in the Hill country south of Hebron' is 3 km (1974: 2). If Kochavi is correct, the average distance between sites north of Hebron and south of Jerusalem must be smaller to bring the overall average down. Perhaps this is natural, since the land becomes rapidly more arid as one moves south in this region.

The nearest-neighbor statistics in Table 3 describe, first, a striking degree of nucleation of settlement in all periods. The statistic varies from 0 to just over 2; values approaching 0 reflect a high degree of clustering; values close to 1 describe a random distribution; and values approaching 2 approximate the most regular pattern (triangular lattice). Given the total area of the survey south of map reference 1450 (2,000 sq. km), c. 100 randomly distributed sites would, on average, be separated by 10 km. The survey data show sites on average as being separated by one-fifth this amount.

Several environmental factors, already mentioned, almost certainly contribute to this pattern of nucleation. Settlements may be seen as making intensive use of small, localized regions of favorable access to water, arable land, trade routes and defensive positions. Given the scarcity of reliable water, marginality of rain for dry-farming and the extremity of the topography in the region under study, large tracts of the region could be said to be unfavorable for settlement. Social factors could also have contributed to the pattern of nucleation; customs of both land tenure and marriage could be imagined that would lead to 'budding' of new sites at a fairly short distance over time and that ultimately could contribute to the pattern of nucleation present in our data. Biases in the manner in which the survey was undertaken could also have contributed; as was mentioned earlier, no attempt was made to gather a truly random sample in the survey used here.

Two shifts in the nearest-neighbor statistic also attract our notice. First, the statistic increases 50% from Iron 2b to Iron 2c; this shift suggests a significant increase in pressure to utilize land in areas apparently not previously considered to be of optimal habitability. Given the stability in the statistic for previous periods, this shift is somewhat dramatic. Just as dramatic is the sharp decline in the statistic in the final period, possibly reflecting a very large drop in pressure to maximize land use. Also, the degree of settlement clustering is all the more striking for this period (Iron 3), as the average distance between sites which were settled during this period rose comparatively slightly to 2.8 km, while the probabilistically expected distance leapt to over 25 km.

Land use around excavated sites. Once we know the size of sites in a region through excavation, we can pictorially approximate the extent of land use around those sites. We accomplish this by estimating the number of inhabitants of a site, then multiplying this estimate by a figure approximating the amount of land needed to sustain each inhabitant in order to to arrive at an area of land needed to sustain the entire settlement at the given size. This procedure enables us to draw a circle around every settlement with an area equal to our estimate of the amount of land needed to sustain each site's estimated population, thus producing a regional map showing intensity of land use.

I became acquainted with the procedure just outlined through its use by Adams (1981), who used 125 persons per hectare as the population-density constant, and 1.5 hectares per person as the constant for land needed to sustain each inhabitant of a settlement. I recognize the very problematic nature of each of these estimates (see the fairly extensive literature on these narrow questions cited in Shiloh 1980, Adams 1981, and Frick 1986) and also the fair degree of consensus which seems to be crystallizing around these figures as satisfactory rough approximations.

For the present purposes I will use the 125 person/hectare estimate in order to facilitate comparison between Adams' results for Iraq and those shown here for Judah. However, the estimate of 1.5 hectares per person is far too low for Judah, for several reasons. First, the unpredictability of rainfall and drought in Judah in comparison to the riverine-based cultivation system of Mesopotamia would have increased both the need for storage and the rate of loss from stored goods very drastically. Second, topsoil replenishment through flooding and silt deposition, unknown in our region, was the rule in Adams'; the fallowing system had to be concomitantly more extensive, and even so loss through erosion was greater in our region. In either case, the quotient of land needed per inhabitant would be influenced upwards. Third, as was mentioned earlier, the extreme topography of Judah in comparison to Adams' region would have rendered significant tracts of land within a circle drawn around many Judean settlements unusable for agriculture. Again, this difference has the effect of increasing the area around a settlement needed to provide an adequate amount of land per inhabitant. I have estimated the effects of these differences between Adams' regime and mine conservatively at 33%, and have thus utilized a quotient of 2 full hectares per person to calculate the area of land needed around Judean settlements.

The regional maps thus generated by period are shown in Maps 8-12. Adams' maps (1981: 90-92, 181, figs. 22-24, 36) show a vastly more extensive utilization of land by larger settlements in his region, with many more sites overlapping in their land utilization; that is, the radii calculated for land utilization are more often greater than the distance between sites in Mesopotamia than in Judah. I suspect that part of this disparity may be due to an underestimate on my part of the discrepancy between Judean and Mesopotamian agricultural productivity. However, it is almost certainly the case that the perceived discrepancy is due to ecological and societal forces as well. The scale of the largest Mesopotamian cities is approximately an order of magnitude greater than that of a similar number of the largest Judean towns in a distribution ranked by site size (Adams 1981: 142, Table 13, and 194, Table 19).

However, we should also recall the implications of our nearest-neighbor analysis at this point: Judean sites in all periods tended to be extremely nucleated in distribution. It is still possible that local Judean environments were as extensively exploited, and local economies as linked, as their Mesopotamian counterparts were, at least for some periods. The areal extent and chronological duration of these increases in pressure on local environments and economies to produce can be seen in the maps of land use.

Several dimensions of the settlement patterns in this region, and the transformations which occurred to those patterns during the period in question, have been articulated thus far. We may now begin to synthesize these results into a preliminary model of regional development and centralization. This, in turn, will enable us to draw some preliminary conclusions regarding the extent, nature and development of administrative control in this region during the period in question.

Synthesis

Summary
The results of the foregoing analyses of settlements may be summarized as follows:

1. *Population shifts.* During the first three centuries of the Iron Age period, population in the region grew fairly slowly overall. The 25% increase from the first two centuries (12th and 11th) to the third (10th) was followed by a redistribution of population in the 10th century to the 9th, tending to concentrate populations in larger settlements (cf. Kempinski and Fritz 1977: 147). Following this redistribution, the rate of population increase nearly doubled over the next two centuries, to 40%. Finally, in by far the most sudden shift of all, the population decreased dramatically, by 70%, over the course of a single century, i.e. from the 7th to the 6th.

2. *Configurations of settlement size.* During the 12th and 11th centuries, the configuration of site sizes seemed to approximate most closely the rank-size model, in which a fairly even gradient in settlement sizes from largest to small-

est is observed. In the 10th century, the area comprised by the largest sites began to increase in proportion to the area comprised by the other site-size categories. This increase in the proportion of area comprised by the largest site-size categories continued until the 7th–6th century boundary, when the largest site-size categories disappeared suddenly and altogether. Meanwhile, beginning perhaps as early as the 9th century but certainly by the 8th, the number of intermediate-sized sites entered a period of decline, never to recover during our period of study. The combination of increase in large site-size categories coupled with a decrease in intermediate site-size categories produced a configuration of settlement sizes which fits best with the primate model, Jerusalem being the primate site in the region surrounded by many smaller sites. The primate model implies that the smaller sites could not have competed with Jerusalem in range and number of central functions.

It was also observed that, in terms of scale, settlements in our region of study occupied site-size categories approximately one order of magnitude smaller than those in Mesopotamia in Adams' study. In other words, the entire settlement pattern is scaled approximately ten times smaller than that occurring in Mesopotamia during roughly the same period of time.

3. *Land use.* Nearest-neighbor analysis revealed a strong tendency toward nucleation of settlement in our region of study. This tendency appeared to remain fairly constant, except during the 7th century, when the clustering pattern lessened. This datum suggests that during the 7th century there was a significant increase in pressure on the society to utilize more land for settlement. Analysis of radii of land required to sustain the estimated population of sites suggests that the nucleation pattern revealed by nearest-neighbor analysis resulted from extremity of topography and a dearth of reliable water sources in the region of study, rendering large tracts of land unsuitable for long-term settlement.

*Preliminary model of regional development
and centralization*

This model is preliminary because of the already observed dangers inherent in constructing such models on the basis of any one kind of data alone. Features of the model will remain to be tested against the public works and luxury items data. At the same time, it is essential to expand our working model in order to be able to generate meaningful hypotheses predicting the values of the key variables mentioned earlier under the changing conditions observed in our data. This will now be attempted.

We have been paying particular attention in our analyses thus far to *shifts in patterns in the data through time*. In the development of this model, it will be seen that, again, shifts from one period to the next bear the primary explanatory burden. At the same time, the proposed models for the explanation of settlement patterns derive significance from 'static', as it were, configurations of settlement data. The rank-size and primate models are examples of this.

For the first two centuries of the Iron Age, then, the data investigated thus far best fit the rank-size model on a small scale, with population growth that is slow in comparison with later rates in the same region. These values for population growth and settlement-size distribution constitute the baseline for later shifts in the settlement data. It is in any case not possible to explain either feature (slow population growth and fairly smooth gradient of site-size categories) without looking even further back to see what this pattern itself developed from. I would guess that the 12th to 10th centuries were characterized by a degree of comparative stability, to judge from the low levels of change (compared to later periods) in the variables assessed, over a significant period of time—two centuries.

The concentration of population apparent in comparisons of data from the 10th century to the 9th into relatively fewer settlements may be at least partly a response to the steady growth in population seen in the preceding period. The significant (25%) increase in population over the preceding period would have stressed, to some degree, the social and technological systems set up to exploit the local ecosystem. If a population increases within a region, and there are no offsetting factors such as technological advancement to increase production and the amount and/or availability of wealth, then the same resources must be shared among more people.

The reorganization of population into relatively fewer settlements seems to have been at least a short-term success, to judge from the near doubling in the rate of population increase over the next two centuries (8th–7th). Such an increase is diagnostic of significantly improved exploitation of local resources, and probably also a marked extension of access to wealth to a supraregional level through trade. Such trade may well have occurred at earlier periods, but during this period it is more likely to have become a significant, integral, and necessary part of the economy.

During this period, Jerusalem emerged as a primate urban state. Concentration of key functions of all kinds in Jerusalem, e.g. administrative, religious, and economic, would be strongly suspected even on the basis of the settlement data alone. Again, this further concentration of resources and functions was probably a necessary societal adaptation to the highly significant increase in population growth seen during this two-century period. Along with wealth, due both to local production and to increased foreign trade, social stratification would also have increased.

This assessment of the centrality of Jerusalem may be further strengthened by reference to the final period considered in our study, the 6th century. The diagnosis here is complete societal collapse. The tendency has been to attribute this collapse to a military strategy employed by the neo-Babylonian empire, namely deportation of population. However, the nature of the local ecosystem and the particular societal adaptation to that ecosystem at the time of the collapse has not been adequately assessed in evaluating the causes and especially the extent of the collapse. If our earlier assessment that the socioeconomic adaptations of increasing centralization were necessary to sustain levels of production adequate to the size and rate of growth of the regional population, then it would only have been necessary to kill or exile members of the controlling elite to sweep away the control and redistribution systems necessary to sustain the larger population. The popu-

lation left behind would have been too large to survive at anything like its pre-existing size, bereft as it was of access to
wealth through trade and administratively enforced levels of
production, both of which had only been possible under the
centralized system. Limitations of various kinds in the
regional ecosystem would then have, over the course of years,
forced population levels back down to earlier levels through
famine or 'voluntary' movement of people to other regions
entirely. In either case, the overburdened local ecosystem
completed the societal destruction catalyzed by the neo-Babylonian removal of the administrative control systems developed over centuries in order to sustain higher and higher
levels of productivity in that region.

Extent, nature and development of administrative control
Thus far, we have utilized settlement data to develop a model
that tentatively explains shifts in population size and concentration seen in our data. The model will now be used to formulate hypotheses about institutions of administrative control
which would be most congruent with the diachronic social
processes outlined in the model.

Again, the period of the 12th–10th centuries functions primarily to establish the baseline from which to evaluate later
periods; and again, without access to the antecedent state
which produced the societal parameters in this period, it is not
possible to assess fully the question of administrative control
systems in this context. However, it may be fair to observe that,
if our assessment of societal change during this period is correct, there is no evidence of strong pressure to modify or
enhance existing administrative controls during the period.
The level of growth and lack of concentration of population at
this time calls not so much for increasing administrative control as for stability in pre-existing administrative systems,
whatever those were. Likewise, the lack of drastic change
over the relatively long period suggests no significant changes
in administrative control systems to enhance agricultural
production or security in response to other forces, whether
from outside the society or within. Given our assumption of
weak (in comparison to urban varieties) and dispersed

administrative controls, there is no reason to posit scribal institutions of any kind for Israel during this period.

Somewhat surprisingly, the next period also offers little in the way of evidence for significantly enhanced administrative control systems. The primary adaptation in this period seems to have been the concentration of population; this concentration, as we argued earlier, actually facilitates administrative control in and of itself. To the extent that population concentration was a successful adaptation, it would have minimized pressure for increasingly powerful administrative systems by facilitating increased control over the means of production via other means, namely, the concentration of the population. Of course, it is necessary to posit some kind of pressure in order to account for the concentration of population itself; however, this concentration need not have been deliberately contrived by the elite. In fact, this is highly unlikely since it would have required a high degree of control which was not possible precisely because the population was previously so dispersed. A more natural explanation is that the population concentration resulted from other forces and was then increasingly exploited by the elite as time passed and mechanisms for control were developed in light of the new situation. What these 'other forces' might have been is not clear from the settlement data themselves.

Mendenhall (1975) has expressed the conviction that the presence of a 'cadre' (1975: 160) of professional scribes was 'required' by the middle of the tenth century. He argues that the ideological basis for the Israelite abhorrence of Canaanite urban administrative control systems was eroded under Saul and swept away finally by David, who needed Canaanite administrative expertise to establish his empire. Mendenhall bases this case primarily on textual evidence, though he also asserts that the archeological record supports his reconstruction (he does not say precisely how). At this point I am most interested in allowing the archeologically based model to speak for itself, so the fuller discussion of this problem must be postponed until a clearer picture arises from further analyses of the archeological data.

I am prepared, however, to offer an alternative reconstruction at this point in order to keep the possibilities open. The questions may be asked: how successful was David in his empire building? And what part did religious ideology play in his success, such as it was? Military victories in and of themselves do not establish enduring states. David's successes in the field merely created the possibility for further administrative consolidation; they by no means required it. Evidence that he failed, or never attempted to set up administrative structures to the extent that has been claimed, may be seen in the political and religious fragmentation which ensued upon his son's death. That fragmentation does not support Mendenhall's contention that David successfully adapted a proven administrative system as the basis for the nascent Israelite state.

I believe it would be easy to furnish evidence for this alternative from biblical texts, for example, David's failed attempt to take a census in 2 Samuel 24; his decision not to build a temple may also relate to this question, insofar as temples are key institutions for economic redistribution and exaction of agricultural 'taxes' from producers by the elite. The short-term success David did enjoy can be explained naturally by his abilities to catalyze widespread support on ideological grounds, personal charisma, and military skill. Far from completing the ideological 'sell-out' begun under Saul, David may have achieved his wide base of support precisely because among other things he reversed the trend toward secularization begun by Samuel's time and accelerated under Saul.

In addition, the Jebusite bureaucracy was, as Mendenhall himself has noted, completely unequipped to handle administrative matters for a region the size of David's conquests. Jebus had been merely the stronghold of a local feudal lord, having some administrative controls but not enough to qualify it as an urban center. Its military value is clear, as is its location as a potential political center for the disunified tribes of the north and south; but why its puny administration should have appeared irresistible to David despite the possibly dangerous political and ideological handicaps it posed for him is not clear.

In short, the textual data allow a range of quite different reconstructions of the development of administrative control during this period. I suspect that Jebus's tiny administrative setup was targeted for explanatory exploitation by Mendenhall and a generation of other scholars partly for the same reason that Mallory climbed Everest: because it was there. At the very least it is justifiable to leave open in the present study the question of the extent to which David followed up his military and political campaigns with extensive administrative consolidation, for which both direct and indirect textual evidence is ambiguous. The archeological data may enable us to speak to this issue from a fresh awareness of the social matrix in which such institutions are always embedded.

Returning to our data, the first clear indication of increased administrative control appears in the next period, when a very large increase in the rate of population growth strongly indicates, indeed virtually demands, a material enhancement in administrative control systems. This would be true even if the development had occurred over a number of larger sites, but in the present instance enormous growth occurred in one site, Jerusalem, eclipsing all former settlement centers. On the basis of this development, we would envision a significantly increased pressure on administrative systems in Jerusalem to expand and broaden their functions. With the decline in intermediate-sized sites we would expect to see a concomitant diminishment in the range of functions required of their administrative systems, and a withering away of such controls outside of Jerusalem, further increasing its administrative burden. In the remaining smaller sites, administrative representatives of the centralized Jerusalemite bureaucracy would manage local administrative functions as part of a regional administrative network, the authority of which extended more and more exclusively from Jerusalem. This administrative dependence on Jerusalem is brought into sharp focus by the failure of the regional system to recreate a center in any other location, despite the presence of at least a significant percentage of the 7th-century population, following the fall of Jerusalem. This failure doomed the remaining population to further decimation.

Turning to the more particular questions of professional scribes and scribal schools, the evidence thus far indicates that little new pressure existed to create a system of professional scribes or administrators prior to the ninth century. Following this time, if professional administrators were systematically trained in an established training center, the training would most likely have occurred in Jerusalem alone. A training center in another locale might have provided another population center with an indigenous group of professional administrators to carry on after the fall of Jerusalem; but there is no evidence for this. Certainly, other settlements besides Jerusalem were militarily reduced during the first decades of the sixth century, raising the possibility that local 'schools' for the training of professional administrative personnel could have been destroyed. However, this is not as likely a scenario as that of a solitary center for such training in Jerusalem, for two reasons. First, the primacy of Jerusalem in the settlement pattern bespeaks a high concentration of regional control over the broadest possible range of functions in that locale, and reduces the need for local training centers. Second, the very 'success' of the neo-Babylonian 'sweep' of the elite class and their professional dependents suggests that the administrative professionals were relatively easy targets. Had they been better dispersed, it would have been far more likely that a critical mass of leadership could have survived to re-establish, however minimally, some of the institutions which originally enabled the local population to develop and grow as it did. Again, however, the absence of any clues that such leadership continued suggests that the centralization of all such functions in Jerusalem is the most workable hypothesis, on the basis of the data reviewed thus far.

Having articulated our model in terms of settlement patterns, we are now in a position to test these results against analyses based on the next data set, public works.

Chapter 3

PUBLIC WORKS

Approach

Introduction
Public works appear to be a key indicator of higher-level administrative control systems. This type of archeological remains appears as a key element in most of the polythetic classification lists for both chiefdoms (Flanagan 1981: 51-52; Peebles and Kus 1977: 431-32; Frick 1987: 33ff.) and states (Frick 1977: 10; Renfrew 1973: 90; Flannery 1972: 404; Childe 1950: 3ff.). The location of public works in these lists is due to their supposed correlation with increasingly high levels of centralized social organization (Trigger 1974: 100).

In this chapter, 'public works' will be defined for the purposes of the present study. Archeologically recoverable aspects of three kinds of public works, namely fortifications, water systems and public buildings, will be specified. Problems relating to the recovery of such data and to the ability of these data to address the questions at hand will be discussed, and the data will be presented. Finally, the results of the analysis of public works data for the period and area in question will be set forth and integrated with the foregoing analysis of settlement patterns. Further preliminary conclusions regarding institutions of administrative control will then be drawn.

Definition of public works
It would be difficult indeed to propose a theoretical definition of the distinction between 'public' and 'private' which would be defensible on all fronts. The definition provided here will be functional and minimalist, designed to meet the needs of the present study only. This definition will assume the form of a

series of criteria that will be used to determine whether a particular architectural artifact may be included in our data as 'public'.

To meet the needs of the present study, the criteria for designating architectural artifacts as public speak to the issues of the nature and extent of administrative control in two distinct ways. First, architectural artifacts reflect the administrative control systems which produced them by manifesting evidence of concentration of labor and natural resources (Price 1978: 165). Frick's comment on Price's contention is that the major expenditure of energy in ancient Israel was clearly agricultural and not monumental public works (1987: 35). Frick goes on to show how the need to manage development of ecological resources indeed contributed to the structural development of social control mechanisms in ancient Israel (pp. 95ff.) However, Price's point is not that public works represent the greatest reservoir of energy expenditure by the society; rather it is that they manifest the ability of central authority to concentrate labor and resources. Energy spent on agriculture is far greater, but also more diffuse, and therefore is not as clear an indicator of the ability of central management systems to concentrate labor and resources.

Public works also reflect administrative control systems not only through their size but also through their function in the society, on both local and regional levels. Evidence for use of a central building as a redistribution center, for example, illustrates the extent of centralized control in a manner independent of the building's size, which only reflects the amount of energy which is 'fossilized' in it, to use Price's term. These two aspects of public works, size and function, bring different yet complementary dimensions of the question of administrative control into focus. Each of these two dimensions of public works, the 'input' and 'output' aspects if you will, can be illuminated by an associated set of archeologically recoverable variables. These variables, which reflect concentration of labor and resources and which we will document and analyze are: manner of construction, scale (size), and quality of workmanship. With respect to function, the variables we will review are first, location, and second, whether there is a concentration of artifacts possibly associated with administrative control:

weights, public documents, artifacts used to standardize commodity redistribution, etc. Each of these variables, and the parameters used to determine whether the values recovered for them qualify the architectural artifact they represent as 'public' for the purposes of this study, will be discussed separately.

Construction
Evidence for manner of construction can bring into focus several issues relating to concentration of labor and resources. How did the ability of the society to concentrate labor vary over the period in question? As was often the case when we analyzed the settlement data, shifts in patterns, in this case of labor concentration as indicated in the public works data, must be accounted for in any model of administrative control. Was this ability to concentrate labor centered in one or a few locales, or was it dispersed? If it was dispersed, was this due to extension of authority from a central source over a wide area, or to the presence of many local, autonomous administrative systems? The more centralized control systems are, and the larger the area over which they are extended, the larger the bureaucracy required to sustain them. This statement is simply a corollary of the emphasis on scale of many of the same variables for distinguishing higher levels of centralized control from lower (Flannery 1972: 412f.; Trigger 1974: 97). Finally, to what extent was the labor thus concentrated part of a trained, professional work force? Public works could be carried out by temporarily conscripted agricultural laborers under minimal 'professional' supervision, or they could be executed by full-time artisans. The development and training of a permanent full-time force of artisans and their continued supply and material support, would have required a far more extensive system of administrative control than would professional supervisors of temporary work forces or corvée labor (Flannery 1972: 406; Frick 1977: 13-14).

Several easily identifiable artifactual traits directly address these issues. *Scale* of the architectural remains is the most direct and obvious trait. 'Work' is defined as force applied over a distance; force, in turn, is directly proportionate to the mass

of the material moved. The most basic and obvious criterion
for definition of public works is therefore scale.

Four kinds of architectural remains are candidates for
classification as 'public' on the basis of scale: fortification walls
around settlements, buildings, water systems, and terraces. Of
these four, the first three, namely encircling walls, buildings
and water systems have routinely been the focus of archeological excavations; so much so that excavators are usually
careful to indicate where such remains were not found. This is
important, since a confirmed absence of such structures for a
particular period is just as valid a datum as presence. Evidence for terrace systems has not been recovered routinely as
is the case for the other three candidates, with the result that
data from too few sites evidencing them are available for
inclusion here. A further difficulty is that terrace systems are
virtually impossible to date with the resolution with which the
other kinds of public works can usually be dated. For these
reasons data on terraces cannot be considered in this study,
though it is recognized that a considerable degree of labor
went into their construction in the period in question (Frick
1987: 35ff.).

Encircling walls are often, though not always, datable with a
fairly high degree of confidence. Also, their dimensions can
often be fairly closely determined, even where they are not
exposed over their entire length, since their design depends to
a large degree on the local topography. However, their evi-
dentiary value is more problematic in periods when the excavator concludes that they were rebuilt. Given the limited expo-
sure of the walls in many cases, even when a rebuilt section is
found and dated it is difficult to know the extent of the rebuild
and, consequently, the amount of labor which was required for
the project. Therefore, the period in which an encircling wall
was founded will routinely be considered in the data. Data on
encircling wall rebuilds, however, will only be included when
the excavators have determined the extent of the rebuilding
operation.

Quality of execution must be considered alongside scale in
any assessment of the amount of labor which went into a particular building project. A less massive structure which was
artistically decorated and carefully executed may have

required more labor than a roughly executed larger structure. This factor has a bearing, then, on the amount of labor concentrated on particular building projects. Quality of workmanship can also aid our analysis in another way: it can directly reflect the presence of full-time artisans working on aspects of the project. This kind of evidence can be mined from excavation reports where these discuss construction methods and describe the quality of decorations. Again, both of these kinds of data are routinely reported on by excavators, which means that these data will be available for a sufficiently wide range of sites to represent adequately all the periods of time in our region.

In addition to enhancing our view of the kind and amount of labor which went into building projects, close assessments of quality of workmanship inform our understanding of administrative control systems on the regional level. When many construction projects occur more or less simultaneously in a region, within the temporal resolution of our data at least, it is sometimes noticed that a similar design for a particular kind of project seems to be reused in different settlements. The question arises: are these similarities due to a centrally controlled regional program of building, or are they the result of local imitation of a successful or popular design? This kind of information can potentially afford great insight into the degree of centralized control in a region during various periods, but determining whether a widespread building pattern is due to centralized control or local imitation can be difficult.

The precision with which the design is imitated, the quality of workmanship, and the nature of the site, whether newly constructed fort or previously inhabited settlement, can help make this determination. A project that precisely imitates a building design on several contemporary sites, is of good quality workmanship, and is located at settlements which would not on other grounds seem capable of executing such work utilizing local resources, may reliably be attributed to some kind of central authority. However, given these guidelines, some regional building programs will escape our notice if variations in local execution are sufficiently great that we cannot with confidence distinguish between them and local imitation. In the case of this variable, we will accept the judgment of the excavators, except where this judgment has been overturned in later discussion.

Function

In addition to scale and technique of construction, the function of public works in their societal context provides some of the most direct insight into the nature and degree of administrative control in a region over time. A key factor in determining whether a particular architectural installation is 'public' in its use is location on the settlement, whether the installation is a water system of some kind or a building.

The public areas of settlements in the ancient Near East were normally the gate of the settlement, where there was often open space in which both economic and legal transactions most frequently occurred, and the acropolis, where a fortress, residence of a local ruler, and/or shrine would usually be located, if any were present at the site. Thus, water installations which supplied the open space near the gate would normally be considered 'public' in their function. This would probably remain true even if the scale alone were not of sufficiently large size to designate the installation as public. Likewise, buildings on the acropolis are normally expected to be public in function. A further indication of the public nature of structures in these two locations is the tendency of artifacts which indicate high social status to be concentrated there; we will return to a fuller discussion of this question in the next chapter.

Summary

Public works are defined for the purposes of this study as architectural remains of sufficiently large scale or high-quality workmanship to reflect aspects of control of human energy in the society: the ability to concentrate it, and the nature of it (full-time professional or otherwise). Public works are also defined in terms of their function in use in the society, as determined not only by scale and quality of workmanship but also by their location within settlements and their distribution regionally. Through analysis of these two dimensions of public works the nature and extent of regional administrative control will be explored.

Approach to the data: limitations

At several points in the foregoing discussion it was noted that this or that type of data was 'routinely recorded'. One of the difficulties in working with a series of excavation reports that have varying goals and methods is that data are not collected in a uniform fashion. In some instances the excavator does not record the information because he or she has had no easy way of recovering it. It is always true, however, that excavators must select what they excavate, select even further what they choose to record, and select even more narrowly what is to be published. Secondary reuses of sets of such reports, insofar as they attempt to compare the data on a collective basis, are restricted to the 'least common denominator' of what is available through publication.

This situation posed no problem in the first chapter, since all excavation reports record at least the location of the site, the location of the fields of excavation on the site, the stratigraphy of the fields, and the dates of the strata. In this chapter and the next, however, the data we use will almost always be a compromise between what is needed to produce results characterized by high confidence-levels and what is available. To use an actual example, while some excavators may record the provenience of stone used to build walls or buildings at their site (e.g. Aharoni 1964: 52; Pritchard 1975: 448; Albright 1943: 15f., in the Bibliography of Sites), others do not. To calculate the actual amount of energy required to erect encircling walls, one would need to know the volume of material moved, the distance from which it was brought, and how much the material was 'worked' prior to installation. Yet the provenience of materials is generally not provided; the original height is never known, though it can sometimes be estimated (e.g. Yadin 1963: II, 323); and the way in which materials were worked prior to installation is recorded variably and subjectively, or was unavailable for recording (as when the only evidence available is a foundation trench).

The problem of variability in recording in the case of public works data will be treated as follows. The energy required to build structures will be discussed as if it were directly proportionate to the surface area, in square meters, covered by the structures. In the case of fortification walls that encircle entire settlements, this figure will be calculated by multiplying the circumference of the wall by its average width. For casemate walls, the width of the inner wall will be added to the width of the outer wall, and this sum will be multiplied by the circumference.

In the case of buildings within settlements, the figure will be the area of the surface between the walls. There is an apparent inconsistency in ascribing to walls energy in proportion to the area covered by a solid mass and to buildings energy in proportion to area covered by a roof. However, the design of buildings is more complex, possibly increasing the amount of energy going into them proportionate to their size. In order to relate buildings and walls to one another in terms of the energy going into their production, it seemed necessary to attempt somehow to take this factor into consideration. There may be more sophisticated ways of determining the comparative difficulty of building these two kinds of structures, but for the present the simplistic approach will serve.

Forts, which are here defined as defensive installations consisting of a perimeter wall with rooms built into the wall on the interior and with some open space within, are handled differently. The area of the perimeter wall is calculated as for encircling walls, and to this is added the portion of the interior space enclosed by interior walls. Forts, in other words, are too small to be considered settlements and too large to be considered buildings, so they are here treated as partaking of both. Existing structures converted to forts on previously occupied settlements are not considered 'forts' in this case; nor are settlements built on the plan referred to above but larger than 0.4 hectares. In both cases the perimeter wall will be handled routinely, as will any buildings qualifying as 'public' according to the parameters specified above.

Water installations will be treated in this chapter, but in a section separate from the other public works data. The patterns of design for each are so individual that no common basis for statistical analysis could be found, and the numbers of installations that are adequately documented are too small to classify and approach in groups. For example, digging a tunnel over 500 meters through solid rock from either end and meeting in the middle (Shiloh 1984: 40) may produce a tiny fraction of excavated rock in comparison with a reservoir; yet it would have required far more labor and almost certainly greater expertise. Volume of rock excavated, as well as an estimate of the engineering difficulties involved, will be discussed when the excavator has mentioned these variables.

Quality of workmanship will also be treated separately from the other public works data, because of the problems mentioned above, except in one case. The 'palace' at Ramat Rahel has preserved uniquely large quantities of artistically crafted stonework around the windows, at the roof line, and on the capitals (Aharoni 1962: 55f.). For this reason, the building (18 meters by 36 meters) was given an artificial energy 'value' by treating it as if it were twice its size. Again, this is a simplistic approach to the problem of estimating energy input; but it can be improved only when excavators better attuned to problems of engineering provide more complete information. In other cases it will be noted when stones were dressed before use, whether the masonry is ashlar or fieldstone, etc.; but no attempt will be made to reflect these factors artificially in the areal statistics.

Further limitations
The focus on area covered by public works is not ideal. These variables do not allow us to distinguish a low wall from one twice as high, though the amount of energy put into building the high wall may be many times as great. Another shortcoming is that structures produced from materials brought in from a great distance require more labor than structures built from local materials; but such data are not included here. Very few sites would be left to compare if only those sites for which such data are available were included in this study. In the case of public buildings and walls, the data which is almost always reported consists of overhead plans drawn to scale which enables us to determine the areal extent of the structures with a fairly high degree of precision. Remarks are sometimes also made about the manner of construction; such data will be used to help reconstruct a rough picture of the quality of labor concentrated on building projects.

The possibility of systematic error in the use of area as a measurement of energy must also be considered. The proce-

dure used in this study depends on an assumption of straight-
line increase, which can be stated thus: as the area covered by
structures increases, the energy required to produce them
increases in direct proportion. This assumption is surely
unwarranted. It seems far more likely that the energy
required to build structures would increase exponentially in
relation to the area covered by the structures. Engineering
problems such as material and design stresses, construction
problems such as raising stones to the top of a high wall where
a low wall requires no special handling, etc., make it inevitable
that additive increases in area of work are associated with
multiplicative increases in amount of energy required. However, the variables which create the error are in this case
complex beyond my ability to estimate on a case-by-case basis.
Substituting a different simple curve for the straight line we
currently have would serve to obscure matters rather than
increase the accuracy of the statistical descriptions. In this
instance, recognizing the problem when we begin to interpret
the statistics is preferable to manipulating the statistics without a secure basis for doing so.

A closely related problem is that of comparing the various
kinds of architectural remains such as encircling walls, public
buildings, and water systems. Although common units of
measurement are used for public buildings and for encircling
walls, both of which are measured in square meters in this
study, it is not possible simply to equate the amount of energy
expended on each on the basis of comparisons between the
square meters covered by each. Different architectural tasks
require different technical approaches, and, ideally, our analysis would reflect the comparative difficulties associated with
each. However, as was mentioned earlier, there is no realistic
way this can be accomplished; the study of it lies in another
area of expertise entirely and would be the object of a fairly
large research initiative in its own right.

The skewing effect of these factors may be confidently dealt
with as follows: we will avoid microanalyzing the data, since
small-scale shifts are likely to have been so influenced by this
factor as to be meaningless for our purposes. Percentage shifts
in areal measurements under 25% will be disregarded as not
statistically significant; percentage shifts higher than this will

be considered as significant enough to demand explanation. The larger the percentage shifts, the greater the confidence with which we may treat them.

Dating is a problem of a very different kind, but just as critical for our study in its own way. Dates for all kinds of architectural remains can be difficult to establish. In a few instances, known structures were not included in the statistics because they were not dated or could not be dated with a sufficient degree of precision (Stern 1975: 1025; Kochavi 1972: 50, 177). Resort is sometimes made to historical (usually biblical) records or to typological considerations in an attempt to pinpoint dates of construction and destruction more precisely (see below). For the present purposes, such dating techniques would introduce an unacceptable element of circularity in the final synthesis, which will attempt to bring together the independent witnesses of historically and archeologically based models, so they are not included here.

The concern about dating on the basis of corroboration with biblical texts has resulted in one significant change in the dating of materials considered in this study. Cross and Milik (1956) dated three forts (Tabaq, Samrah and Maqari) in the Judean foothills to the ninth century, despite the following facts: the material was not stratified, which led them to conclude that the forts were settled for only one occupational level; the material in them dated primarily to the 8th and 7th centuries, with some material as early as the 9th century and some as late as the 5th; absolutely no material dating to the 10th century or earlier was found. The building of the forts was attributed to Jehoshaphat, in the mid-9th century, partly because he was credited in the biblical record with building forts and because this interpretation does not conflict with the archeological evidence (1956: 16f.). However, this does not seem to be the best interpretation on the basis of the archeological evidence alone, and there is nothing in either the biblical record or the remains of the forts to connect them with Jehoshphat, other than rough chronological coincidence. It seems unusual that no 10th-century material whatever would have appeared in any of the forts if they were settled in the mid-9th, and the three-century single occupation phase also seems long. The archeological evidence alone would seem to point to a construction in the early-to-mid-eighth century. In the absence of more conclusive evidence tying these structures to Jehoshaphat, their founding date has been entered as the 8th century in the data used here.

A final problem is the absence of data for public buildings at Jerusalem. This vital information is currently preserved only in historical records rather than excavation reports. This information is too important to overlook, but it is also inappropriate simply to include this information alongside our other data in this instance given our desire to discuss the archeological remains separately from the written record (see the discussion in Chapter 1). I will address the written information in the concluding synthesis to be found at the end of Chapter 4, on luxury items, rather than include it here; final judgment on tenth-century building trends will therefore have to await the inclusion of this information at that later point.

With these concerns in mind, we may proceed to a consideration of the public works data.

Presentation and Analysis of Data

In the first section, we will consider the encircling wall and public building data. Then, the water systems data and the evidence for skilled artisanship will be considered and integrated with the more quantified building data. Concentration of labor will be mapped geographically through time. Finally, evidence for regional building patterns will be presented and discussed.

The areal coverage of encircling walls is provided in Table 9: Encircling Walls; areal coverage for buildings and forts is provided in Table 10: Public Buildings; combined area is given in Table 11: Encircling Walls and Public Buildings—Combined Area; and descriptions of manner of construction of all of these, plus data on water installations and evidence for skilled artisanship, are provided by period in Table 8: Public Works Catalogue. These data sheets constitute the statistical basis for the charts, graphs and maps to be discussed in this section. Our primary interest will be the intensity of shifts in the public works variables outlined above: scale, local concentration vs dispersion, quality of craftsmanship, and extent of evidence for regional building programs.

Each datum represents at least one reference in an excavation report, and very often several in more than one piece of literature (if, e.g., some aspect of it, such as the date, has been debated). In order to simplify the documentation, a Bibliography of Sites has been provided. Data will not be individually referenced unless the excavator has made a subjective judgment regarding some aspect of the data, such as whether the workmanship was performed by professional craftsmen.

Encircling walls and public buildings
The number of building projects in the region and period of our study are plotted by century against the number of settled, excavated sites in Chart 6: Public Works: No. of Sites, Walls, and Buildings. This chart provides a transition of sorts from the settlement patterns of the previous chapter to the public works data explored in this. These data suggest a fairly steady increase in the initiation of public works projects in the early centuries of our study, jumping to a peak in the eighth century and followed by a rapid decline in the sixth century. This pattern contrasts only slightly with that recognized in the case of the settlement data, which is characterized by a tremendous acceleration from the ninth/eighth to the seventh century, and an even steeper decline from the seventh to the sixth.

Actually, the public works curves are smoothed somewhat by virtue of the scaling of the graph required to include the site data, obscuring large percentage shifts. The combined number of public building projects triples from the 11th to the 10th century (3 to 10), and increases again roughly 25% from the 9th to the 8th (11 to 14). In the 7th century, the number of public building projects initiated in our sample falls by nearly half; and, in our sample, there is no archeological evidence for any public building projects having been initiated in the 6th century.

The shift from the 11th century to the 10th accords well with the settlement data from the previous chapter. There we saw a concentration of population from dispersed, smaller settlements to fewer larger ones in this same period. It is natural, then, to find an increase in building activity in the

sites which show growth over that same period: Arad, Beersheba, Gibeon, Lachish, Jerusalem and Malhata all grew in
size and undertook building public works over this period. Tell
el-Ful was reduced to the status of a fort, and Tell Beit Mirsim,
while not extending the outer limit of its settlement, apparently grew by increasing the intensity of population within the
limits of its walls (Albright 1943: 1, 25). Interestingly, of the six
largest sites which did not grow in this period, five have no evidence of new public works in the 10th century (Ashdod,
Azekah, Gezer, Nasbeh and Sharuhen; Tell Beit Mirsim is the
only possible exception, but that apparently grew by increasing
in density rather than expansion, as was just noted). The
regional expansion in building activities in the 10th century
seems to have been localized almost exclusively in the newly
large towns, the same settlements which accepted the population influx from the countryside during this period, according
to the model developed in the previous chapter.

However, the settlement and public works curves do not
continue to parallel each other very closely after the 10th century. The next large shift in the settlement data, the 8th century increase, is paralleled by a barely significant increase in
the number of public works projects. Again, when we arrive at
the 7th century, we notice a sharp decline in the number of
new building projects, while the number of settlements experi-
ences only a slight dip. The drop off in the number of settlements does not occur until the 6th century, at which time the
number of public works initiated declines to zero, as was mentioned earlier.

Light may be shed on the discrepancy between the activity
of the 'number of settlements' variable and the public works
variables by referring to the bar graphs which register area of
walls (Chart 7), area of public buildings (Chart 8), and combined area (Chart 9). Here what we are measuring is not
merely the number of building projects undertaken but their
size, or 'scale'. These graphs provide a more direct measurement of the amount of energy generated in public works by
weighting building projects statistically according to the
amount of area they cover.

Chart 7, Area of Walls, registers a 180% increase from the
11th century to the 10th, a 265% increase from the 9th cen-

tury to the 8th, and a fourfold decrease (400%) from the 8th
century to the 7th; the variations between other periods are
not statistically significant. Except for the decline in the 7th
century, these shifts mirror those in the settlement data. The
area of new public buildings, shown in Chart 8, approximately
doubles every century from the 11th to the 8th, and then
remains constant through the 7th before declining to zero in
the 6th. By taking scale into consideration, then, a different
relation between the public works variables emerges: regional
energy invested in the building of encircling walls multiplied
dramatically in the 8th century, then declined even more
dramatically in the century following. Energy invested in
public buildings within settlements remained high and steady
over the same period, paralleling the settlement data.

The actual pattern of regional energy expenditure on public
works is brought into even sharper focus when the number of
each kind of project initiated over the same period is considered together with the total energy expenditure. The number
of new walls decreased from the 9th to the 8th century,
whereas the energy expended in this area *increased* 265%;
this fact reflects a focusing of greater energy on relatively
fewer sites. This impression is strengthened by the fact that
three-quarters of the energy expended on walls in the 8th
century occurs on only two of the five sites (Jerusalem and
Lachish). A focusing effect appears in the public buildings data
as well, only a century later. The 7th century public buildings
data shows a 40% decrease in the number of new projects
begun; but there is no concomitant decrease in the energy
expenditure in this period, as measured by the areal coverage
of the buildings. In other words, the same amount of energy as
was spent in the previous (8th) century on nine new public
building projects was spent on but *five* in the seventh; the labor
and natural resources directed into this kind of work was concentrated in fewer sites.

The patterns of dispersion and concentration of energy in
public building projects has been mapped for the periods of
major shifts. This series of maps (Maps 13–17) was generated
by plotting the map reference points on the x-y plane against
'elevations' in the z plane given by the area, in square meters,
of public works on the site during a given century. The z-

coordinate data is provided in Table 8: Public Works Catalogue.

The first period which is mapped, the 12th, is provided as a baseline for comparison. The period of the first major shift, the 10th century, shows broad regional expansion in new public works programs at nine sites. No new programs were undertaken in sites along the coast in this period, and a somewhat higher expenditure of energy seems to have been concentrated in Jerusalem and Gibeon, scarcely ten kilometers distant from one another.

The next major shift in public works energy expenditure occurs in the 8th century, producing a very different map. We may note the scale of the z-axis coordinates; the values for Jerusalem and Lachish are so high that the scale had to be increased fivefold to keep them on the map. The distribution of energy for public works is less dispersed in this period, with most of it concentrated in the two primary sites. Also of note in this map are the two clusters of forts which appear in this period. One consists of three forts just above the Dead Sea below Jerusalem; the other is also a three-fort cluster, appearing halfway between Jerusalem and Lachish on our map. The fort clusters are discussed below.

In the final shift mapped in this way, the regional emphasis on building seems to have shifted primarily to the coastal plain. The one central hill site with a large building program in this period is Ramat Rahel, a suburb of Jerusalem.

Several apparently meaningful shifts in various aspects of the public works data have been isolated thus far. First, we noticed a correlation between the sites at which public works were begun and those which were growing in size in the 10th century. Second, there also seemed to be a general correlation between the shifts in numbers of excavated sites which were settled in any one period and the initiation of new public works, up until the 7th century. At that point, the amount of energy spent on founding new walls or completely rebuilding old ones declined sharply, whereas the number of inhabited settlements and the amount of energy invested in new buildings remained high. Third, we noticed a statistically significant concentration of public works energy, both for encircling walls and buildings, in fewer and fewer sites beginning in the

8th century. We shall return to these issues, but first we need to consider other information which will have a bearing here and raise other questions as well.

Water systems data
The dating of these structures is notoriously difficult. Several water systems (Albright 1943: 47-48, Iron II drain through public square at Tell Beit Mirsim; Aharoni 1974: 38-39, 1975: 149, system of drains and cisterns at Beersheba, including one 15 m across by 10 m deep just inside the gate; Grant and Wright 1939, drain in main street, 'huge' cistern; Pritchard 1961, the Iron II tunnel, 130 m long) which were very appreciable in size could not be included in the discussion for this reason, but in a handful of cases water systems have been sufficiently well dated to contribute meaningfully and significantly to the discussion here. They are: the 12th-century spiral staircase to pool at Gibeon (Pritchard 1961); the early 9th-century channel at Jerusalem (Shiloh 1984); the 8th-century tunnel at Jerusalem (Shiloh 1984: 40); the 8th-century 'great shaft' at Lachish (Tufnell 1953: 162-63); and the 8th-century water-dispersion structures at the Judean forts explored by Cross and Milik (1956).

None of these structures were constructed merely to contain water. Instead, they conducted it (as at Jerusalem), conducted people to it (as at Gibeon and Lachish), or dispersed it (as at the Judean forts). The structures are minimally described in Table 8, Public Works Catalogue; the amount of areal coverage is listed and totalled in Table 2: Water Systems (below).

Measurements are given in cubic meters in each case; for the low retaining wall/dam structures at the forts, it is arbitrarily assumed that they were one meter high. Since we do know the volume of material excavated in the case of the water systems, we can come closer to reconstructing the amount of 'work' done (as this term is used in classical physics; see above) in building them than we could with the structures we considered earlier, when only the surface area could be reliably ascertained. However, the conclusions we can draw from these data remain somewhat limited. The variations in engineering and technical difficulties mentioned above in connection with the building of encircling walls vs public buildings are probably even more significant.

It is possible to compare directly the figures given here for water systems with the figures given earlier for buildings and encircling walls by imagining that the surface areas covered by those structures are exactly one meter high. This allows the surface-area units, given in square meters, to be viewed as volume units in cubic meters. Since buildings and encircling walls are several times higher than one meter (Yadin 1963: II, 323 estimates the height of Nasbeh's four-meter-wide wall at 12 meters), one could mentally multiply the public buildings or encircling walls data by whatever factor one was comfortable with to make the structures as tall as one imagines them to be, and then compare those figures directly with the water systems data.

However, we will attempt no such conversion here. Combining the figures from the different kinds of public works quantitatively would produce a false sense of precision, given the limitations of our data. Also, we have thus far generally eschewed 'conversion factors' in order to keep our quantitative analysis focused on actual measurements from excavation reports rather than partially contrived measurements wherever possible. We will therefore restrict our integration of the data from water systems with that of other types of public works to the conceptual level.

Despite these limitations, the water systems data shown in Table 2 provide a striking contribution to our understanding of public works in this period.

Century	12	9	8
Site			
Abu Tabaq (fort)			1086
Gibeon	848		
Jerusalem		212	1066
Lachish			9500
Samrah (fort)			612

Table 2. Water Systems: Volume of Rock Excavated (in m³)

Several points may be made on the basis of these figures. First, the 'Great Shaft' at Lachish, which Tufnell dated to 730 BCE in construction and 700 BCE for filling in (Tufnell 1953: 162-63), represents an enormous concentration of labor. The 8th century is the period to which most building activities of this kind are dated, both in terms of number of projects and in terms of volume of material excavated or built.

It should be pointed out that the tunnel at Jerusalem and the dam system at Abu Tabaq, though approximately equal in volume of material, are not comparable in terms of engineering difficulty and labor. The dam system is merely a set of very long, low walls built across a wadi bed to disperse water issuing from the hills to cultivated fields (Stager 1976: 146ff.). The tunnel in Jerusalem, in contrast, is an engineering marvel, excavated through 533 meters of solid rock.

It is evident that the most remarkable water system structures were built in the 8th century, in the very period and at the very locations that already display the largest building projects of any period in our study: Lachish and Jerusalem. The focusing of labor in the 8th century at these two sites, noted in connection with the encircling walls data, is strongly confirmed by the water systems data.

Evidence for skilled artisanship
For several reasons, evidence for skilled artisanship in public works is difficult to locate in excavation reports. Sites tend be reoccupied with building materials being reused; even foundation trenches are often robbed of stone blocks by later builders. Artistic decorations of public works, being on the outside of buildings, are among the first sources of data to be lost to human destruction and natural erosion. Consequently it is easier to find evidence of skilled artisanship in luxury items such as those found tomb caches, which we will consider in the next chapter. Here, as we seek evidence for skilled artisanship from public works, we are forewarned that the handful of evidence recovered in excavations represents but a fraction of what originally existed.

In addition to artisanship we must consider architectural standards. Some structures may have been so complex from an engineering standpoint that professional architects or builders may have been required to design the structures and/or supervise the execution. Regrettably, while excavators sometimes estimate the quality of artistic decoration and construction, both positively and negatively (see below), estimates of the need for professional construction expertise does not exist in the excavation reports used in this study. The structures which invite attention in this regard are the 9th-century podium at Lachish, possibly the smaller 9th-century one at Hesi, and the 8th-century tunnel at Jerusalem. The absence of speculation about professional engineering or architectural planning does not constitute evidence for the absence of such expertise in any specific site; the question has simply not been addressed by the excavators. However, it may be fair to wonder whether this is so because no clear archeological evidence for professional building design, which would provide a basis of comparison with other architectural remains and force the issue more broadly, has been found.

The evidence for professional artisanship is, therefore, as follows. As has already been noted, the construction of the fortified palace at 7th-century Ramat Rahel used the 'finest building techniques of the period' (Aharoni 1964: 51f.) Its ornamental window-balustrades represent a level of ornamental design which is unparalleled at any other site in our region or period. Two other sites are possible candidates for professional workmanship. At Beersheba (Aharoni 1974: 36) in the 9th-century levels and Jerusalem (Avigad 1984: 43) in the 8th, fortification walls were built of well-dressed, squared ashlar masonry.

Three other structures, all from the 9th century, were, according to the excavators, evidently not built by professional artisans. Palace B at Lachish is not square on one corner; the excavator believes that this is due to a design error (Tufnell 1953: 31f.). Kochavi (1974: 5f.) has noted a similar problem at Rabud in the fortification wall, which is built in unequal segments that do not meet squarely. Finally, in the case of 9th-century Nasbeh the excavator interpreted the non-uniform quality of the wall construction as evidence 'that the wall was erected by groups of corvée laborers, who were compelled to fulfill set quotas of work imposed on them' (Broshi 1975: 915). Lachish (4.2 ha), Nasbeh (3.2 ha) and Rabud (5.0 ha), it should be noted, were all fair-sized towns in this period.

This evidence, limited as it is, provides information about the presence of skilled artisanship in the Iron 2 period. The only possible evidence for it comes from the 9th, 8th and 7th centuries, and the predominant and most convincing evidence is from the 8th and 7th centuries at Jerusalem and Ramat Rahel. The latter site, which lies less than three kilometers distant from Jerusalem, is essentially a suburb of Jerusalem. Otherwise, even in the largest towns, building projects were carried out by local non-professionals, perhaps under professional supervision, though there is no direct evidence of this. It is also possible that professional involvement in the 9th-century projects mentioned above was limited to occasional visits rather than a permanent or semipermanent professional presence.

Evidence for regional building patterns
In five instances, excavators of Judean sites have proposed that certain aspects of the public structures they uncovered betray evidence of centralized planning. One of these is dated to the 11th–10th century, two are associated with 10th-century strata, and two occur in 8th-century levels.

Meshel and Cohen (1980) suggested that two structures in the northern Negev were Iron age forts whose 'position within the network of Negev strongholds shows they were built under central authority and royal initiative'. Herzog (1983) and Finkelstein (1984) disagreed, noting that the 'forts' have no common architectural pattern, and that their construction is relatively poor. Finkelstein proposed instead that the 'forts' were enclosures constructed by pastoral nomads during a brief period of relative economic prosperity (1984: 201f.). Finkelstein has cast sufficient doubt on the hypothesis of Meshel and Cohen that the burden of proof must fall on those wishing to claim that these structures are of royal origin. Such a claim will not be maintained here.

The excavators of Beth Shemesh noticed that the dimensions of walls and casemates at that site and the dimensions of the contemporary structures at Tell Beit Mirsim, 33 kilometers distant, were 'so close that one must presume the erection of both under common direction' (Grant and Wright 1939: 252; cf. Albright 1943: 14). It should also be noted that the 10th-century construction at Beth Shemesh consisted of adding an inner wall and transverse dividing walls to a pre-existing, 13th-century solid wall.

Aharoni has made a similar claim about the 10th-century gate complex at Beersheba: 'The similarity of the gates at Dan and Beersheba makes it probable that the two cities were fortified under the control of a single ruler' (1974: 38; 1975: 147). Slightly more than 200 kilometers separates these sites.

Cross and Milik (1956) have suggested that the construction of several 8th-century forts (my date) were carried out as part of a centrally controlled building program. They discovered three contemporary sites within five kilometers of one another in the Judean foothills above the Dead Sea. Three similarly designed dam/water dispersion structures were located in the same vicinity and considered to be contemporary. The dimensions of the forts were quite different, varying from 32 × 32 m to 68 × 40 m; but the contemporaneity of founding and similarity in design of associated water structures suggests a centralized building program behind the forts (1956: 15f.). These forts were dated to the 9th century by the excavators, but for reasons given above, an 8th-century date is used for them here.

Another set of three forts was investigated by Mazar (1982). In this case the forts were all located within six kilometers of one another. The designs of the three were similar, though one (30 × 30 m, 900 m²) was twice the size of the other two (20 × 20 m, 400 m² each). These forts were located five kilometers north and thirty kilometers west of the trio above the Dead Sea. (See the 8th-century three-dimensional map of public works plotted against geographical locale.) Again, Mazar asserts that these structures were the product of a centralized authority (1982: 87ff.).

The characters of the building programs claimed for the forts just discussed may be classified in two distinct categories. The 10th-century building programs were refortifications of pre-existing settlements; the 8th-century fort complexes were built anew. To project labor and other resources into previously unsettled sites seems to be evidence for a greater degree of regional authority and a larger capacity to concentrate energy than utilization of resources and personnel at a pre-existent site. Minimally, all that is required of a building program of the 10th-century type is local acknowledgment of a central authority, and a common plan. Local labor and possibly local expertise were used. In the construction of new settlements, labor and expertise, and probably some material support, all had to be routed from one area to another, requiring greater administrative support.

This is not to say that the evidence for the 10th-century building programs precludes the presence of a central authority as strong as that in the 8th century. Rather, the archeological evidence presented here suggests a stronger central control system in the 8th century than in the 10th century.

Summary
We have thus far presented public works data that relate to the issue of administrative control mechanisms. These data are: public buildings and walls, water works, evidence for skilled artisanship, and evidence for building programs. We must now attempt to draw this material together into an integrated model.

Synthesis

The public works data provide evidence of four major shifts in regional concentrations of labor and resources. These shifts can now be analyzed in terms of their relationship to changing patterns of administrative control.

Summary of the evidence
1. *10th century.* A reallocation of public works energies from a few older, larger settlements to more numerous and newly large settlements. Energy devoted to public works is fairly evenly distributed in the hill country in this period, though the area around Jerusalem already in this period receives significantly more resources than do other areas. Overall labor output for public works in the region as a whole approximately doubles.

2. *8th century.* A very large (roughly 300%) increase in regional energy and natural resources allocated to the building of walls, water installations and forts. Building projects are

more often centrally planned and less dispersed in this period, with energies concentrated in Jerusalem, Lachish and the two constellated fort systems.

3. *7th century*. Building of new encircling walls dropped sharply (400%), while construction of public buildings remained as high as the previous period but was concentrated in far fewer sites (three as opposed to eight for the 8th century).

4. *6th century*. No building projects or programs were initiated in this period in our sample of excavated sites.

The surface area comprised by encircling walls and major water installations experienced very significant increases in the 10th and 8th centuries BCE. These periods coincide with regional political turmoil involving Philistia and Egypt (early and late 10th century, respectively) and Assyria (late 8th century). The monumental water installation projects at Jerusalem and Lachish in the 8th century are as much a defensive response to the threat of Assyrian invasion as was the building of walls in the same sites in this century (Yadin 1963: II, 320). The ability of the Israelite society to respond to external political pressures on a regional level in these two eras (8th and 10th centuries BCE) differs markedly: in the 8th century, the capacity to muster resources was much greater, but most of the increase was focused in two primary sites. In the 10th century the energy devoted to public works was considerably smaller but was distributed more evenly.

Most of the evidence for labor and resource energy and skilled artisanship at this time comes from Ramat Rahel in the environs of Jerusalem. In fact, skilled artisanship in public building projects is virtually non-existent outside the urban area of Jerusalem at any period. Indeed, before the excavations at Ramat Rahel, Kenyon (1967: 50) claimed that no evidence for professional masons appears anywhere in monarchic Israel.

Preliminary conclusion

The settlement data provided indirect evidence about the nature and extent of administrative control systems in the region and period of our study. The public works data now provide more direct support for those inferences. The first direct evidence of regional administrative control appears in the 10th century, via the duplication of building plans at widely dispersed sites (Dan and Beersheba, and Tell Beit Mirsim and Beth Shemesh). However, the degree of administrative control required by this evidence is relatively low. While Jerusalem and Gibeon, a close neighbor, contain evidence of somewhat higher levels of public building activity than the rest of the region, the relatively even distribution of energy is consistent with a model of a comparatively high degree of local management of labor and resources.

The picture changes when we move to the 8th century, however. The gap between labor expended on the two major sites and the rest of the sites has increased from 40% to 500%. Also, clear evidence of a central administration able to project labor and material regionally appears for the first time in this century with the construction of the two three-fort clusters. Clear evidence for skilled artisanship in public works appears for the first time in the following century, the 7th, in the neighborhood of Jerusalem. These findings are entirely consonant with the 'primate' model proposed for Jerusalem in Chapter 3 of this study. They are also consistent with the findings (1) that little evidence for strong centralized control in our region appears in our data prior to the 8th century, and (2) that there is solid evidence for such control projected from Jerusalem beginning in the 8th century and continuing into the 7th.

The public works data may also add a feature to the portrayal of the regional administrative matrix formulated on the basis of our study of settlement patterns. The resurgence of public works on the coastal plain in the 7th century may indicate a retraction of the influence of Jerusalem to the central hills in this period. If this is the case, we would expect a bifurcation between the material culture of sites along the coastal plain and that of sites in the central hills during this period. Unfortunately, this hypothesis cannot be tested on the basis of the data collected for this study. What information we do have indicates that the pattern of centralized control in our period seems to vary from longer-range but weaker influence in the 10th century to shorter-range and stronger influence over other sites in the 7th.

Ramifications for scribes and scribal schools

Since I intend to discuss this question much more fully in the light of the luxury items data as well as the data presented here and in the previous chapter, a full integration of the public works data with the other two analyses will wait until the next chapter. Here, I will content myself with a few general remarks. The analysis of public works data tends to refine and confirm, albeit very indirectly and still tentatively, the picture of scribes and scribal schools drawn on the basis of the settlement data in Chapter 1. The manifold increases in both the quantity and quality of public works in the 8th century constitute direct evidence for the need for very significantly stronger and more complex administrative systems to manage those programs at that time than had been the case at any previous period in our study. At the same time, the focusing of those energies at Jerusalem and Lachish in the 8th century, and at Jerusalem alone in the 7th, suggests that the range of the expected increase in permanently based administrative activity relating to public works functions, at least, was primarily focused in those areas during those periods.

This draws our preliminary synthesis of public works data and its integration with the settlement data to a close. It is now time to turn our attention to the final area of data analysis, luxury items.

Chapter 4

LUXURY ITEMS

Introduction

In this chapter we will define luxury items for the purposes of this study; address some of the problems inherent in this type of data, and discuss how these problems will be managed in the analysis; and present and discuss the luxury items data.

Definition of Luxury Items: Approach

Luxury items may generally be defined as objects to which, for various reasons, access is more or less limited. The materials of which the object is made may be of limited availability, whether naturally or because of monopolistic control; the workmanship of the object may be highly valued; or the object may have come from such a distance that access to it is limited to those who control the trading relationship which brought the object to the local area. Each of these reasons finds a parallel in the lists of indicators for both ranked and stratified societies (Webster 1975: 469; Flanagan 1981: 51-52; Peebles and Kus 1977: 431-32; Frick 1987: 33ff.; Frick 1977: 10; Renfrew 1973: 90; Flannery 1972: 404; Childe 1950: 3ff.). However, luxury items will be defined more broadly in the present study, and will include any artifactual evidence that can provide insight into the societal variables relating to administrative control systems. These variables are summarized from the indicators for ranked and stratified societies documented above:

1. the presence of full-time artisans, whose livelihood depends on the ability of an elite to provide them with

foodstuffs, thus liberating them to pursue their craft full-time;

2. the extent and nature of control over both raw materials and manufactured goods; or

3. the extent and nature of regional trade, and degree of centralization of that trade.

Our definition, then, will include all artifacts fitting the general description given in the first paragraph, but will also include some others as well (see below).

In order for luxury items to provide the necessary information, at least some of the following data must be available for each item:

1. provenience (of production)
2. raw materials: their provenience and abundance/scarcity
3. quality of production (workmanship)
4. technology used for production
5. evidence for possible direct use in economic or political control systems: e.g. standardized weights, some inscribed sherds, jar-handles impressed with an ownership stamp, ring- or cylinder-seals, etc.

Artifacts which may provide any of the above data are, for the purposes of this investigation, categorized as 'luxury items'. This definition, like that given for public works (above), is a functional socioeconomic one, adopted for convenience in the present context and not intended to be generally applicable. While the word 'luxury' usually indicates market value, this association is not always maintained under the present definition. For instance, in the case of precious metals such as silver and gold, the common understanding of 'luxury' corresponds fairly well to the use of the term here. However, in two related instances the common connotation of the word 'luxury' would be misapplied in our study.

First, industrial installations used by specialists, such as that used for balsam production at En-gedi in the last decades of the 8th century BCE (see below,) are not themselves 'luxury items', yet they provide insight into the class of skilled artisans which produced luxury items, and they also key the discussion of centralized control of both skilled labor and rare (for whatever reason) raw materials. Thus, they will be considered in this chapter. Second, for analogous reasons, material evidence of writing (inscriptions, ostraca, and some seals) will also be included. While these materials are perhaps treasured above all by the archeologist (Avigad 1984: 41), this valuation is completely unrelated to their market value in the period whence they derive. Nevertheless, such materials can provide evidence of specialized skills, as for instance when the quality of the writing suggests the work of a professional scribe. As in the case of industrial installations, materials associated with writing provide insight into the distribution of skilled labor and, consequently, the management of that labor. Perhaps most importantly, such evidence affords us our most direct contact with the information processing institutions upon which the 'managerial superstructure' (Flannery 1972: 412) was dependent. The study of luxury items will contribute to an analysis of these institutions through time and across our region. This analysis in turn will bear on what we will be able to say about scribal education and general literacy in our final synthesis of the luxury item data with the settlement and public works analyses.

The material will be presented as follows. First, an overview of the distribution of various classes of luxury items through time will be provided. Evidence for precious materials, imported goods, and centralized control of industry will be presented and discussed. Also included will be a discussion of the distribution through space and time of skilled artisanship. This discussion will enable us to discuss the question of skilled artisanship generally, and scribal skills particularly, more directly than was possible in the case of settlement and public works data.

The results of our presentation and evaluation of the luxury items data will then be used to amplify the diachronic model of regional management of natural and human resources that was developed in the discussion of the public works data. This evaluation will next be integrated with those of previous chapters in order to augment our archeologically based model of the development of regional administrative control in our period of study.

Finally, the direct evidence for writing, in this case ostraca and inscriptions reported in our sample of excavation reports, will be discussed and correlated with the model of administrative control developed on the basis of the other data. Our discussion of this data will seek to locate this phenomenon within the broadly based model of administrative control. The model thus generated will then be compared with that developed via historical and other data in the next (concluding) chapter.

Limitations in the Data

The limitations in the luxury items data may be characterized as paralleling those already discussed in regard to public works, but dramatically increased in degree of limitation in almost every case: variability of reporting, variability in excavation, dating, and subjectivity of reporting. Each of these areas of difficulty, and the manner in which it is handled, will be discussed in turn.

Variability of reporting

In our discussion of the public works data we noted a degree of variability in the way in which architectural remains were recorded. This variability is even greater in the case of luxury items. First, even preliminary reports almost always include the data needed for the present study to examine settlement and public works. In contrast, 'small finds' that should be included in our 'luxury items' discussion are usually included only in full preliminary or final reports, which have been completed for slightly less than half (15 of 31; see below) of the excavated sites in our sample. Occasionally, when such finds are considered by the excavator to be of sufficient significance to the scholarly community, they are published separately (e.g. Diringer 1947; Negbi 1967). These examples are the exception rather than the rule. The reporting of luxury items is so much less frequent than is the case for settlement and public works data that our sample of sites is greatly reduced.

The most significant, and disappointing, example of this problem is that of Jerusalem. A great deal of excavation and discussion has firmly established both the settlement size and the nature of the fortifications of Jerusalem through time during our period (e.g. Avigad 1984; Mazar 1975; Shiloh 1984). However, although several large-scale excavations have exposed extensive areas on the hill of Ophel, around the temple mount, and on the western hill, *not a single excavation in Jerusalem has systematically or comprehensively published the small objects.* Tantalizing glimpses of finds appear in general works by the excavators, but excavation reports proper have simply not been done for this major site. In the present instance, this means that Jerusalem falls into the category of sites which will not be discussed in the quantitative analysis sections of this chapter, since the data that would enable its inclusion are not available. That information that can be gleaned from the preliminary or general works on Jerusalem will be presented in later sections as appropriate; but the lack of full information remains highly regrettable.

The reduction in our sample size has two other immediate and serious effects on the analysis of data in this chapter. First, the reduction in sample size significantly lessens the confidence with which we can draw conclusions regarding regional trends. As has been the case in previous chapters, our explanatory efforts will be directed towards detecting shifts in the data from one period to the next. However, in this chapter, because the sample size has been reduced, the shifts must be much larger in order to permit a degree of confidence in interpretation similar to that which was possible with the settlement and public works data. Since the luxury item data will be analyzed by artifact groups of quite varying sizes, the percentage shifts that will be considered significant will vary from group to group. The larger the number of sites reporting the particular type of artifact, the smaller the percentage shift required to be considered significant.

The second serious effect will occur in our mapping of regional distributions of artifacts. For classes of artifacts which are not well represented in our sample, such mapping will not be done. Too many of the variations in small samples are due simply to accidents of recovery by the excavator (Hodder 1976: 18). A relatively small cache of an item at a particular site can numerically overwhelm the data for that entire class of artifact in the statistical analysis, producing large percentage shifts without being meaningful. We will look at regional distributions with the awareness that an absence of data at a site during any given period should not be interpreted as an absence of the class or type of artifacts represented by that data.

In addition to reduction of sample size, incomplete reporting affects our data in a second way. Even where small finds (or 'objects', as the chapters describing such artifacts are frequently entitled) are reported, there is practically no standardization of discussion from report to report. The phrase 'small finds' covers many classes of artifacts, each with its own set of functional and decorative attributes.

The lack of standardization in presentation comes as no surprise (cf. e.g. Clarke 1978: 155f.), but it is nonetheless a formidable obstacle to regional studies such as this one. In scattered instances, small objects are fully discussed in the text, with provenience, dating, description and discussion of comparative materials provided. Usually, however, details about the artifacts are found in tables and locus lists. Since the format of such lists varies considerably from report to report, as does the information actually provided, we are reduced to a 'least common denominator' situation in much the same way as we were with the public works data. As it happens, the number of reported artifact variables consistently shared by excavation reports is fairly small. This may be considered a higher-order parallel of the problem Clarke noticed in connection with archeological terminology (1978: 23f.).

In the case of luxury items, the traits or variables which minimally must be known in order to make an artifact usable for the purposes of this study are date and composition. Probable function is usually known as well, and will be considered when it is known; but in the case of badly corroded metals or materials whose provenience is known the artifact can provide important information even when its original use cannot be reconstructed. 1642 artifacts have been included in the quantitative section of the present study using these guidelines (see Tables 12–15). Other variables, such as quality of workmanship and technology of production, are discussed much less frequently in the excavation reports. When they are discussed, so many variables are operative in the discussion of so few cases that presentation in a quantitative format would be overly complex and misleading as well. In order to incorporate data of the latter kind into the discussion, non-quantitative anecdotal sections will be included as the appropriate forum for this kind of information. The descriptive statistics will serve as a backdrop and check against over-interpretation of the few cases of this kind.

Variability in extent of excavation

Variability in the extent to which sites have been excavated also impede our efforts to compare information from different sites. Even if two comparably sized sites are excavated by the same person and reported in the same manner, a more fully excavated site can be expected to produce more finds, and a larger range of finds, than a site of which only a fraction has been excavated. This situation in fact often arises when sites are overlaid by modern settlements, sharply restricting the area accessible to excavation (e.g. Amiran 1970: 10, in reference to Jerusalem). However, even among sites that can be freely excavated, some will be more fully excavated than others. This causes problems for a regional study attempting to compare remains from site to site; the quantities of remains will vary not only according to the size and nature of the original settlement in any given period, which would be meaningful, but also according to the size of the excavation.

It is possible to factor the excavation size out of the data, however. The amount of surface area excavated can be determined from top plans, and the percentage which this area constitutes of the overall settlement size for each period calculated. Then, the number of artifacts can be divided by that percentage to provide an estimate of the number of artifacts that would have been recovered had the entire site been excavated. This is not a perfect solution by any means; the precision of the approximation depends on the degree to which the part of the site which was excavated is representative of the whole. It assumes that the rate of recovery of artifacts from the excavated area would remain constant for the whole site, an assumption that may be unwarranted when a very small sample of the site has been excavated. However, this procedure nonetheless improves the comparability of the data among sites by correcting for extent of excavation.

Dating

The need to date the finds precisely is critical for our purposes, as has already been mentioned. In order to compare the data in this chapter with those in earlier ones, the resolution of dating for luxury items must be as high as was the case with settlement and public works data. However, dating of artifacts presents unusual difficulties. The preferred method of determining the date of an object is through its location in a stratified context. However, objects of the type under consideration here are sometimes preserved in use for great lengths of time (e.g. Mazar 1966: 56-57). Their presence in a clearly stratified ceramic context does not indicate original temporal provenience, only deposition. A further problem is that excavators finding such objects outside a stratified context (e.g. in surface debris) will in some cases date them typologically, on the basis of comparison with materials discovered at other sites. It is not always clear on what basis the artifacts were dated, even after searching through serial number and locus lists. Although typological dating increases the quantity of data available to us, it diminishes the confidence with which we can draw conclusions on its basis, since similar artifact characteristics can vary in date from region to region due to the time required for the characteristic in question to 'travel'. In a region as small as that considered in the present study, this difficulty is probably minimized but cannot be ignored entirely.

Problems relating to dating of artifacts will be handled here as follows. First, only materials found in stratified contexts, or materials which can be typologically dated with a very high degree of confidence because of a large and well-documented corpus of comparative materials, are included as data. A considerable amount of data has been excluded from consideration in this report because of inadequate resolution or lack of certainty in dating of materials. This is in no way intended as a criticism of excavators; quite the contrary. This limitation is due to the relatively small number of loci in any excavation that are clearly stratified and also contain sufficient materials of a kind that enable that stratum to be precisely dated. The majority of any type of find will be found outside such key contexts, among unstratified or mixed remains. The more important consideration is that excavators distinguish clearly between objects found in closely datable strata and those found in other contexts, thus enabling secondary reports such as this one to determine which data are usable for their purposes. This has generally not been a problem, testifying to the quality of care taken in reporting.

The second approach to the limitations in dating artifacts will be to increase the volume of pertinent data by decreasing the resolution required in dating it in the first part of the analysis. Two degrees of resolution in dating will be utilized. The span of our report, the 12th to the 6th centuries BCE, is generally held to cover two ceramic periods in our region of study: Iron 1, which will include the 12th–10th centuries in this case; and Iron 2 (9th century to the decade of the 6th century). A large amount of material in excavation reports is dated to the general period rather than the precise century. This material will be treated separately as a supplement to the more precisely dated materials (Tables 12 and 14). Excavation reports utilizing a different nomenclature for 'Iron 1' and 'Iron 2' have been standardized to such usage.

Subjectivity in reporting
The final way in which the strength of the data presented here must be questioned concerns the role of professional artisans in the manufacture of the artifact. This problem routinely arises in connection with the third criterion, 'quality of production', listed at the beginning of this chapter. In many cases, excavators or secondary researchers have concluded that a particular artifact is so well executed that only a full-time professional artisan could have attained the necessary skill. Interestingly, this class of determinations includes deciding whether an inscription was executed by a full-time 'scribe' or a non-professional. Such conclusions, when made in the absence of explicitly stated and well-defined criteria, remain subjective no matter how indubitable they appear in many cases.

These subjective determinations will be discussed alongside the less debatable kinds of data. I have decided to do this because of the importance of the information, because there is presently no other way to get it, and because I judge that the reliability of the discussions on at least some of the various artifact types, subjective as they may be, is still high enough to contribute convincingly to the present study. I will in no case reverse the judgment of excavators unless others have done so in the literature. However, it is hoped that the present study will both show the need for and contribute to further discussion on the issue of 'material isomorphs' (attributes of artifacts that correspond to specific societal traits) of full-time professionalism in artifact production. The question must be asked for each artifact-type: precisely which criteria, and what values for those criteria, can most meaningfully locate artifacts on a manufacturing continuum extending from full-time professional artisanship to 'homemade'? For the time being, we must rely on the professional judgment of those who publish the artifacts, since that is the present state of the discussion, while continuing to hope that the discussion moves to a more objective footing.

Conclusion
Despite some serious limitations in securing the luxury items data, the picture is not entirely bleak. Excavators have a strong tendency to make a special effort to find, tabulate and explain special artifacts because such items provide direct evidence for numerous important questions: the degree of social stratification, the nature of trade and the economy, the extent of professional artisanship, etc.; cf. Albright's 'patient search' for ostraca (1943: 73). This bias works in our favor in the present instance by maximizing coverage and discussion of the very artifacts which provide us with the most pertinent information, though the same bias would work against us in a disastrous way if we were attempting to address many other questions. The objects and items upon which we shall focus here are in fact reported relatively often and fully despite the variability; they are sometimes the subject of discussion both in the excavation reports themselves and in secondary discussions of the reports. Even excluding the data which cannot be used here because of imprecise or uncertain dating or function (e.g. the lack of clear distinction between stone weights, gaming pieces, and rubbing stones), there remains sufficient information on which to base our examination of scribalism in the context of administrative control.

Presentation and Analysis of Data

Introduction

Data from fifteen excavated sites (all in our sample that provide data meeting our requirements for precision and type of
information; see above) is collated in two catalogues and one
spreadsheet by period and century (Tables 12–14). The sites in
our sample for which data of this kind was available were
Arad, Tell Beit Mirsim, Beth Shemesh, Beth Zur, Beersheba,
En-Gedi (Tell Jurn), Tell el-Ful (Gibeah), Gezer, Gibeon,
Meṣad Hashavyahu, Jerusalem, Lachish, Tell en-Nasbeh,
Ramat Rahel and Tell Sippor. This list does not include sites
for which only stamped jar-handle data exists (e.g. Judeideh;
see below). The excavation reports and supplementary articles
used to compile these data are presented by site in the Bibliography of Sites.

The first of the two catalogues, Table 12: Luxury Items by
Period, lists summary descriptions of number of finds, material, function, whether the item was inscribed, and whether it
was imported, by period and site. 'Iron 1' is used here for 12th
through 10th centuries, and 'Iron 2' represents the 9th century through the first decade of the 6th century. The second
catalogue, Table 13: Luxury Items by Century, lists the same
information by century rather than by period.

In some cases, the number of a particular item could not be
ascertained from the excavation report, plates, or lists. In such
instances, the phrase 'no count' is included in the description
(see, e.g., 'Jerusalem' in the 7th century). Items for which
there was no count are not included in the quantitative data or
the charts and graphs generated from that data, but they will
in many cases be included in the discussion.

The data catalogued in this way have been compiled in a
spreadsheet entitled Table 14: Luxury Items—Aggregate
Counts by Type, Class, Century and Period. Twelve kinds of
artifacts are listed. Most of the artifact types are self-explanatory, but a few are not. First, the 'imported' category consists primarily of samples of wood; but a handful of seals and
scarabs known to have been produced in Egypt are also
included. No doubt more of the artifacts listed in our spreadsheet were also imported, but this information is in such cases

not available or uncertain. The imported seals are thus counted twice, once in the 'imported' section and once in the 'seals' category. Second, the artifact type 'jewelry' includes many pieces also included in the 'metals' section. These are the only two examples of overlap in the data listed. The total number of *artifacts* represented in this spreadsheet is 947, but considered as items of *information*, some 200 of them do double duty, resulting in the totals of over 1100 at the foot of the spreadsheet. Stamped jar-handles occur only in the 8th and 7th centuries, and will be treated separately (see below).

Also note that the 'Periods' column includes all the data from both catalogues: the data from centuries 12, 11, and 10 are added to the 'Iron 1' data to produce the totals in the 'Periods 12–10 IR1' column. Likewise, the 'Periods 9–7 IR2' column totals the information from Table 12 (Luxury Items by Period) for Iron 2 and the data from the 9th century through the first decade of the 6th.

In the lower section of Table 14: Luxury Items—Aggregate, data are provided by class as follows. 'Jewelry' includes cosmetic pallettes as well as the jewelry proper. 'Metals' includes bronze, iron and silver. 'Statuary' includes both the terracotta figurines and the stone statuettes. The 'writing' class includes inscriptions, ostraca (ink on potsherd), and inscribed seals and scarabs. The 'Class Totals' are in some cases smaller than the totals for the twelve artifact types listed above because the 'Imported' artifacts and 'weights' are not included in any of the classes; the classes, therefore, represent only ten of the twelve artifact types discussed here. In order to facilitate the location of patterns in the data, the information in the luxury items spreadsheet has been plotted in the form of a series of bar charts and maps. These plots will serve as the starting point for our discussion in this section.

Overview by period and century

In the first chart for this section, Chart 10: Luxury Items by Class and Period, we notice a tremendous increase in all classes of finds from Iron 1 to Iron 2. The smallest percentage increase is in 'Metals', and even there it is over 400%. The increase shown in this chart is too large, and occurs over too many artifact types, to be explained by recourse to accidents of recovery. All items for which a count was available in the excavation reports in our sample of sites and which were dated to a precise century are included here. The most natural explanation of this pattern in the data is that the regional economy represented by our sample of sites was much more productive over the range of artifact types represented here in the Iron 2 period than it was in the Iron 1 period. This chart does not permit us to be precise as to the character of this increase either temporally or geographically, but the fact that it was a large increase is undeniable.

Chart 11 (Luxury Items by Class and Century) includes fewer items, as discussed earlier, but enables us to achieve greater temporal definition of the increase observed in the data by period. These data seem to indicate that the abundance of luxury items in strata datable to these centuries began a significantly steeper increase in the 8th century than had been seen in the centuries previous, climbed even more steeply to a peak in the 7th, and declined precipitously in the following century.

We should not leap to the conclusion that the increase that began in the 8th century is directly reflective of an increase in production or circulation of such items in the economy. This is one explanation, and a simple one at that; but other factors may also be operative. What these data directly reflect is an increase in the rate of *deposition* of such items. Tools being made obsolete by technological innovations, fashions going out of style, and destruction of sites are all possible explanations of an increase in the rate of artifact deposition in a particular period.

The most likely explanation among those listed above can be determined by using each to generate a prediction of artifact distribution, and checking our data to see which fits best. A hypothesis of obsolescence would be the best fit to a large increase in the rate of deposition of a very few types of artifacts; if most or all artifact types increase in rate of deposition in the 8th century, chances are small that obsolescence or change of fashion is the cause.

The hypothesis of destruction of sites as the cause for increased deposition rates would predict increased rates for destroyed sites but not for undestroyed ones. Also, the hypo-

thesis of site destruction would predict the increase only for
the century in which the destruction occurred; continued high
deposition rates beyond that century would not be accounted
for by this explanation.

The hypothesis of increased productivity can be checked by
correlating the 8th-century increase in luxury item deposition
with the settlement and public works data. We would expect
an increase of the magnitude (manifold) seen in our data to be
associated with substantial increases in population and productivity as measured in other areas, such as public works.
Also, a large increase in productivity generally would predict
an increase in a broad spectrum of artifact types rather than a
few.

In this particular instance, several factors argue in favor of
a general increase in productivity and circulation of such
objects in this century as at least a primary cause for the
increase in deposition. First, review of the stacked-bar charts
for each of the artifact classes (Chart 12: Jewelry; Chart 13:
Metals; Chart 14: Statuary, Weights and Imports, and Chart
15: Evidence of Writing) shows that the range of artifact types
whose rates of deposition followed the pattern noticed above
for the artifact classes generally, in this period, includes most
of those covered by our survey. Obsolescence cannot account
for this broad range of increase in deposition rate for the artifact types covered in our survey; this datum, rather, is consonant with the hypotheses of increased productivity and of site
destruction.

The focus on numbers of finds in the quantitative analysis is
in some instances misleading. For example, Albright (1943:
79) noted that, during the period covered in this study, iron
quickly became more commonplace than bronze, eclipsing it
as the material of choice for most agricultural and household
uses. Bronze continued to be used primarily for ornamental
purposes. However, far more *pieces* of bronze were recovered
in the 9th-, 8th- and 7th-century strata of sites than were
implements of iron. Albright's characterization of the relationship between bronze and iron for our period in this region is
probably consistent with our data. The reason for this is
twofold: because bronze was preferred for ornamental purposes, bronze artifacts are more frequent in burials than iron;

and iron was comparatively rare as an ornamental material, almost always being used for agricultural tools or weapons.

The two artifact types that fail to fit this pattern are iron, which shows no significant increase in the 7th-century deposits (Chart 13), and seals (see Chart 16, Evidence of Writing). In the case of iron, the statistics may be the result of a reporting bias. For two sites, Tell Beit Mirsim and Beth Shemesh, Albright (1943) and Grant and Wright (1939) do not provide counts of the iron artifacts from this period because they were too numerous; instead, they present the best-preserved examples of types of iron artifacts in the plates. No counts of iron artifacts are given for Lachish from this century either. The data for iron are probably depressed because the material became too commonplace: too commonplace to be deposited in ancient tombs where it could be preserved, and too commonplace to be recorded routinely by modern excavators (cf. Albright 1943: 79, and the discussion above).

Seals, on the other hand, increase in deposition in the 9th century and peak in the 8th. That is, they show roughly the same temporal pattern as the other artifact types but are one century ahead. Most of the scarabs (39) from well-dated deposits were recovered at Lachish. The higher 8th-century deposit rate at Lachish could be due to the military conquest of this site at the end of the 8th century. However, another explanation may be more likely. At Lachish, the 8th-century tomb deposits show a gradual lessening of Egyptian artistic influences (Tufnell 1953: 47). It may be that scarabs indeed went out of fashion, possibly also losing any functional value as seals as well, and were 'thrown away' during this period.

In addition to Lachish, Beersheba also appears to have been abandoned at the end of the 8th century, perhaps because of military pressure. However, the rest of the sites recording increases in artifactual data continued to be settled at the same or larger settlement sizes in the 7th century. Thus, while some of the increase in rate of deposition of luxury items in the 8th century may be accounted for by site destruction, most of it cannot.

Finally, a striking correlation is discovered among the 8th–7th-century patterns of settlement, public works initiated, and deposition of luxury items. In each case, very large increases appear in the 8th century. In the 7th century, settlement sizes and numbers remain high, as does the rate of new buildings initiated. The amount of energy put into construction of fortification walls decreases from the 8th to the 7th century. It may be that energies dedicated in the 8th century to warding off the Assyrian threat turned in the 7th to the production of commodities. We shall return to this point in our synthesis. At present we note that this datum matches the prediction generated on the basis of a hypothesis of a regional, large increase in productivity beginning in the 8th century and reaching its zenith in the 7th, and that it does not accord well with predictions generated by the other hypotheses outlined above. What Pritchard noted for Gibeon, namely that 'the major period of prosperity [occurred] toward the end of the 7th century' (1961b: 39) seems to be true for our region generally.

A regional, large-scale increase in labor productivity for the kind of artifacts represented here may indicate that the management systems involved in production and perhaps also in redistribution of such items may have had to increase at the same time. In order to test this possibility we must attempt to ascertain the degree to which this pattern of production was concentrated locally or distributed evenly across the region; the degree to which it was centrally controlled; and the degree to which production of the items listed here was accomplished by professional, skilled artisans.

Regional Distribution and concentration

Having examined the development of luxury item production temporally, we will now produce a similar degree of refinement geographically. In this section, we wish to see whether there is strong evidence of local concentration of luxury items or fairly even distribution, and how these variables change through time. We can address these issues by plotting the number of artifacts at each site, by century, against the geographical location of the site as given by the map reference coordinates of that site. As was mentioned above, the number of artifacts recovered and recorded at each site has been weighted according to the excavated percentage of the settlement size during each century. These plots appear as Maps 18–22. The maps have been produced for aggregates of all items recorded in the catalogue by century, and including the stamped jar-handle data.

In these maps, the vertical or z-axis scale 'elevation' changes depending on the number of finds; the more finds that need to be mapped, the larger the intervals on the z-axis scale. The Dead Sea, at c. −400 m, is the low point; the shore of the Mediterranean is at 0 m; and the weighted values of artifact counts are positive integers, plotted as 'elevations' above sea-level.

Several of the data limitations should be kept in mind as the maps are discussed. Generally, the sample of sites for which the maps were produced is much smaller than for the similar maps produced to illustrate the settlement and public works data. Only very large shifts (100% or more) in either the number of sites or the number of artifacts represented at them will be considered as meaningful. Also, Jerusalem is notable for its absence from this part of the analysis; the reasons for this absence are given in greater detail above. We shall incorporate Jerusalem into the discussion later, since the luxury item data does provide some means for direct assessment of the importance of this site. The questions regarding its centrality have been raised in both the settlement and public works data, and we hope to clarify the picture in this chapter. However, the luxury item data is very poorly represented in publications for Jerusalem; and such data as do exist are poorly quantified. Thus the site is not included in the maps we shall discuss here.

With these caveats in mind, we turn to the set of maps which total all types of items by site and century. Little change is seen from the 11th to the 9th century; the changes in the number of sites (3–5–3) and in the scale (100–200 weighted items) are hardly large enough to be noticed, given the limitations of the data. However, when we come to the 8th century, the picture changes dramatically. The upper limit of the z-axis scale jumps from 200 to 2600 to accommodate the data from one site, Lachish. Also significant is the large increase in the number of sites represented (9). Aside from Lachish, the sites continue to fall in the 1–200 range for number of artifacts weighted by percentage excavated. Judeideh appears

solely on the basis of stamped jar-handles found there by excavations that produced little other data suitable for our purposes; the jar-handles were dated securely on typological
grounds and counts were done by type and date for the quantitative analysis (see below for fuller discussion of stamped jar-
handles). Finally, in the 7th century Judeideh appears again
as a result of jar-handle data; but Lachish, Ramat Rahel, Gibeon and Nasbeh all show weighted artifact-counts of 300–500.
Twelve sites, even more than in the 8th century, are represented.

Within the resolution of our data, the only site at which
deposits of luxury items are unusually concentrated is
Lachish in the 8th century. At other times, the site with the
largest weighted artifact totals is less than 100% larger than
the next largest site or sites. Judeideh, which in the 7th century has the second most concentrated deposits after Lachish
in the 8th century, is less than 50% larger than four other
sites. Given the resolution of our data, this difference is not
significant. What is significant in the 7th century is the size-
able increase in scale for several sites in comparison to the 9th
century and earlier.

In connection with the evidence for writing, it should be
noted that the increase in the number of ostraca dating to the
7th century is not clearly indicative of an increase in writing
generally at this time. This phenomenon could also be
explained as an increase in the use of less perishable potsherds
in place of papyrus as the material of choice for writing. A
decrease in the supply of papyrus, for example, could result in
an increase in use of ostraca for writing and show up as an
increase in our figures and thus not bear any meaningful
relation to an increase in writing generally during this century. Our data may provide circumstantial evidence for the
latter hypothesis. A decline in connections with Egypt beginning at least in the 9th century has already been noted at
Lachish (Tufnell 1953: 47f.). If this phenomenon occurred
regionally, such evidence would suggest diminishment in ties
with Egypt in the 8th century, possibly resulting in a reduction
in papyrus trade and an increase in the use of other materials
for writing. Our data unfortunately are inadequate to address
this problem, which would require a more focused study. We

will return to the issue of the development of writing as it relates to administrative control systems later in this chapter.

As a result of these data, we can draw several conclusions with a fair degree of confidence. First, luxury items were highly concentrated in Lachish in the 8th century. Second, there is no evidence of such concentration at any other site in our sample for the period covered by our data. Except for Lachish in the 8th century, our maps strongly indicate regional dispersion of the increase in aggregate luxury item production rather than local concentration. We concluded in the previous section that the peak production of the objects discussed in this study was in the 7th century, and in that century there is no evidence of concentration at any site in our sample.

Kenyon (1967) presented evidence that Jerusalem is an exception to this picture of our region in the 7th century in at least two cases. While not counted, the fragments of 'hundreds' of figurines dating to this century and found in her excavations, which cover a tiny fraction of 50 ha 7th-century Jerusalem would place Jerusalem many times 'higher' than any other site for this artifact type in our 7th-century maps (1967: 101). In addition, Kenyon found 41 weights, 22 of which were inscribed, in strata dating to the 7th century (1967: Pl. 51, and discussion there). Again, this corpus would place 7th-century Jerusalem many times higher than all other 7th-century sites for this artifact type. At the time, Kenyon noted, this find approximately doubled the entire corpus of weights for all sites in Palestine, including the north. The possible bearing of this particular artifact type, the function of which was to standardize one aspect of the exchange system, on the issue of degree of centralization of economic control will also be discussed below. The point to be noted here is that such evidence as exists for Jerusalem indicates that it was the only site in our region in the 7th century at which concentration of the greatly increased levels of artifact deposition occurred. This finding is based on so little evidence that it could hardly be considered strongly supportive of the picture of the centrality of Jerusalem during this time as revealed by the settlement and public works data. However, it is at least not inconsistent with the other data.

With these quantitative studies as a backdrop, we can consider the question of regional administrative control of certain aspects of the economy in our period, namely evidence for imported goods, centralized control of industry, and skilled artisanship.

Evidence for imported goods
The earliest evidence for imported goods in our region is that of Egyptian-made scarabs. Two dating to the 12th–11th century were recovered from Beth Zur, and one each dating to the Iron 1 period were found at Tell Beit Mirsim and Beth Shemesh. At Lachish, a 10th-century example and four 9th-century ones have been found. Also found in 9th-century Lachish were five local copies, and after this time Egyptian-style seals continued to be produced locally (17 scarabs, 20 scaraboids, and 16 faience amulets from 8th-century Lachish are all locally produced).

Wood was apparently a significant import beginning at least in the 9th century. According to Homsky and Moshkovitz (1976: 47), Beersheba in the 9th–8th centuries imported cedar of Lebanon, 'providing evidence of trade relations between Judaea and Phoenicia' at this time. Tufnell (1953: 61) notes that acacia wood for 8th-century wood doors at Lachish had been brought a 'considerable distance' from the south, though she does not suggest a possible trading partner.

For the 7th century, Naveh (1975) cites 'large quantities' of Greek Cypriote pottery at Meṣad Hashavyahu. Naveh explained the presence of the pottery at this fort by positing the existence of a contingent of Greek mercenaries there, hired by Josiah. This fort was built in the latter half of the 7th century, and was occupied only for the last two or three decades of that century.

Also dating to 7th-century deposits are two Assyrian beakers at Ramat Rahel. Interestingly, eleven fragments of locally manufactured imitations of Cypriote pottery were also found at this site. The excavator interpreted these finds as evidence for 'local acceptance of foreign artistic styles despite regional non-admission' (Aharoni 1964: 100; cf. Albright 1960: 47).

This latter remark of Aharoni's is a kind of 'damning with faint praise' insofar as imported goods are concerned: these very minimal data represent all references by excavators to datable imported objects in the sample of sites included in this study. The primary conclusion to be drawn is that there is precious little evidence that any of the sites in our sample undertook significant foreign trade relations during the period covered by our survey. As has been mentioned before, we must be wary of drawing negative inferences based on our limited sample. Nevertheless, we can at least state that we lack positive evidence to support contentions of ongoing, significant regional or local trade between foreign trading partners and sites in the luxury items portion of our survey during this period. The evidence from the Lachish tombs, representing the closest situation to long-term and significant levels of trade as reflected in large quantities of imported goods, indicates a tapering-off of such trade relations as there were between that site and Egypt during the 9th century.

However, there is one positive remark that can be made regarding the evidence for imported items presented here. During the 8th and 7th centuries, all evidence for imports comes from forts, with the possible exception of Lachish. Meṣad Hashavyahu and Beersheba were both fortified citadels, built not with local resources but as part of a regional defensive network (see above, 'Evidence for regional building projects' in Chapter 3). Ramat Rahel was evidently built as a royal residence (Aharoni 1964). None of these sites, in other words, were local settlements capable of developing independent trade relations of the kind which would have brought the imported materials found at them to the sites. They all owed their existence to the direction of labor and materials from an outside source. It is almost certain that the economic relations resulting in the deposition of foreign-made materials or timber at those sites were handled by the 'mother' site which also provided the resources to fortify them. Even Lachish may have had its acacia wood brought up from the south with outside assistance, which may also be responsible for the construction of the massive citadel built there in the 8th century.

Hardly a shred of evidence exists for significant foreign trade relations being carried on by independently established settlements in our survey during this period. However, there is a not inconsiderable amount of evidence to suggest that a site not included in the survey in this chapter did have significant foreign contacts and was capable of redistributing such materials at secondary sites. Our settlement and public works data strongly suggest that this site was Jerusalem. Direct evidence of imported goods deposited at Jerusalem during this period is lacking in the material published to date, so the suggestion made here must await positive proof. However, our limiting remarks stand: there is no evidence for lasting foreign trade relations being carried on by settlements other than Jerusalem; and even the evidence for such trade as did occur only begins to appear in the 9th century, with the predominant evidence coming from the forts and fortified sites established under outside control, presumably Jerusalemite, in the 8th and 7th centuries.

Evidence for centralized control of industry
Two kinds of evidence may possibly point toward centralized regional control of industry in our region during the period covered by our study. The first kind of evidence is that of stamped jar-handles; the second is the existence of sites dedicated to a single industry. Each possibility will be discussed in turn.

Stamped jar-handles. 695 stamped jar handles are distributed in 8th and 7th century deposits in seven of the sites covered in our survey. The majority of the stamps picture a scarab, a word meaning 'belonging to the king', and the letters of the name of one of four towns: Hebron, Ziph, Sokoh and MmsT. The location of the last site has yet to be determined, but the provenience of the clay of which the MmsT-stamped handles are formed is known to be Marisa (Yeivin 1958: 10-11). Fully a third of the stamps (216) are in such poor condition that the city name can no longer be made out. In addition, 12 examples of a stamp featuring another pattern, the rosette, have been discovered. The numbers of each kind of stamp, and their temporal provenience, are shown in Chart 16: Stamped Jar-Handles.

There is some debate as to the function of these stamps. Albright (1943: 75) suggested that the four towns mentioned in the stamps were 'royal store-cities, in which taxes in kind were stored'. Pritchard (1959: 16) proposed that the marks 'identify jars for return to one of four vintners'. Pritchard's suggestion was based in part on his discovery of two local stamp-seals at Gibeon—one had an erroneous Hebrew letter *nun* on it. Albright's explanation would place the function of such handle-stamped jars in the context of a centrally controlled, regional redistributive system. Pritchard's concept, on the other hand, could fit a centrally controlled system but would nestle comfortably into other regional patterns of trade as well, such as the existence of competing towns with only nominal crown control over the economic context in which the jars were used. However, the fact that while the city names varied the basic scarab design did not, implies that the four cities were involved in some kind of centralized system governed by 'the king' to which the stamps refer. Pritchard (1962: 118) later noted that some jar handles from Nasbeh, Lachish, Gibeon and a Shephelah tell were all stamped with precisely the same seal, indicating that the vessels bearing such stamps were traded between sites. If this was the case, the vessels were not being returned directly to the vintners.

Silver (1983: 30ff.) maintained that the stamped jar-handles were reflective of private enterprise, with the *lmlk*, scarab and rosette stamps all representing promotional efforts by the local producers. However, Silver's analysis seems to regard private enterprise and royal management as mutually exclusive systems, and he consequently makes no attempt to address the extent of royal involvement in the economy at this point. It is possible that private enterprise existed in the 8th and 7th centuries, but the limited and indirect evidence Silver adduces for this hypothesis falls far short of supporting a portrayal of commodities production in 8th–7th-century Judah as dominated by the private sector. My guess is that temple, crown and private forces all existed in tension with one another throughout the monarchy, with ebbs and flows in the balance between each and constantly shifting allegiances. Further detailed study of the textual and archeological data pertaining to this matter is required before a final verdict can be rendered, but, until clearer and more substantial evidence for Silver's hypothesis can be found, the best explanation for the *lmlk* jar handles continues to be that they functioned as part of a centrally managed system (thus also Cross 1969 and Rainey 1982).

How extensive this system was, and what commodities were managed under it, remains unclear. Our data do not enable us to address these questions with much precision, but it seems evident from the large number that have been recovered at sites other than those named on the stamps (695 from our sample of sites) that these jars were quite prevalent and well-distributed in our region. Again it should be noted that these stamps first appear in the late 8th century and continue in use through the 7th (Stern 1975: 49-50). This datum comports well with the hypothesis that the general rise in productivity seen in our data in these two centuries may have been associated with centrally based efforts at regional control over the increased production. Our data provide circumstantial evidence for a manifold-commodity utilization of the jars, such as was proposed by Albright, though a single-commodity use as discussed by Pritchard is not ruled out.

Single-industry sites. Single-industry sites may indicate the presence of a centrally managed system in some cases. Several characteristics of such sites would increase the likelihood that they formed part of a regionally managed system. The dedication of all labor energies at a site to a single industry can imply the presence of a system to redistribute food so that skilled workers can devote all their energies to a specialized craft. This would more likely be the case if the industry required special skills that could only be developed by full-time dedication on the part of the workers. Also, we might expect to find a contemporaneous network of such sites, each with its own specialized industry, in a regionally managed system (Peebles and Kus 1977: 432). Increasing specialization, or 'segregation' to use Flannery's term (1968: 409), along with increasingly centralized control of more and more diverse functions, should correlate strongly with increasingly powerful bureaucratic institutions and information processing support.

Three sites from our sample, namely Tell Beit Mirsim, Engedi and Gibeon, have been identified as possible single-industry sites. In one other instance, Grant and Wright (1939) identified an Iron 1 metal industry at Beth Shemesh; however, there is no evidence that this site at this time was dedicated primarily to the production of the one commodity, as may have been the case at En-gedi, Gibeon and Tell Beit Mirsim.

Albright (1943: 56ff.) says that scores of basketfuls of loom weights and the presence of dye vats distributed evenly throughout the area excavated by him indicate the existence of a dye industry at Tell Beit Mirsim. The founding date for this industry is not certain, but it apparently does not predate the 8th century (1943: 59). The dye vats, measuring approximately half a cubic meter (see his Pl. 11) occur in 'considerable numbers'; Albright thus concluded that 'the inhabitants of the town must have specialized in the manufacture of textile goods' at this time.

Mazar's excavations at En-gedi (1966) revealed the existence of vats and other artifacts which, he felt, indicated the presence of an industry in balsam production. This industry can be very precisely dated to the last few decades of the 7th century since the site was inhabited only for this short period. Mazar asserts that specialized skills were involved in the balsam industry, which he says was carried on by families organized in guilds and dependent on the crown (1966: 20-21).

Pritchard (1961b) counted 63 rock-cut wine cisterns, with an average capacity of 1500 US gallons, in his excavations at Gibeon. He also discovered 40 clay stoppers and one clay funnel which fit the 56 stamped jar handles he found very well. He concluded that there was a wine industry at Gibeon dating to the Iron 2 period. As was the case at Tell Beit Mirsim, the date of establishment is not precisely known and could fall anywhere from the 9th to the 7th centuries. This industry seems to underlie Pritchard's remark that 'the major period of prosperity [at Gibeon] was toward the end of the 7th century' (1961b: 39).

Of the three sites discussed above, En-gedi is the most likely candidate for an industry dependent on outside support. The techniques involved seem to be the most specialized (see Mazar's discussion), though dyeing and wine production involved skills that were nearly as specialized. Mazar's portrayal of En-gedi as a crown dependency organized into familial guilds does not seem to be justified on the basis of the evidence at En-gedi itself. However, the fact that three distinct industries apparently existed contemporaneously during the 7th century may be additional evidence that Tell Beit Mirsim and Gibeon, along with En-gedi, were specialized members of a regional network of industries at this time. Such a degree of interdependence would imply a bureaucratic infrastructure to manage the redistribution of products between sites that were no longer economically autonomous. Also, the loss of economic autonomy could imply a greater degree of political and military dependence on other settlements in each case. Thus, while the evidence from the individual sites is not particularly striking, the probable contemporaneity of this phenomenon at three sites may be more than a coincidence.

Evidence for skilled artisanship
Aside from what was presented in the preceding section, there is little evidence for skilled artisanship. Rather, workmanship seems to be poor. In looking at the small finds he recovered from Gibeon, Pritchard (1959: 122-23) was doubtful about the existence of craft specialists at his site. Tufnell (1953: 375) found that the pillar-based terracotta figurines that are so plentiful at Judean sites were manufactured by a two-step process: the heads were made centrally from a common mold, and the bases were of local make, generally of poor quality. Negbi (1967) studied over 200 terracottas from Tell Sippor and concluded that they had been made locally by non-professionals. Kenyon (1967: 50), noting that Solomon had to import skilled Tyrian laborers to build the public works with which he was credited in biblical sources, commented that there is little evidence for professional masonry to be found in all Israel throughout the monarchic period. This was before the publication of excavations at Ramat Rahel, however. In addition to the window-balustrades there (see above in Chapter 2), two painted sherds represent the sole evidence for this form of art from this period in our region of study (Aharoni 1975). Also dating to the seventh century is a flat seal, one centimeter square, from En-gedi (Mazar 1966: 37-38). Mazar comments that 'the workmanship is excellent and there is no doubt that the object was made by an experienced craftsman'. Avigad (1984: 41) found two 7th-century ostraca in his excavations at

Jerusalem which he felt were undoubtedly the work of a skilled scribe.

The scanty evidence for indigenous craft specialization for the items and sites covered in our survey dates no earlier than the 8th century and comes mostly from the 7th. Such evidence as there is comes from the two sites claimed by the excavators to have been crown dependencies: En-gedi and Ramat Rahel. This corroborates the findings of our analyses of other artifact attributes: the 8th, and especially the 7th centuries provide virtually all the evidence we have for craft specialization and consequently for the comparatively sophisticated control systems which made craft specialization possible.

Having presented several kinds of data for luxury items and suggested how each may relate to the issue of administrative control systems through time in our region, we are ready to integrate these analyses with one another. The resulting synthesis can then be compared with the results of syntheses of settlement data and public works data analysis, and our model of regional development of administrative control can thus be further refined.

Summary of Luxury Items Results

The quantitative data revealed a manifold increase in the deposition of ten of the twelve artifact types covered in our study beginning in the 8th century and accelerating in the 7th. The most likely explanation for the increased rate of artifact deposition during this period was determined to have been an increase in the production of a broad spectrum of non-agricultural goods rather than regional military conquest or artifact obsolescence in most cases.

This increase in deposition rates for many artifact types is characterized geographically by a lack of concentration at any site and balance among an increasing number of sites during the 8th and 7th centuries. Two possible exceptions to this pattern were noted. Lachish in the 8th century appeared to concentrate deposits more than twice as large as any other 8th-century site for many of the artifact types represented in this study. The other exception was Jerusalem in the 7th century, at which time the deposition rates for two kinds of artifacts, weights and statuary, were many times higher than corresponding rates at any other site in that century.

The evidence for systematic, sustained foreign trade was mostly non-existent. No site in our sample contained material remains of such trade, with the possible exception of Lachish prior to the end of the 9th century. However, the small amount of material determined to have been imported in the 8th and 7th centuries was highly concentrated in secondary sites constructed and supported not by an indigenous population but by another, primary settlement. It was suggested on the basis of the settlement and public works data that the leading candidate for the primary settlement among the sites covered in our survey of excavation reports was Jerusalem.

There was significant evidence for centralized management of some aspects of the regional economy, primarily in the 7th century but perhaps beginning as early as the 8th. The pattern of distribution of the 'belonging to the king' stamped jar-handles suggested that several commodities, rather than just one, were redistributed among sites under centralized auspices utilizing jars thus stamped. These stamped jar-handles appear in the 8th century and continue through the end of the 7th. A few examples of standardized weights, which probably represent another form of regional management of redistribution of goods, were found at several of the sites in our sample (6 of 12). McCown (1947: 260) found that the range of measurements for weights inscribed with the same name was too great to justify claims for a standardized system. However, on the basis of new evidence, Kenyon (1967: Pl. 51) concluded that Hezekiah had attempted to standardize the weight system in the late 8th century. Over 90% of the weights found in stratified contexts at our sites dated to the 7th century; most of these were uncovered in Jerusalem, but their broad distribution regionally reflects widespread use. Finally, the existence of contemporary single-industry sites in 7th-century Tell Beit Mirsim (dye industry), En-gedi (balsam production) and Gibeon (wine production) reveals another possible dimension of intrasite management of production in our region in that century.

Evidence for skilled artisanship, paralleling that for import-ed artifacts, was minimal and concentrated in the 7th cen-tury, and it appeared only in Jerusalem dependencies.

This analysis of the luxury item data leads to the following conclusions. First, evidence for any kind of regional manage-ment of the economy only begins to appear in the luxury item data in the 8th century, coinciding with a sharp and geo-graphically dispersed increase in production of a broad range of non-agricultural goods. In this century, Lachish concen-trates deposits of the items covered by our survey at a rate more than twice as high as any other represented site. How-ever, an abundance of the 'belonging to the king' stamps that began to appear in this century were also found at Lachish, and since the king was not there, Lachish was at best a secon-dary player in the nascent stages of such management. Sec-ond, the evidence for regional management becomes much stronger in the 7th century. In this century Lachish dimin-ished significantly in regional importance, while Jerusalem was apparently the focal point of further broad-based and manifold increases in regional production, founding of new sites, and management of foreign exchange relations and a minimal amount of indigenous, full-time professional artisan-ship.

In the next chapter, Chapter 5, we will integrate this analy-sis of luxury items data with that presented in Chapters 2 and 3 on settlement and public works data.

Chapter 5

CONCLUSION

In this chapter we will, first, integrate the results of analyses of luxury items, settlement, and public works data, and consider the matter of schools and writing in ancient Judah by correlating the direct evidence for writing with the synthesis of the settlement, public works and luxury items data. A model of writing as a key and developing part of information processing systems functioning within a network of administrative control of public works, production and redistribution of commodities will thereby be generated from the archeological data. Then, this archeologically based model will be used as the basis for re-evaluating the cross-cultural and biblical data which was the focus of discussion in Chapter 1.

The final section of this conclusion will provide suggestions for further research. Our goal in this study has been to develop a model which integrates two branches of archeological research that are too often unrelated: collection of archeological data, and testing of models based on that data. Consequently, we will present suggestions for further research of the second variety, of which the present study is an example, and also for improvements in data collection in archeological field work so that archeology can contribute information especially appropriate to the kind of secondary research represented here.

Integration of Settlement, Public Works and Luxury Items Analyses

We must be wary of attempting to integrate the results of the settlement, public works and luxury items analyses too simplistically. The data on which the analyses were based varied significantly in character, as we have shown in the 'Limitations in the data' sections in each case. The settlement data was the best-preserved and most consistently reported of the three, but in terms of analytical value it provided the most indirect evidence for intrasite relations and suprasite management of those relations. The luxury items data provided the most direct view of these societal variables, but it was more subject to the vicissitudes of time and vagaries of reporting than were the other two kinds of data. Public works data struck a median position between the extremes of settlement and luxury items data both in terms of survival rate of the structures from which the data were gathered and the consistency with which they were reported.

The distinct values of each of these kinds of data bear on the issues at hand in a complementary fashion. The settlement analysis, presented and discussed in detail in Chapter 2, will function as a framework for the interpretation of the other two kinds of data and also as a check against their over-interpretation. The public works and luxury items data will provide complementary insight into the management of labor, natural resources, and exchange for this region and period. Where they appear to conflict, the analysis based on public works data will generally be considered more reliable than that based on the data described in Chapter 4. The public works data are drawn from a broader sample of sites, and recovery of such data from the sites was superior to that in the case of luxury items.

With these reservations in mind, we can consider whether the analyses presented in Chapter 4 fit, or fail to fit, with the model proposed and refined above. The first thing to observe is that analysis of the luxury items data provides striking confirmation of the model of regional administrative development formulated on the basis of public works and settlement in most of its aspects. The sharp and broadly based increase in the production of certain artifacts, beginning in the 8th century, coincides temporally, geographically and in terms of degree of dispersion with the values of these variables predicted by our model. The picture of Jerusalem's primacy based on its size and control of building programs was confirmed and functionally refined. Regional management of commodities, craft specialization, and foreign exchange were all handled exclusively by Jerusalem, again beginning in the 8th century and reaching an apex in the 7th.

However, in at least two cases, a prediction based on the model was not fully confirmed by the luxury items data. First, while we successfully predicted the large increase in productivity in the 8th century on the basis of settlement patterns alone, it was anticipated that a significant portion of that increase would be related to increased foreign exchange in this period. While most of the evidence for imported goods does come from the 8th–7th centuries, the level at which it occurred should be characterized as negligible. Second, the evidence for skilled artisanship was likewise non-existent. This situation is surely related to the dearth of published data on Jerusalem. However, the available data do not permit us to be certain about this. All that can be said is that the prediction of significantly increased levels of imported goods for the 8th–7th centuries was not confirmed, and that the prediction of similarly increased levels of skilled artisanship received weak confirmation at best.

Despite these instances in which the predictions were not borne out, all the evidence at our disposal confirms Jerusalem's increasingly prominent role as the central place in 8th–7th-century Judah. The presence of a broad range of functions had its centre exclusively at Jerusalem, including increasing influence moving to complete control (as was apparently the case at En-gedi) over other sites. Evidence of increasing economic dependence of other settlements on Jerusalem also underscores this. The negative evidence for such centralized regional management prior to the 8th century and following the 7th is also compelling in the luxury items data, as it had been for the settlement and public works data.

The Judahite monarchy: when did it become a state?
Although examination of the nature of the state in 10th-century Judah is not an explicit goal of this study, the negative portrayal of that entity may be, to some, the most controversial finding presented here. There is little evidence that Judah began to function as a state at all prior to the tremendous increases in population, building, production, centralization

and specialization which began to appear in the 8th century. The limited quantity of data could only account for this finding if a reason could be found for differential recovery of 10th- and 8th-century materials. Lacking such an explanation, the disparity in rates of recovery of 10th- and 8th-century materials is best explained as reflecting the rates of deposition of those materials. A comparison of the listings of societal traits expected to be found in stratified societies (see above) with our data will show that these traits are almost completely absent from our region in the 10th century. Even in the 8th and 7th centuries, the period of greatest development seen through the lens of our data, evidence for some of the traits, namely professional, skilled artisanship, inter-regional trade, and population of the scale expected to characterize a state (100,000+; cf. Flannery 1972: 412f.; Trigger 1974: 97) must be characterized as weak. In the 10th century systematic evidence of the kind we would expect from a state is even more difficult to come by. The primary problem is one of scale: the levels of production and population were just too small in 10th-century Judah to suggest the presence of the full-scale state; they seem more appropriate to a chiefdom, generally (see the discussion below). However, even if we were to ignore this fact and evaluate the society in this region on the basis of complexity alone, the amount of evidence for material centralization or full-time craft specialization is small indeed. Under our polythetic classification scheme, Judah was a small state in the 8th–7th centuries, but not before.

The picture portrayed through study of our data contrasts quite sharply with what must be described as a strong consensus that the Judahite monarchy became a state at some point in the 10th century (thus Flanagan 1981; Frick 1987; Alt 1967; Demsky 1971; Mettinger 1971; etc.). The only conflict on this point seems to be whether the state came into being under Saul (Alt 1966: 185), David (Frick 1987: 188, 191) or Solomon (Flanagan 1981: 58). This general consensus and the data presented in this study seem to me to be incompatible; a hypothesis of statehood for Israel in the 10th century would predict the recovery of values of archeological evidence of all kinds in the 10th century similar to that which we found only in the 8th and 7th centuries.

This problem has a critical bearing on our discussion of the education of those who functioned as the officials in Judah's administrative control systems. Perhaps the key attribute of a state in contrast to less highly organized forms of social organization is the nature and strength of such controls.

> In states, the managerial superstructure becomes... more elaborate, multilevel, and centralized; and the royal bureaucracies who process data for hundreds of thousands of souls must be supported by costly tribute, corvee labor, and often the pillaging of less powerful neighbors. In the case of some ancient civilizations, such as the Classic Maya, such a superstructure was supported in spite of agricultural practices believed to be no more sophisticated (except in rare cases) than those of egalitarian tribes. Looked at in this way, the most striking difference between states and simpler societies lies in the realm of decision-making and its hierarchical organization, rather than in matter and energy exchanges (Flannery 1972: 412).

In order to determine the cause of the disparity between the conclusions to which the evidence presented above leads and the consensus regarding the advent of the state in Judah, it is necessary to consider the evidence for the transformation of Judah into a state in the 10th century. Several important studies (Frick 1987; Flanagan 1981; Gottwald 1979) have focused on the development of Israel in the 12th–10th centuries from a set of loosely confederated tribes to a more integrated society. Unfortunately for the present need, their analysis stops short of consideration of the development from chiefdom to statehood, though, as we saw, this does not deter them from asserting that this development occurred in the 10th century. This is especially surprising in view of the title of Frick's book.

T.N.D. Mettinger's study (1971) of this problem deserves more attention than can be given here, but the evidence upon which he bases his analysis is so different in character from the evidence we have used that to address his points in detail would carry us very far afield indeed. However, since the results of his careful study of a quite different set of data are among those which vary so greatly from the evidence presented here, some effort must be made to relate the two. I will limit myself to some general remarks.

First, Mettinger appears to use the term 'state' rather
loosely. He never draws his use of this term into the technical,
sociological context in which it has been used here; see, e.g., his
discussion of 'state annals' (pp. 36ff.). The phrase 'state
annals' seems to be used synonomously with 'official archives'.
In this connection, it should be noted that his explication of the
lists of titles of officials of the united monarchy (10th century)
includes an analysis of the relation of these roles to 'tribal
institutions'. This, and his subsequent discussion, suggests that
he should be using the term 'chiefdom' rather than 'state'
since one aspect of the distinction between chiefdom and state
is that other institutions supplant kinship as the primary basis
for social organization (thus e.g. Flannery 1972: 403ff.; Frick
1975: 97ff.).

A second point which should be noted is Mettinger's occasional application of evidence from later materials to his discussion. His presentation (pp. 89ff.) of the Samaria ostraca,
which he dates to the 8th century, and of the stamped jar-
handles (dating, as we saw, exclusively to the 8th–7th centuries) on are examples of this. His study, to properly include
such materials, should be more diachronic than it in fact is.
There is no sense of the development and transformation of
administrative institutions in his presentation. His approach
(though not, I believe, his data) implies that the Solomonic
apparatus continued to operate on approximately the same
level throughout the monarchic period. This problem makes it
impossible for him to distinguish 10th-century administrative
control systems from later developments. It is also obvious that
Mettinger's information could be re-evaluated with an analysis of such development in mind, by paying closer attention to
the dating of his materials, biblical as well as epigraphic (see
below). I believe such a procedure would have a high probability of good results. It is regrettable that this was not done in the
first place.

A third difficulty encountered in Mettinger's analysis is his
seemingly uncritical use of comparative materials from Egypt
and Mesopotamia; see, for example, his 'question of foreign
prototypes' (p. 2). His rationale for the use of such materials is
that

...the tribal confederation could not offer an appropriate basis for the development of the apparatus for the central administration of the kingdom. This makes it necessary to pay special attention to the possibilities of borrowing (1971: 2).

Mettinger offers no evidence for or even discussion of the first assertion. The latter assertion, and the subsequent discussion, betrays no sociological sensitivity to the very problematic nature of cross-cultural comparisons (Talmon 1977; Golka 1983). Under the circumstances, his failure to notice this area of potential difficulty undermines the credibility of his evaluation of this type of data.

Mettinger's assessment of schools in Israel will be discussed below. If his analysis were untangled temporally, and included critical evaluations of the comparative materials, it would produce results which could be fruitfully compared with those produced here. The detail of insight into administrative institutions possible through textual analyses is far greater in some respects than that afforded by our data. The present state of the discussion, however, renders comparison of the results produced here with Mettinger's problematic. The best that can be said is that Mettinger's analysis, in its present state, provides no sound basis for modifying the conclusion reached here, namely that Jerusalem began to function as the primate center of a 'state' (in the technical sense) only in the 8th century, and then on a relatively small scale, for a state (cf. Crenshaw 1984: 611).

It may be useful to compare the trait lists for 'chiefdoms' and 'states' to clarify what may be merely a terminological problem. First, according to Flannery,

Chiefs have divine connections, not just noble birth... Frequently, they build up elaborate retinues of followers and assistants (often relatives)—the chiefly precursors of later state bureaucracies. Often, chiefdoms have not only elaborate ritual but even full-time religious specialists; indeed, the chief himself may be a priest as well.
    ...chiefdoms have large populations, with villages of paramount chiefs sometimes running into the thousands...They also have a higher degree of craft specialization, both in necessities and luxury goods...Yet, although there are village specialists, there is usually as yet no class of craft specialists, no occupational castes as in stratified societies (197   402-403).

According to Flannery, states are characterized by a far higher number of institutions, very large population, frequent warfare, complex agricultural systems, more highly developed crafts, intense exchange, and the regulation of thousands of persons through the establishment of a highly diversified and specialized set of offices (1972: 412).

To this list Peebles and Kus add public works and part-time craft specialization, defensive organization and management of intersocietal trade (1977: 431-33). Flanagan (1981) mentions all these and also territorial expansion, reduction of internal strife, pervasive inequality, ecological diversification (perhaps the same as Flannery's increasingly complex agricultural systems), centers which coordinate social, religious and economic activity, and the absence of 'a true government to back up decisions by legalized force'. It is this final criterion (alone) which he calls upon as evidence for the transition from chiefdom to state.

Some of the features which have been used to characterize Solomon or David as statebuilders in fact appear here as distinguishing lower-order societies from chiefdoms. For example, Solomon is given credit for organizing intersocietal trade (1 Kgs 9.26ff.; 1 Kgs 10.11, 22, 28). Yet, properly speaking, if Solomon was the leader to initiate this, he should be considered as the one who moved Israel from a lower-order society to a chiefdom, as far as this particular trait is concerned. Likewise, his building activities and establishment of a royal retinue do not distinguish his role from that of a paramount chief. As Service puts it,

> The great change at the chiefdom level is that specialization and redistribution are no longer merely adjunctive to a few particular endeavors, but continuously characterize a large activitiy of the society (1962: 143).

Another point must be considered as well. According to Frick (1987), Hopkins (1981) and Flanagan (1981), the process of evolution from lower-order society to chiefdom (Saul) was a lengthy process, taking place over the course of the 12th through early 10th centuries. If this time scale is at all accurate, then it is somewhat surprising that Israel should pass through the 'chiefdom' phase so rapidly. Flanagan calls both

David and Saul 'chiefs' (1981: 69), while Frick calls Saul a chief, and David a chief and then the first ruler of a state (1987: 191). At least, the contrast in the rapidity of this transition needs to be explained in comparison with that of the previous stage of development.

The fact of the matter is that the transition from chiefdom to statehood for Israel has been assumed often and explained seldom. The data presented here challenge certain assumptions about this transition and indicate that the transition from chiefdom to state in ancient Israel should be studied much more carefully on a textual and archeological basis. The evidence provided in this study, and the technical definition of 'chiefdom' as it appears in the sociological literature, seem to indicate that this term may be the one most applicable to the level of administrative control present in 10th-century Judah. There was significant evidence, as we saw, of administration involvement on a regional scale, but the level and quality of control implied in our evidence was qualitatively different from that for which evidence was found in the 8th–7th centuries (see above, on public works: evidence for regional building patterns, and the synthesis in that chapter). The model which places the achievement of full statehoood for Judah in the 8th century allows time for the transition from chiefdom to statehood to occur on a scale which corresponds more closely to the temporal scale implied in the ecological models of Frick and Hopkins. Rather than metamorphosing suddenly, the institutions established by Solomon evolved and developed over time into a full-blown state by the 8th century (cf. Silver 1983: 5-7, 52; Pritchard 1974: 35f.). Solomon, by this account, should be credited with setting in motion the institutional forces which eventually resulted in state bureaucratic controls, accompanied by an intensity of settlement and levels of regional economic activity appropriate to a state.

However, the restriction of the areal extent of our study to Judah renders conclusions made on the basis of the data presented here tentative where they concern the period of the united monarchy. Analysis of data from Ephraim, the Galilee, and Transjordan as well as Judah is necessary in order to address fully the problem of the transition of Israel to a state. Also, transitions from one system state to another can happen with great rapidity, even on a regional scale. The model of a slow transition to statehood is not predicated on an assumption that such transitions are more likely to occur slowly. Rather, it is based on the archeological evidence from that region and period.

The end of the Judahite state: a pathology
We have already noticed the striking collapse of the Judahite state in the 6th century; and we suggested in the synthesis of the settlement data that the model of Jerusalem's primacy, if confirmed by later data (as it has been), might help explain the extent of the societal collapse following the fall of Jerusalem and the deportation of its leading citizens in the early 6th century. Before we seek to explain this phenomenon, we need to consider a debate which is currently unresolved in the anthropological-archeological literature, and that is the conflict between multivariant and 'prime mover' varieties of explanation (Flannery 1972: 406). Carneiro (1970: 734) calls them 'voluntaristic' and 'external coercion' explanations. The multivariant approach seeks explanations in terms of the interaction between multiple parts of a system via mechanisms such as feedback, homeostasis, etc. (Clarke 1977: 45ff.) Carneiro (1970) and Athens (1977: 358-59) assert that phase shifts in a system, such as a shift to or from a state, cannot be explained in terms of the internal workings of a system alone. The approach taken by Frick (1979: 233; 1987: 95f.) follows Flannery's model; the present study will incorporate aspects of both, in this particular case, though on the whole it is closer to Flannery's (see Chapter 1).

We may begin our attempt to explain the 6th-century collapse of the Judahite state by recalling that the key *functional* indicator of primate sites is the arrogation of most central functions to it, and the disappearance of intermediate-sized sites (see the discussion of Ziph's 'rank-size rule' by Adams [1981: 72-73], cited above). Flannery describes a condition apparently similar to this, which he terms 'hypercoherence':

> This highly centralized but sometimes unstable condition results from the breakdown of whatever autonomy the various small subsystems (or institutions) in a larger system may have; one by one, they are coupled more closely to each other and/or to

the central hierarchical control until... change in one does in fact affect all others too directly and rapidly... too great a degree of coherence can be as lethal as too little (1972: 420).

This condition may describe Jerusalem in the 7th century. Perhaps in part because of the Assyrian reduction of Lachish, and perhaps other intermediate-range sites, and the survival of Jerusalem, it was thrust into an even more central role than it might otherwise have assumed. So many functions were arrogated exclusively to Jerusalem that secondary sites were ill equipped to assume control of a complex and in some cases industrially specialized regional economy including several sites which were apparently not self-sustaining. The boom in population visible in the settlement data, which began in the 8th century and escalated in the 7th, was dependent on a concomitant and similarly scaled boom in wealth, which we were able to detect and characterize through the luxury items data. Without the functions carried on at Jerusalem, this economic pattern could not persist.

The complete disappearance of settlement at most Judean sites during the 6th century, documented in our settlement data, may appear in a rather different light as a result of this interpretation. Many of the smaller sites, even if they had been self-sufficient in their past, may not have been self-sustaining apart from their participation in the regional economy based in Jerusalem at this point in time. The neo-Babylonian reduction of Jerusalem catalyzed a phase shift from a state system to a much lower-level system.

The institutions of information storage, processing and transmission may have played a key role in this pathology. Centralized coordination of resources, human and material, is completely dependent on these institutions, perhaps more so than on any others; Flannery suggested that this might prove to be true (1972: 411). It was the loss of the interregional communication and coordination on which it had come to depend which finally doomed the regional social system to almost complete dissolution. Military reduction of Jerusalem as a central site certainly initiated this process, but the development of Judah as an increasingly complex state in the period prior to this was very likely a primary reason that the devolution in social complexity which resulted from the military incursion was so drastic.

Our archeologically based reconstruction of some of the societal transformations in monarchic Judah brings population growth, external military impact and ecological limitations into the explanatory framework. However, the primary dynamic for change in monarchic Israel was seen to be none of these on an individual basis. Rather, such change was explained in terms of dynamic feedback between these variables and another which was considered to be central: the development of societal institutions for managing resources and labor to respond to variations in some of the other, aforenamed variables. The development of the Judahite bureaucracy into a higher-level system managing a greater range of economic and legal transactions in an ever more centralized fashion was for two centuries a positive development for the regional economy, measured in terms of productivity and population growth. A heavy price was apparently paid in terms of adaptability and survivability.

Ramifications for writing and schools
The conclusions reached here will once again diverge from what appears to be a fairly solid consensus. First, the conclusions on this issue will be set forth on the basis of a straightforward reading of the data. Then, some alternative views on this issue will be presented and discussed in the hope that the disparities between these views and the model developed here can be better understood, and perhaps resolved.

The luxury items data provide some direct evidence on several points which corroborates tentative conclusions reached by inference earlier in this study; but evidence is also lacking precisely where we would most like to have it. In the first place, the luxury items data strongly confirm the absence of a general knowledge of writing in Judah prior to the 8th century. Reference to the map of evidence for writing shows this; and it also shows evidence of this knowledge beginning to spread in the 8th century (four sites) and continuing to do so in the 7th (seven sites, half of our sample).

At the same time, it should be noted that all of the seven sites in the 8th–7th centuries containing direct evidence of writing have been discussed in various connections in terms of their dependence on Jerusalem. Lachish, Arad and Meṣad Hashavyahu were essentially forts built and maintained as part of a defensive network by Jerusalem in this century. Gibeon, Tell Beit Mirsim and En-gedi were the three sites which were discussed in this chapter as showing evidence of industrial specialization and economic dependence on the regional redistributive network maintained by Jerusalem. Finally, Ramat Raḥel was simply a royal suburb of Jerusalem and, like En-gedi and Meṣad Hashavyahu, was built and maintained by Jerusalem.

It could hardly be a coincidence that every site outside Jerusalem containing direct evidence of writing was to some degree administratively dependent on Jerusalem. The conclusion to which this evidence points is that professional administrators were trained in Jerusalem, and only in Jerusalem. Further, specialized training in administrative skills was apparently needed on a broad basis only in the 8th–7th centuries, when the administrative demands of managing a regionally interdependent economic network would have required a concomitant quantum leap in regional communications. The question of whether this education took place in schools or not will be discussed in the next section.

Finally, it is possible to make some remarks, for the first time, about the 'democratization' of writing among the general populace. Our evidence shows that even local, nonprofessional examples of writing are limited to sites which show the strongest evidence of professional administrative involvement through one of several forms of dependence on Jerusalem. Even with a simple alphabet, it may have been unlikely that literacy could be passed on without some form of abiding presence of a person trained in that skill. Sites that, because of their close ties with Jerusalem, merited ongoing involvement in its administrative network, which was likely to have included legal and religious as well as economic aspects, would have an ongoing, indigenous 'stake' in mastering the skill of written communications. Further, the existence of intrasite relations of the kind described here increases the likelihood that a representative from Jerusalem may have been in permanent or semipermanent residence as a local ruler or governor in the

8th–7th centuries at the sites noted above. Both of these possibilities would inevitably increase the probability that residents of sites with significant economic and political ties to Jerusalem would have both the opportunity and the motivation to learn to read and write during this period. However, there is no evidence that writing, much less institutions established for formal training in it, existed in every village and hamlet.

With these remarks our definition of an archeologically based model of administrative control mechanisms, scribal schools and writings draws to a close. We will now compare this model with other kinds of evidence: biblical, cross-cultural, and epigraphic (speaking here of the written content of sherds which we only counted) to see how our model can contribute to a more broadly based discussion.

Re-evaluation of Schools in Monarchic Judah

Introduction
In this section we will re-evaluate the matter of schools in ancient Israel in light of the three kinds of data considered in the first section of Chapter 1: biblical, cross-cultural and epigraphic. We asserted that each of these kinds of data alone afforded little opportunity for unambiguous interpretations of scribal institutions in monarchic Israel. Under such circumstances, we decided to postpone looking at these data collectively until a sound interpretive framework could be established for them.

These kinds of data may now be reviewed in light of our analyses of archeological data from monarchic Judah. The degree to which biblical, cross-cultural and epigraphic data function comfortably within the interpretive framework established here will be briefly assessed in each case. If a datum must be interpreted in an unnatural way in order to fit it into our model, we must consider modifying or overhauling the model. However, the comparison of these data with our model may also work in a different manner. Because the historical data were ambiguous standing alone, the primary value of hearing them within the interpretive framework of the archeologically based model will be to see the direction in which the ambiguities in the cases reviewed will be resolved, given our prior assumptions.

A detailed analysis of each of these data sets, namely biblical, cross-cultural, and epigraphic, will not be attempted here. The data available in each case deserve a great deal more attention than can be devoted to them here. However, for our purposes detailed analyses are not necessary. The broad outlines of the relation of our findings to these data can be meaningfully sketched in a brief space, and we can then make general observations as to how the data might be integrated with the archeological model constructed above.

The biblical evidence

The following 19 passages have been singled out as possibly providing 'circumstantial' (Crenshaw 1984: 602) evidence of schools: Deut. 24.3; Josh. 18.9; Judg. 8.13-17; 2 Sam. 8.17; Isa. 8.16; 10.19; 28.9-13; 29.11-12; 50.4-9; Jer. 8.8; 32.12; Hab. 2.2; Prov. 3.3; 4.1-9 (especially 4.5); 7.3, 8.32-36; 17.16; Job 31.35-37. In order to consider these passages in the context of our model, we would first need to date them as closely as possible. This has not been done in the analyses of Lemaire (1981, 1985), Golka (1983), Crenshaw (1984), or Mettinger (1971), yet to utilize these passages as a basis for discussing schools in Israel without being sensitive to their temporal provenience robs these texts of any potential for providing us with a developmental picture. Mettinger, for example, should have utilized only such texts as may be dated to Solomon's period to support his claims about Solomon's bureaucracy; but, as with the ostraca, he fails to notice this problem, and texts from the eighth century and later are used as evidence for Solomon's system of administration (1971: 144; and see above).

While biblical texts are notoriously difficult to date, the eight prophetic examples cannot be dated prior to the latter half of the 8th century. Four of the five examples from the book of Proverbs are from the first nine chapters, which are at least in some quarters claimed to be later than the rest of the book (e.g. McKane 1970: 4ff.). The final editing of the 'Deuteronomic History' is known to date to the 6th century, raising at least the possibility of a late (post-8th century) date for those passages as well (Gray 1970: 6). In other words, eight of the nineteen passages are securely dated to the 8th century or later, and, except for one, the rest may date to this period or later as well. However, the degree of difficulty in dating these texts greatly reduces their value in any discussion of the development of Israel's state administration.

Even if the texts were to be more securely dated, we would still face the task of attempting to decide whether these texts place the education they may refer to into a school context, or not. Mettinger's discussion of this issue (1971: 143ff.) is very unconvincing on several points. First, he draws support from Egyptian and Mesopotamian models in a rather uncritical fashion (see his discussion of the first point on pp. 143-44). Second, his statement that 'the development of a royal administration in Israel created a need for educated officials and thereby also a need for a scribal school' (p. 144) is not supported by any evidence. He does not address problems such as the scale of administrative requirements of the society and the possibility of other forms of education besides schools, not to mention the comparative ease of learning an alphabetic script (cf. Gelb 1963: 260). All of these variables are critical in any evaluation of the kind of education administrators would appropriately receive in any societal context. Third, his biblical references (p. 144) in no instance make any mention of a school, as we observed (in Chapter 1) and as he himself notes (p. 143). Since he does not consider the possibility of education by tutoring or apprenticeship vs. school education, and since he makes no distinction between texts referring to Solomon's time and those of a later date (see above), his conclusions regarding schools must await further confirmation.

The archeologically based model developed on the basis of settlement, public works and luxury items data perhaps clearly, even dramatically, portrays a localization of scribal activity to Jerusalem-dependent sites. Formal scribal training would, therefore, take place primarily if not exclusively in Jerusalem. Crenshaw's careful assessment that 'for a chosen few, specialized scribal training may have been provided in Hezekiah's [late 8th-century] court' (1984: 614) is quite close to the position our archeological materials suggest.

Cross-cultural comparisons: Mesopotamia and Egypt
We can use our model to examine the issue of comparability of Judah with other societies. Our model is based on an assumption that the institutions of societal control, which are the context in which we are viewing the institutions of scribalism and schools, are embedded in a larger societal framework. This larger framework has been characterized by correlating our theoretical model to various configurations of archeological remains. If our assumptions are valid in this case, it follows that we may also usefully compare the configurations of archeological remains of different societies as a means of determining how comparable they really are.

However, we must be cautious. Temporal or spatial proximity was not seen as an adequate basis from which to infer that institutions in primary states such as Egypt or Mesopotamia must have parallels in a secondary state such as Israel (see Chapter 1). As a result of Price's (1978) analysis, even the degree to which Judah (and Israel) developed as secondary states from Egyptian and Mesopotamian primary states should be seriously questioned.

A basis for comparing institutions from one culture with those from another could be established in harmony with our assumptions, as follows. According to our model, closely parallel configurations of archeological remains correlating with key societal variables in different societies would strengthen the case for parallel institutions relating to those variables. We cannot compare what we can see in one society and not another; we can only compare what we can see in both. Given our functionalist assumptions, the archeological data interpreted within the framework of the model developed earlier would enable us to attempt a comparison to other regional contexts on a meaningful, and validatable, level. This, indeed, is a vital ultimate goal of research such as the present study (see below, 'Suggestions for further research').

In this case, let us say that we wish to compare the values of key aspects of settlement, public works and luxury items as compiled in this study with values for parallel data in contemporary Egypt and Mesopotamia, where scribal schools are attested in written documents dating as early as 1900 BCE (Mettinger 1971: 140ff.; Gadd 1956: 3). Our task is made easy by the fact that in every case all values of key variables studied here are an order of magnitude higher or more for Egypt and Mesopotamia than for our region. The largest site in our area at any time, Jerusalem, was at fifty hectares only 15% the size of central cities in Mesopotamia (Adams 1982: 72). The number of settlements larger than ten hectares, Adams' arbitrary cutoff for designation as 'urban', was in Mesopotamia more than ten times the number of such sites in Judah (and, almost certainly, Israel as well; cf. Shiloh 1980: 29ff.) for every period after the Uruk. Comparable disparities are so readily observable in the area of public works for both Egypt and Mesopotamia that it is pointless to enumerate them. Finally, while intrasite relations appeared in Judah, evidence for intraregional trade was minimal, as was the evidence for skilled artisanship of all kinds. Again, the analogous picture for Egypt and Mesopotamia is completely otherwise.

Without wishing to belabor the obvious, a conclusion must be drawn which is apparently not so obvious. We have assumed that the functional context of writing and professional scribalism in these or any other societies may be perceived in the same archeologically observable material isomorphs. Since these variables for Egypt and Mesopotamia assume values so much higher than was the case in Judah in our period, the need for information transfer to manage the tremendously greater amount of traffic of every kind was correspondingly greater for Egypt and Mesopotamia than for Judah.

In point of fact, cross-cultural comparison on any material basis results in a resounding conclusion of lack of comparability between monarchic Judah on the one hand and Egypt and Mesopotamia on the other (cf. Demsky 1972: 391).

We should also observe that the incomparability of our region with these others extends to the technique of writing to a significant degree. The art of producing hieroglyphic and cuneiform scripts was far more demanding than was the case with the syllabic scripts which characterized our region throughout this period (Gelb 1963: 255ff.). It would be imprudent to assume that such different writing systems would function or be institutionally promulgated similarly in different societies even if the societies were quite comparable on other grounds. It also cannot be assumed that governmental structures or institutions of any kind which utilized such different systems of information transfer would develop similarly, even if other external conditions were identical. The syllabic script is simple enough that functional knowledge of it could be passed on from one person to another in a comparatively short time (Demsky 1972: 391). Schools would hardly have been necessary, unless other skills that demanded an educational setting were being taught alongside literacy.

In the present instance, we must conclude that the evidence from Egypt and Mesopotamia provides no basis for supposing that schools to train scribes ever operated in monarchic Judah. On the contrary, the evidence suggests that institutions for teaching writing as an integral part of information management and regional control in our period would have been quite different from those which developed in Egypt and Mesopotamia.

Epigraphic evidence for schools and scribalism

As is the case with so many archeologically recovered artifacts, epigraphic materials (by which we mean here ostraca as well as inscribed materials, to which the description 'epigraphic' properly refers) provide more than one level of information (Clarke 1978: 155). Two levels in particular are of interest here. First, the mere fact that they have writing on them provides information that can be used directly in an archeologically based model. Thus epigraphic evidence was utilized in the 'luxury items' chapter, where a discussion of the regional distribution of this artifact type through time was incorporated into the model along with studies of other artifact types. However, at that point in the discussion we ignored the content of the epigraphic remains, which is a second level of information provided by written records. This level has evoked much discussion, especially when the content of inscriptions relates to the question of scribes and scribal schools (see the literature cited in Chapter 1). This second aspect of epigraphic remains, their written content, deserves comment as it relates to our archeologically based model.

To begin, let us review the situation reconstructed in this study. Using our functionalist model of writing as part of an information network embedded in a larger socioeconomic context, we predicted that artifactual evidence for writing would correlate highly with other variables indicative of regional economic interdependence and centralized control. This prediction was strikingly confirmed in every aspect for which we analyzed our data. Evidence for writing showed a strong correlation, both temporally and in terms of scale, with the increases in regional economic productivity observed in the 8th and 7th centuries. Evidence for writing also showed a strong geographical correlation with evidence for trade, skilled artisanship, and centralized control during the same period. Finally, all evidence pointed toward Jerusalem as the locale of such centralized management. In synthesizing these results we conscientiously avoided the issue of the historical content of the epigraphic materials. We postponed this question until we had formulated a broadly based model of the socioeconomic context within which the minimal and often ambiguous historical (written) data might best be interpreted.

Now we can illustrate how epigraphic evidence might be interpreted in light of the larger socioeconomic matrix with two examples, one of which works well and the other of which does not. First, let us consider an inscription uncovered on a step of the palace at Lachish, alongside an inscribed lion. This inscription, dating to the 8th century, contains the first five letters of the Hebrew alphabet. Tufnell (1953: 357) claimed at the time that this find represented 'the earliest archeological evidence for the order of the alphabet in Palestine *and systematic learning*' (italics mine). The evidence for systematic learning was the poor quality of the script, the order of the letters, and the location near the palace.

The excavator's interpretation of the Lachish inscription is corroborated by our research. Lachish was the largest, best-defended, and richest site in terms of public works and luxury items outside Jerusalem in our sample of sites during the 8th century. At a site of the regional position of importance that Lachish occupied, it is not unnatural to find evidence that people may have been learning to write. Some people were certainly being exposed to the information systems used to manage the considerable legal and economic traffic at this site. The phrase 'systematic learning' is also perhaps carefully imprecise: 'systematic' could refer to anything from scribal schools to the fact that the letters were written in order. In this case, our analysis suggests that this abecedary should not be interpreted as evidence for a school. Schools would be located in Jerusalem, if schools even existed. The level of expertise and knowledge, and the presence of the inscription on what could hardly have been a systematic location for teaching (a step), do not permit us to infer the presence of anything more at Lachish at this time than an interest in learning to write by someone with access to the environs of the palace.

Our second example is exceptional in many respects, and it may be especially illustrative to deal with it for that reason. Our model, and most models based on descriptive statistical analyses, are developed in the first place from evidence of the typical or average sort. It is difficult to develop models which deal successfully with extreme cases, but it is also helpful to see how they handle such cases once they have been set forth. The curve we will throw at our model is the 'Gezer calendar', which is a small limestone slab found in late 10th-century deposits at Gezer. Albright (1943), Rathjen (1961), Lemaire (1981) and others have interpreted this artifact as a schoolboy's rhyme practicing the seasons of the year. The evidence for this interpretation is the poor quality of the writing, the meter of the Hebrew words, and the simple level of the content of the text. Accordingly, this artifact has been taken as evidence for general literacy and the presence of schools in the 10th century.

The approach taken here looks first at societal context. The questions we would ask are: was 10th-century Gezer known from other evidence to have been involved in socioeconomic activities at levels which would have required knowledge of writing? How extensive was this requirement? How does this find fit in with the regional picture of writing at this time? Gezer was a prosperous settlement in the 12th–11th centuries, was destroyed at approximately the time the 'calendar' was deposited, and is believed to have been the beneficiary of a rebuilt gate and encircling wall in the late 10th century. This building activity, and the slow recovery of settlement, may indicate that the site was reoccupied as a fort at this time (Finkelstein 1981: 136ff.). The artifactual remains from this period at Gezer are somewhat minimal. There is no clear evidence at the site or in the region of extensive intrasite relations, and the evidence for writing in this period is extremely minimal and not at all widespread, mostly taking the form of seals and scarabs (see Tables 12–13). It seems unsound on the basis of the overall picture to maintain that children were being taught to read and write in a school in 10th-century Gezer. This stone may have been produced by someone learning to write, but it goes several steps beyond the evidence at hand to say that the person was a child, that there were schools, and that literacy was general.

Suggestions for Further Research

In the present study I have attempted to show how anthropological theory can function as an interpretive matrix utilizing data from extant excavation reports to advance our understanding of specific institutions in their regional and temporal settings. The model articulated in this particular study has focused on institutions of information management within the spatial and temporal framework shared by the data on which the model was based. However, the particular focus of this study is no less important than are the possibilities for the broader application of the techniques used here. This work demonstrates that serious and far-ranging secondary research of an integrative kind can be fruitfully conducted using already-published information. Clarke (1978: 1ff.) has asserted that analysis is not keeping pace with excavation. One of the major goals of this study has been to establish that the data are available, and usable. Because of my strong personal interest in the overarching methodological aspects of this study, my suggestions for further research will not be limited to the particular questions regarding scribes and schools we have put to the region and period represented in the data in this case, though they will begin there. Instead, my concluding remarks will move in the direction of guidelines for future archeological research.

In the first place, then, the region of study used here could and should be expanded to include the hill-country north of Gezer to the Jezreel valley, the Galilee, and the Transjordan. Application of this approach to the larger region would permit us to establish regional baselines for our key variables and then compare the behavior of these variables from subregion to subregion within our overall region. In fact, this approach would have been preferable here, but the amount of data proved too vast at this stage. Other institutions besides information management should be studied, and results integrated with those produced here. Such institutions could include, for example, mechanisms for economic redistribution such as taxation, sacrifice, and worship-offerings. Among other things, this broadening of focus is needed to help make a determination about the level of social complexity of Solomon's united kingdom, a question which was raised here but not satisfactorily resolved.

The inclusion of larger regions and more institutions points toward another, critically important direction for future research, namely the development of more general models (Clarke 1978; Binford 1977). Ultimately, such models are needed in order to be able to explain the development of institutions in a variety of cultural settings. More general theories should be tested and calibrated by correlating their projected values with written attestation and archeological data over a range of societies, past and present. They may then be used to study societies for which only partial input values are available, as for instance in the present case. Development of such theories would enable the manifold thrusts of archeological research, both geographical and conceptual, to communicate better with one another. This integrative dimension should motivate and direct both secondary research into already-excavated sites and future excavation efforts. Narrower studies such as the present one are needed, but they increase in value when a section seeking integration with other such studies into a larger regional and societal framework is included.

Future research in this area would also benefit greatly from several improvements in the prosecution and recording of field excavations. In the field, higher resolution in determining site size through periods can be achieved without much damage to the sites if cores are collected via sampling techniques. This technology, much utilized in other branches of science, has not been developed for archeological purposes to a sufficient degree. Also, site size by periods has never been a focus of systematic and deliberate field study. The first chapter of this study has shown what use can be made even of limited data of this kind. Regional analysis of settlement patterns provides a framework within which to interpret the architectural and artifactual evidence, and it is too often ignored as an analytical technique with the result that sufficiently precise data are not collected and reported.

Another area of field excavations which should be standardized is keeping records of volume of sherds, by weight if not by counting. This enables study of density of occupation by locus, and facilitates quantitative regional study. Moreover, keeping track of this kind of data will require excavators to remain sensitive to the importance of quantitative data and may positively influence both their excavation strategy and their recording technique.

Finally, and most important of all, field study should in every case be integrated with the analytical and theoretical side of archeological research. Sites should be excavated as minimally as possible, in order to address specific questions which arise from a theoretically sensitive examination of previously excavated sites. Research on the theoretical side needs significant emphasis if it is truly to guide future excavations, both in terms of the questions asked and in terms of the excavation and analytical techniques used. In a healthy scientific discipline, theory and technology are constantly engaged in a neck-and-neck race. In archeology, theory has a tremendous amount of catching up to do.

Table 3. Nearest-Neighbor Statistics—Sites South of Map Reference 1450

Total site population: 151   Surveyed area: 2,000 km^2

Symbol	Meaning	Formula	Iron 1	Iron 2a	Iron 2b	Iron 2c	Iron 3
		Formulae			*Values by Survey Period*		
n	number of sites	—	85	(96)	88	(135)	40
P	site density	n-1/Area	0.04	0.05	0.04	0.07	0.02
r	average distance between sites (km)	sum(r)/n	2.10	2.00	2.10	2.00	2.80
r_e	expected r if sites distributed randomly	1/2P	11.90	10.53	11.49	7.46	25.64
R	nearest-neighbor statistic	r/r_e	0.18	0.19	0.18	0.27	0.11

Table 4. Settlement Size—by Century

Name of Site	Map Reference Points	Elevation (meters above MSL)	Centuries BCE						
			12th	11th	10th	9th	8th	7th	6th
ARAD	770	578	0.5	0.5	0.0	0.0	0.0	0.0	0.0
AREINI	1133	152	0.0	0.0	0.6	0.6	0.6	0.6	0.0
ASHDOD	1295	52	0.0	0.0	0.0	0.0	0.0	0.7	0.0
ASHDOD-YAM	1330	25	0.0	0.0	0.0	0.0	0.0	0.0	0.0
AZEKAH	1230	400	0.6	0.6	0.6	0.6	0.6	0.6	0.0
B. MIRSIM	950	497	0.0	0.0	0.0	0.0	0.0	0.0	0.0
B. SHEMESH	1280	205	0.0	0.0	0.0	0.0	0.5	0.0	0.0
B. ZUR	1100	1000	0.0	0.8	0.8	0.0	0.5	0.0	0.0
BEERSHEBA	720	300	0.2	0.2	0.8	0.8	0.8	0.0	0.0
EN GEDI	986	-336	0.0	0.0	0.0	0.0	0.0	0.6	0.6
FUL	1370	840	0.5	0.5	0.0	0.0	0.2	0.6	0.6
GEZER	1400	230	10.0	10.0	10.0	0.0	0.0	0.0	0.0
GIBEON	1393	850	3.0	3.0	7.0	0.0	0.0	0.0	0.0
GILOH	1264	835	0.8	0.0	0.0	0.0	0.0	0.0	0.0
HASHAVYAHU	1462	25	0.0	0.0	0.0	0.0	0.0	0.6	0.0
HESI	1060	130	0.0	0.0	0.0	0.0	0.0	0.0	0.0
JEMMEH	880	0	0.8	0.8	0.8	0.8	0.8	0.8	0.8
JERUSALEM	1315	800	0.4	0.4	13.0	20.0	60.0	60.0	0.0
JUDEIDEH	1150	398	0.0	0.0	2.5	2.5	2.5	2.5	0.0

Table 4 (continued)

Name of Site	Map Reference Points	Elevation (meters above MSL)	Centuries BCE						
			12th	11th	10th	9th	8th	7th	6th
LACHISH	1350	274	0.0	0.0	1.0	4.2	4.2	1.0	0.0
MALHATA	1530	450	0.0	0.0	0.5	0.5	0.5	0.8	0.0
MASOS	1460	400	0.0	0.0	0.0	0.0	0.0	0.0	0.0
MOR	1240	25	0.6	0.6	0.0	0.0	0.6	0.0	0.0
NAGILAH	1270	200	0.0	0.0	0.0	0.9	0.9	0.0	0.0
NASBEH	1720	784	0.0	0.2	0.2	0.2	0.2	0.2	0.2
R. RAHEL	1707	819	0.0	0.0	0.0	0.0	0.5	0.6	0.0
RABUD	1515	660	0.0	0.0	0.0	0.0	0.0	0.0	0.0
SAFI	1359	232	0.0	0.0	0.0	0.0	0.0	0.0	0.0
SERA'	1190	170	0.0	0.0	0.6	0.6	0.0	0.6	0.6
SHARUHEN	1000	100	0.0	0.0	0.0	0.0	0.0	0.0	0.0
SIPPOR	1250	84	0.5	0.0	0.0	0.0	0.0	0.0	0.0
Totals			49.9	52.6	70.6	70.7	116	115	7.2

Table 5. Occupied Sites from the 'Israelite Period'
(Judaea, Samaria and Golan Survey)

Survey Number	Survey Area	Map Reference Points		Meters above MSL	Iron 1	Iron 2A	Iron 2B	Iron 2C	Iron 3
004	JUDAH	1628	1264	680	1.0	1.0	1.0	1.0	1.0
007	JUDAH	1678	1265	860	1.0	0.0	0.0	1.0	1.0
008	JUDAH	1626	1255	700	0.0	0.0	0.0	0.5	0.0
013	JUDAH	1617	1244	780	10.0	10.0	10.0	10.0	10.0
014	JUDAH	1616	1241	794	0.0	0.0	0.0	0.0	10.0
017	JUDAH	1627	1244	801	0.0	0.0	0.0	0.5	1.0
024	JUDAH	1647	1235	909	0.0	0.0	0.0	0.0	10.0
026	JUDAH	1665	1231	888	0.0	0.0	0.0	0.0	1.0
028	JUDAH	1594	1228	718	0.0	10.0	10.0	0.0	0.0
030	JUDAH	1594	1220	575	0.0	0.0	0.0	0.0	0.5
032	JUDAH	1607	1215	675	0.0	0.0	0.0	1.0	10.0
035	JUDAH	1671	1212	675	1.0	1.0	1.0	1.0	1.0
036	JUDAH	1573	1203	663	0.0	0.0	0.0	0.0	0.5
039	JUDAH	1653	1202	850	0.0	0.0	0.0	10.0	10.0
040	JUDAH	1677	1208	956	0.0	0.0	0.0	1.0	1.0
046	JUDAH	1641	1193	924	10.0	10.0	10.0	10.0	1.0
049	JUDAH	1710	1195	675	0.0	0.0	0.0	0.5	0.0
054	JUDAH	1636	1178	950	1.0	0.0	0.0	0.0	0.0
066	JUDAH	1631	1161	976	10.0	0.0	0.0	0.0	0.0

Table 5 (continued)

Survey Number	Survey Area	Map Reference Points	Meters above MSL	Iron 1	Iron 2A	Iron 2B	Iron 2C	Iron 3
058	JUDAH	1502	1158	479	0.0	0.0	0.0	0.0	10.0
060	JUDAH	1588	1156	922	10.0	10.0	10.0	10.0	10.0
062	JUDAH	1700	1157	825	1.0	1.0	1.0	1.0	1.0
070	JUDAH	1504	1135	435	10.0	10.0	10.0	10.0	10.0
079	JUDAH	1602	1127	980	0.0	0.5	0.0	0.0	1.0
085	JUDAH	1651	1121	934	1.0	1.0	1.0	1.0	1.0
100	JUDAH	1637	1102	950	0.0	0.0	0.0	1.0	1.0
104	JUDAH	1665	1092	900	0.0	0.0	0.0	0.5	0.0
111	JUDAH	1636	1083	1013	1.0	1.0	1.0	1.0	0.0
113	JUDAH	1477	1076	525	10.0	10.0	10.0	10.0	1.0
115	JUDAH	1531	1072	784	10.0	10.0	10.0	10.0	1.0
118	JUDAH	1621	1078	965	0.0	0.0	0.0	0.5	0.0
121	JUDAH	1589	1063	975	0.0	0.0	0.0	0.5	0.0
123	JUDAH	1623	1064	1010	10.0	10.0	10.0	10.0	1.0
132	JUDAH	1513	1057	653	1.0	1.0	1.0	1.0	1.0
133	JUDAH	1545	1052	800	0.0	0.0	0.0	1.0	1.0
135	JUDAH	1464	1044	452	0.0	0.0	10.0	10.0	0.0
136	JUDAH	1472	1048	450	0.0	0.0	0.0	10.0	0.0
147	JUDAH	1597	1036	944	1.0	1.0	1.0	0.0	0.0
149	JUDAH	1572	1022	899	1.0	1.0	1.0	1.0	1.0
152	JUDAH	1452	1018	450	0.0	0.0	0.0	0.0	1.0

Table 5 *(continued)*

Survey Number	Survey Area	Map Reference Points		Meters above MSL	Iron 1	Iron 2A	Iron 2B	Iron 2C	Iron 3
154	JUDAH	1526	1016	860	0.0	1.0	1.0	1.0	0.0
162	JUDAH	1645	1005	850	10.0	10.0	10.0	10.0	0.0
165	JUDAH	1460	993	545	0.0	0.0	0.0	0.0	0.0
166	JUDAH	1485	996	740	1.0	10.0	10.0	10.0	0.0
168	JUDAH	1523	996	874	10.0	10.0	10.0	10.0	1.0
175	JUDAH	1532	986	879	0.0	0.0	0.0	0.0	0.5
176	JUDAH	1551	985	815	10.0	10.0	10.0	10.0	0.0
178	JUDAH	1628	982	880	1.0	1.0	1.0	1.0	1.0
190	JUDAH	1634	972	852	0.0	0.0	0.0	0.5	0.0
193	JUDAH	1532	967	700	0.0	0.0	0.0	0.5	0.0
213	JUDAH	1487	932	675	0.0	0.0	0.0	1.0	0.0
215	JUDAH	1515	934	698	1.0	1.0	1.0	1.0	0.0
216	JUDAH	1519	932	775	0.0	0.5	0.0	0.0	0.0
222	JUDAH	1628	925	800	1.0	1.0	1.0	1.0	0.0
225	JUDAH	1458	912	625	0.0	1.0	1.0	1.0	0.0
229	JUDAH	1508	903	650	10.0	10.0	10.0	10.0	1.0
231	JUDAH	1627	909	863	1.0	1.0	1.0	1.0	0.0
233	JUDAH	1429	897	615	0.0	0.0	0.0	0.5	0.0
236	JUDAH	1606	893	790	0.0	0.0	0.0	0.5	0.0
238	JUDAH	1525	882	625	0.0	0.0	0.0	0.5	0.0
246	JUDAH	1557	862	710	0.0	0.0	0.0	1.0	0.0

Table 5 (continued)

Survey Number	Survey Area	Map Reference Points		Meters above MSL	Iron 1	Iron 2A	Iron 2B	Iron 2C	Iron 3
248	JUDAH	1575	854	730	0.0	0.0	0.0	1.0	0.0
249	JUDAH	1432	843	430	0.0	0.0	0.0	1.0	0.0
250	JUDAH	1562	846	730	0.0	0.0	0.0	1.0	0.0
105	BENJAMIN	1768	1431	650	1.0	1.0	0.0	0.0	0.0
108	BENJAMIN	1762	1425	625	1.0	1.0	1.0	1.0	0.0
109	BENJAMIN	1764	1423	625	0.0	0.5	0.5	0.5	0.0
110	BENJAMIN	1632	1419	650	0.0	0.0	0.0	0.0	1.0
111	BENJAMIN	1653	1411	750	0.0	0.0	0.0	0.0	1.0
112	BENJAMIN	1660	1418	775	0.0	0.0	0.0	0.0	1.0
114	BENJAMIN	1716	1413	775	0.0	1.0	1.0	1.0	0.0
115	BENJAMIN	1755	1418	525	1.0	1.0	1.0	1.0	0.0
117	BENJAMIN	1778	1415	500	10.0	0.0	0.0	0.0	0.0
118	BENJAMIN	1772	1414	618	0.0	1.0	1.0	1.0	0.0
125	BENJAMIN	1749	1405	675	0.0	1.0	1.0	1.0	1.0
144	BENJAMIN	1691	1374	700	0.0	1.0	1.0	1.0	0.0
145	BENJAMIN	1743	1378	650	1.0	0.0	0.0	0.0	0.0
147	BENJAMIN	1773	1373	583	1.0	1.0	1.0	1.0	0.0
150	BENJAMIN	1678	1367	829	1.0	1.0	1.0	1.0	1.0
151	BENJAMIN	1679	1365	725	0.0	0.5	0.5	0.5	0.0
152	BENJAMIN	1760	1369	638	1.0	1.0	1.0	1.0	0.0
156	BENJAMIN	1696	1359	769	0.0	1.0	1.0	1.0	0.0

Table 5 (continued)

Survey Number	Survey Area	Map Reference Points		Meters above MSL	Iron 1	Iron 2A	Iron 2B	Iron 2C	Iron 3
057	JERICHO	1933	1432	-225	1.0	1.0	1.0	1.0	0.0
059	JERICHO	1940	1420	-270	1.0	1.0	1.0	1.0	0.0
061	JERICHO	1917	1413	-208	1.0	1.0	1.0	1.0	0.0
080	JERICHO	1921	1342	-80	1.0	1.0	1.0	1.0	0.0
081	JERICHO	1923	1340	-80	1.0	0.0	0.0	0.0	0.0
082	JERICHO	1923	1338	-80	1.0	1.0	1.0	1.0	1.0
083	JERICHO	1920	1330	-80	1.0	1.0	1.0	1.0	0.0
085	JERICHO	1927	1313	-100	1.0	1.0	1.0	1.0	0.0
089	JERICHO	1889	1285	-25	1.0	1.0	1.0	1.0	0.0
091	JERICHO	1874	1276	40	1.0	1.0	1.0	1.0	0.0
092	JERICHO	1886	1277	-40	1.0	1.0	1.0	1.0	0.0
093	JERICHO	1921	1278	-100	0.0	0.5	0.5	0.5	0.0
094	JERICHO	1929	1277	-110	1.0	1.0	1.0	1.0	0.0
095	JERICHO	1878	1262	20	1.0	1.0	1.0	1.0	0.0
098	JERICHO	1930	1260	-375	1.0	1.0	1.0	1.0	0.0
099	JERICHO	1868	1252	20	1.0	1.0	1.0	1.0	0.0
100	JERICHO	1870	1250	20	1.0	1.0	1.0	1.0	0.0
102	JERICHO	1872	1249	20	10.0	10.0	10.0	0.0	0.0
108	JERICHO	1857	1217	42	0.0	0.5	0.5	0.5	0.0
113	JERICHO	1907	1207	-175	1.0	1.0	1.0	1.0	0.0
114	JERICHO	1910	1208	-325	1.0	1.0	1.0	1.0	0.0

Table 5 (continued)

Survey Number	Survey Area	Map Reference Points	Meters above MSL	Iron 1	Iron 2A	Iron 2B	Iron 2C	Iron 3
117	JERICHO	1844	1191	120	1.0	1.0	1.0	1.0	0.0
121	JERICHO	1811	1184	360	1.0	1.0	1.0	1.0	0.0
124	JERICHO	1850	1183	180	1.0	0.0	0.0	0.0	0.0
126	JERICHO	1900	1180	-275	1.0	0.0	0.0	0.0	0.0
128	JERICHO	1895	1172	-60	1.0	1.0	1.0	1.0	0.0
131	JERICHO	1840	1160	275	1.0	1.0	1.0	1.0	0.0
135	JERICHO	1830	1150	215	1.0	1.0	1.0	1.0	0.0
145	JERICHO	1887	1129	-384	0.0	1.0	1.0	1.0	0.0
147	JERICHO	1718	1115	710	1.0	1.0	1.0	1.0	0.0
152	JERICHO	1585	1109	140	1.0	1.0	1.0	1.0	0.0
154	JERICHO	1710	1090	500	1.0	1.0	1.0	1.0	0.0
156	JERICHO	1759	1090	549	1.0	1.0	1.0	1.0	0.0
159	JERICHO	1730	1080	525	1.0	0.0	0.0	0.0	0.0
161	JERICHO	1750	1080	500	1.0	1.0	1.0	1.0	0.0
163	JERICHO	1781	1089	450	1.0	0.0	0.0	0.0	0.0
165	JERICHO	1760	1070	430	1.0	0.0	0.0	0.0	0.0
167	JERICHO	1780	1070	385	1.0	1.0	1.0	1.0	0.0
168	JERICHO	1790	1076	365	1.0	1.0	1.0	1.0	0.0
169	JERICHO	1793	1074	421	1.0	1.0	1.0	1.0	0.0
172	JERICHO	1732	1069	586	1.0	1.0	1.0	1.0	0.0
174	JERICHO	1750	1060	557	1.0	1.0	1.0	1.0	0.0

Table 5 *(continued)*

Survey Number	Survey Area	Map Reference Points	Meters above MSL	Iron 1	Iron 2A	Iron 2B	Iron 2C	Iron 3
175	JERICHO	1776	1067	430	1.0	1.0	1.0	1.0	0.0
182	JERICHO	1761	1048	445	1.0	1.0	1.0	1.0	0.0
186	JERICHO	1819	1041	350	1.0	1.0	1.0	1.0	0.0
193	JERICHO	1799	1020	400	0.0	1.0	1.0	1.0	0.0
196	JERICHO	1875	1019	-300	1.0	0.0	0.0	0.0	0.0
197	JERICHO	1791	1008	300	1.0	1.0	1.0	1.0	0.0
198	JERICHO	1819	1009	340	1.0	1.0	1.0	1.0	0.0
199	JERICHO	1816	1005	370	1.0	1.0	1.0	1.0	0.0
201	JERICHO	1809	999	390	1.0	1.0	1.0	1.0	0.0
202	JERICHO	1820	990	310	1.0	1.0	1.0	1.0	0.0
204	JERICHO	1835	986	265	1.0	1.0	1.0	1.0	0.0
207	JERICHO	1829	979	200	1.0	0.0	0.0	0.0	1.0
236	EPHRAIM	1522	1422	275	0.0	0.0	0.0	0.0	0.0
238	EPHRAIM	1541	1420	310	0.0	0.5	0.5	0.5	10.0
241	EPHRAIM	1524	1386	310	1.0	1.0	1.0	1.0	1.0
242	EPHRAIM	1526	1386	300	1.0	1.0	1.0	1.0	0.0

Table 6. Nearest-Neighbor Sites and Distances—
Sites South of Map Reference 1450

Primary Site Code	Map Reference Points		Distances to Nearest Neighbor by period (km)					Survey Code for Nearest Neighbor				
			Ir1	Ir2a	Ir2b	Ir2c	Ir3	Ir1	Ir2a	Ir2b	Ir2c	Ir3
J004	1628	1264	2.3	2.3	2.3	0.9	2.0	J013	J013	J013	J008	J017
J007	1678	1265	5.0			5.0		J004			J004	
J008	1626	1255				0.9					J004	
J013	1617	1244	2.3	2.3	2.3	1.0	0.3	J004	J004	J004	J017	J014
J014	1616	1241					0.3					J013
J017	1627	1244				1.0	1.0				J013	J013
J024	1647	1235					1.8					J026
J026	1665	1231					1.1					J027
J027	1674	1237					1.1					J026
J028	1594	1228		2.8	2.8		1.4		J013	J013		J032
J030	1594	1220					1.4					J030
J032	1607	1215				3.1	0.7				J013	J040
J035	1671	1212	3.6	3.6	3.6	0.7		J046	J046	J046	J040	
J036	1573	1203					2.7					J030
J039	1653	1202				1.5	1.5				J046	J046
J040	1677	1208				0.7	0.7				J035	J035
J046	1641	1193	1.6	3.6	3.6	1.5	1.5	J054	J046	J046	J039	J039
J049	1710	1195				3.6					J040	
J054	1636	1178	1.6					J046				

Table 6 (continued)

Primary Site Code	Map Reference Points		Distances to Nearest Neighbor by period (km)					Survey Code for Nearest Neighbor				
			Ir1	Ir2a	Ir2b	Ir2c	Ir3	Ir1	Ir2a	Ir2b	Ir2c	Ir3
J056	1631	1161	1.8					J054				
J058	1502	1158					2.3					J070
J079	1602	1127		2.5			3.2		M152			J060
J085	1651	1121	4.1	4.1	4.1	2.4	2.4	J111	J111	J111	J100	J100
J088	1608	1117				2.4					M152	
J096	1511	1104					3.2					J070
J100	1637	1102				1.9	2.4				J111	J085
J104	1665	1092				3.0					J100	
J111	1636	1083	1.9	1.9	1.9	1.6		J123	J123	J123	J118	
J113	1477	1076	4.1	3.5	3.5	3.5	4.1	J132	J135	J135	J135	J132
J115	1531	1072	2.3	2.3	2.3	2.3	2.3	J132	J132	J132	J132	J132
J118	1621	1078				1.6					J111	
J121	1589	1063				2.8					J147	
J123	1632	1064	1.9	1.9	1.9	1.8	3.8	J111	J111	J111	J118	J100
J132	1513	1057	2.3	2.3	2.3	2.3	2.3	J115	J115	J115	J115	J115
J133	1545	1052				2.4	2.4				J115	J115
J135	1464	1044		3.5	3.5	3.5			J113	J113	J113	
J136	1472	1048										
J147	1597	1036	2.9	2.9	2.9	2.8	4.0	J149	J149	J149	J121	J133
J149	1572	1022	2.9	2.9	2.9	2.9	6.3	J147	J147	J147	J147	J113
J152	1452	1018										

Table 6 (continued)

Primary Site Code	Map Reference Points	Distances to Nearest Neighbor by period (km)					Survey Code for Nearest Neighbor				
		Ir1	Ir2a	Ir2b	Ir2c	Ir3	Ir1	Ir2a	Ir2b	Ir2c	Ir3
J154	1526 1016		2.0	2.0	2.0			J168	J168	J168	
J162	1645 1005	2.9	2.9	2.9	2.9		J178	J178	J178	J178	
J165	1460 993										
J166	1485 996	3.8	3.8	3.8	3.8		J168	J168	J168	J168	
J168	1523 996	3.0	2.0	2.0	2.0	1.4	J176	J154	J154	J154	J175
J175	1532 986					1.4					J168
J194	1609 966				2.5					J178	
J205	1545 945				2.6					J193	
J213	1487 932				2.8					J215	
J215	1515 934	3.2	0.5	3.2	2.8		J229	J216	J229	J213	
J216	1519 932		0.5				J215				
J222	1628 925	1.6	1.6	1.6	1.6		J231	J231	J231	J231	
J225	1458 912		5.1	5.1	3.3			J229	J229	J233	
J229	1508 903	3.2	3.1	3.2	2.7	8.6	J215	J216	J215	J238	J175
J231	1627 909	1.6	1.6	1.6	1.6		J222	J222	J222	J222	
J233	1429 897				3.3					J225	
J236	1606 893				2.6					J231	
J238	1525 882				2.7					J229	
J246	1557 862				1.7					J250	
J248	1575 854				1.5					J250	
J249	1432 843				5.4					J233	

Table 6 (continued)

Primary Site Code	Map Reference Points	Distances to Nearest Neighbor by period (km)					Survey Code for Nearest Neighbor				
		Ir1	Ir2a	Ir2b	Ir2c	Ir3	Ir1	Ir2a	Ir2b	Ir2c	Ir3
J250	1562 846				1.5					J248	
B105	1768 1431	0.9					B108				
B108	1762 1425	0.9	0.3	0.3	0.3		B105	B109	B109	B109	
B109	1764 1423	0.3	0.3	0.3				B108	B108	B108	
B110	1632 1419					2.2					B111
B111	1653 1411					1.0					B112
B112	1660 1418					1.0					B111
B114	1716 1413		3.4	3.4	3.4			B125	B125	B125	
B115	1755 1418	1.0	1.0	1.0	1.0		B108	B108	B108	B108	
B132	1649 1388		2.5	2.5	2.5			B142	B142	B142	
B142	1672 1378		1.2	1.2	1.2			B150	B150	B150	
B144	1691 1374		1.5	1.5	1.5			B150	B150	B150	
B145	1743 1378	1.9					B152				
B147	1773 1373	1.4	1.4	1.4	1.4		B152	B152	B152	B152	
B150	1678 1367	6.6	0.2	0.2	0.2	5.1	B145	B151	B151	B151	B111
B151	1679 1365		0.2	0.2	0.2			B150	B150	B150	
B152	1760 1369	1.4	1.4	1.4	1.4		B147	B147	B147	B147	
B156	1696 1359	1.6	1.6	1.6				B144	B144	B144	
M057	1933 1432	1.4	1.4	1.4	1.4		M059	M059	M059	M059	
M059	1940 1420	1.4	1.4	1.4	1.4		M057	M057	M057	M057	
M061	1917 1413	2.4	2.4	2.4	2.4		M059	M059	M059	M059	

174

Table 6 (continued)

Primary Site Code	Map Reference Points	Distances to Nearest Neighbor by period (km)					Survey Code for Nearest Neighbor				
		Ir1	Ir2a	Ir2b	Ir2c	Ir3	Ir1	Ir2a	Ir2b	Ir2c	Ir3
M080	1921 1342	0.3	0.5	0.5	0.5	0.5	M081	M082	M082	M082	
M081	1923 1340	0.2					M082				
M082	1923 1338	0.2	0.5	0.5	0.5	0.5	M081	M080	M080	M080	
M083	1920 1330	0.9	0.9	0.9	0.9		M082	M082	M082	M082	
M085	1927 1313	1.8	1.8	1.8	1.8		M083	M083	M083	M083	
M089	1889 1285	0.9	0.9	0.9	0.9		M092	M092	M092	M092	
M091	1874 1276	1.2	1.2	1.2	1.2		M092	M092	M092	M092	
M092	1886 1277	0.9	0.9	0.9	0.9		M089	M089	M089	M089	
M093	1921 1278		0.8	0.8	0.8			M094	M094	M094	
M094	1929 1277	1.7	0.8	0.8	0.8		M098	M093	M093	M093	
M095	1878 1262	1.4	1.4	1.4	1.4		M099	M099	M099	M099	
M098	1930 1260	1.7	1.7	1.7	1.7		M094	M094	M094	M094	
M099	1868 1252	0.3	0.3	0.3	0.3		M100	M100	M100	M100	
M104	1862 1231	2.1	1.5	1.5	1.5		M102	M108	M108	M108	
M108	1857 1217		1.5	1.5	1.5			M104	M104	M104	
M113	1907 1207	0.3	0.3	0.3	0.3		M114	M114	M114	M114	
M114	1910 1208	0.3	0.3	0.3	0.3		M113	M113	M113	M113	
M117	1844 1191	1.0	2.9	2.9	2.9		M124	M108	M108	M108	
M121	1811 1184	3.4	3.4	3.4	3.4		M117	M117	M117	M117	
M124	1850 1183	1.0					M117				
M126	1900 1180	0.9					M128				

Table 6 (continued)

Primary Site Code	Map Reference Points		Distances to Nearest Neighbor by period (km)					Survey Code for Nearest Neighbor				
			Ir1	Ir2a	Ir2b	Ir2c	Ir3	Ir1	Ir2a	Ir2b	Ir2c	Ir3
M128	1895	1172	0.9	3.7	3.7	3.7		M126	M113	M113	M113	
M131	1840	1160	1.4	1.4	1.4	1.4		M135	M135	M135	M135	
M135	1830	1150	1.4	1.4	1.4	1.4		M131	M131	M131	M131	
M145	1887	1129		4.4	4.4	4.4			M128	M128	M128	
M147	1718	1115	2.6	2.6	2.6	2.6		M154	M154	M154	M154	
M152	1585	1109	4.7	2.5	4.7	2.4		J060	J079	J060	J088	
M154	1710	1090	2.2	2.6	2.6	2.6		M159	M147	M147	M147	
M156	1759	1090	1.4	1.4	1.4	1.4		M161	M161	M161	M161	
M159	1730	1080	1.1					M172				
M161	1750	1080	1.4	1.4	1.4	1.4		M156	M156	M156	M156	
M163	1781	1089	1.6					M168				
M165	1760	1070	1.4					M161				
M167	1780	1070	0.5	0.5	0.5	0.5		M175	M175	M175	M175	
M168	1790	1076	0.4	0.4	0.4	0.4		M169	M169	M169	M169	
M169	1793	1074	0.4	0.4	0.4	0.4		M168	M168	M168	M168	
M172	1732	1069	1.1	2.0	2.0	2.0		M159	M174	M174	M174	
M174	1750	1060	1.0	1.0	1.0	1.0		M180	M180	M180	M180	
M182	1761	1048	0.8	0.8	0.8	0.8		M180	M180	M180	M180	
M186	1819	1041	3.2	2.9	2.9	2.9		M198	M193	M193	M193	
M193	1799	1020		1.4	1.4	1.4			M197	M197	M197	
M196	1875	1019	5.2					M204				

Table 6 (continued)

Primary Site Code	Map Reference Points	Distances to Nearest Neighbor by period (km)					Survey Code for Nearest Neighbor				
		Ir-1	Ir2a	Ir2b	Ir2c	Ir3	Ir1	Ir2a	Ir2b	Ir2c	Ir3
M197	1791 1008	2.0	1.4	1.4	1.4		M201	M193	M193	M193	
M198	1819 1009	0.5	0.5	0.5	0.5		M199	M199	M199	M199	
M199	1816 1005	0.5	0.5	0.5	0.5		M198	M198	M198	M198	
M201	1809 999	0.9	0.9	0.9	0.9		M199	M199	M199	M199	
M202	1820 990	1.4	0.4	1.4	1.4		M201	M201	M201	M201	
M204	1835 986	0.9	1.6	1.6	1.6		M207	M202	M202	M202	
M207	1829 979	0.9					M204				
E236	1522 1422					1.9					E238
E238	1541 1420		3.7	3.7	3.7	1.9		E242	E242	E242	E236
E241	1524 1386	0.2	0.2	0.2	0.2	3.6	E242	E242	E242	E241	E236
E242	1526 1386	0.2	0.2	0.2	0.2		E241	E241	E241	E241	

Table 7. Nearest-Neighbor Program:
Identification and Triangulation Program
(Written in Ashton–Tate's dBASEIII+)

```
CLEAR ALL
CLEAR
SET TALK OFF
SET SAFETY OFF
STORE '1' TO AGE1
STORE '2A' TO AGE2
STORE '2B' TO AGE3
STORE '2C' TO AGE4
STORE '3' TO AGE5
STORE '_NN' TO SUFF1
STORE '_NN_CO' TO SUFF2
STORE 1 TO COUNT
STORE LTRIM(STR(COUNT)) TO CNT
SELECT 1
USE JSGNN
GO TOP
DO WHILE .NOT. EOF()
   **This part selects only those sites occupied in each period, one
   **period at a time, to speed calculations
      STORE AGE&CNT TO AGE
      COPY TO D:JSG FOR IRON_&AGE > 0.1 .AND. Y_AXIS < 1600
      SELECT 2
      USE D:JSG
      COUNT FOR IRON_&AGE > 0.0 TO AGETOT
      SELECT 1
      GO TOP
   **This loop sets the initial parameters for the calculations for
   **each site, one site at a time
      DO WHILE .NOT. EOF()
      STORE X_AXIS TO XOR
      STORE Y_AXIS TO YOR
      STORE SURVCODE TO SC
      CLEAR
      @5,5 SAY ;
'Now calculating nearest-neighbor distances for Iron&AGE'
      @6,5 SAY ;
'Number of sites remaining: 'GET AGETOT
      SELECT 2
      GO TOP
      IF SURVCODE=SC
         SKIP
```

Table 7 (continued)

```
    ENDIF
    STORE SQRT(((XOR-X_AXIS)*(XOR-X_AXIS)) + ;
((YOR-Y_AXIS)*(YOR-Y_AXIS)))*.1 TO  NN
    STORE SURVCODE TO NNCODE
    SELECT 1
    REPLACE IR&AGE.&SUFF1 WITH NN
    REPLACE IR&AGE.&SUFF2 WITH NNCODE
    SELECT 2
    SKIP
  **This loop checks each site to see if it is the nearest neighbor; if it
  **is, the code and values are entered
    DO WHILE .NOT. EOF()
        STORE SQRT(((XOR-X_AXIS)*(XOR-X_AXIS)) + ;
((YOR-Y_AXIS)*(YOR-Y_AXIS)))*.1 TO  NNP
        IF NNP<NN
            STORE NNP TO NN
            STORE SURVCODE TO NNCODE
            SELECT 1
            REPLACE IR&AGE.&SUFF1
            REPLACE IR&AGE.&SUFF2 WITH NNCODE
            SELECT 2
        ENDIF
        SKIP
    ENDDO
    SELECT 1
    SKIP
    STORE AGETOT-1 TO AGETOT
    ENDDO
    SELECT 2
    USE
    SELECT 1
    STORE COUNT-1 TO COUNT
    STORE LTRIM(STR(COUNT)) TO CNT
ENDDO
RETURN
```

Table 8. *Public Works Catalogue*
Excavated Sites South of Map Reference 1450

CENTURY: 12

Site Name: ASHDOD
mud-brick wall surrounding acropolis only

Site Name: GIBEON
wall; local stone
11.3 m diameter by 10.8 m deep cylindrical cutting to water pool

Site Name: GILOH
double wall, outer = 1.9 m, inner = 1.9 m, no partitions found so not
'casemate', built of unhewn stone facing with rubble cores

CENTURY: 11

Site Name: ASHDOD
mud-brick wall surrounding 'lower city'

Site Name: FUL
casemate wall, rubble masonry, rubble core, outer wall = 1.2 m, inner
wall = 1 m.

CENTURY: 10

Site Name: ARAD
fort 50 m^2, casemate wall, outer wall = 1.6 m, inner = 1.4 m, 2 meters
between, 12 projecting towers, gate had three double-piers

Site Name: B. MIRSIM
casemate wall of local stone (quarry found on site), 1.5 m outer wall,
1m inner wall

Site Name: B. SHEMESH
casemate wall of small, unhewn stones

Site Name: BEERSHEBA
solid stone foundation with glacis, header–stretcher construction,
brick superstructure

Site Name: FUL
casemate wall, 1.2 m outer wall, 1 m inner wall, reused old foundation
trench, hammer-dressed small stones (counted as rebuild)

Table 8 (continued)

Site Name: GIBEON
rubble fill, headers with fill atop to level courses

Site Name: JERUSALEM
casemate wall

Site Name: LACHISH
32 × 32 m, 2 m thick brick walls

Site Name: MALHATA
4–4.5 m thick encircling wall

CENTURY: 9

Site Name: ARAD
solid wall, 4 m thick

Site Name: AREINI
casemate wall

Site Name: B. MIRSIM
outer casemate wall strengthened to 2 m, piers on east gate strengthened, gate and tower added on west approach (considered as rebuild)

Site Name: BEERSHEBA
casemate wall of well-dressed ashlar stone alternating with rows of brick
2.2 m wide gravel and brick glacis plastered with white chalk

Site Name: GEZER
some 'Solomonic' ashlar rebuild of LB walls, inner casemate (1.7 m thick) added (counted as rebuild)
Solomonic fortress on acropolis 'possible'

Site Name: HESI
upper defensive and lower retaining mud-brick walls

Site Name: JERUSALEM
400 m part rock-hewn, part stone-covered tunnel

Site Name: LACHISH
'largest, most massive and impressive building of Iron Age known in the land of Israel', 30 × 70 m 'palace' raised on foundation podium, 3 m thick brick walls, supporting ramps of hammer-dressed blocks all around except N. side

Table 8 (continued)

Site Name: MALHATA
3–3.5 m thick encircling wall

Site Name: NASBEH
slightly chipped stones set in clay mortar, coated with plaster, surrounded by glacis, 4 m thick, 9–10 towers, quality of construction uneven, gate = 2 pairs of piers, also uneven construction

Site Name: RABUD
4 m large boulder wall, rubble fill, unequal segments of wall do not join squarely, joined by header–stretcher, at least one tower

CENTURY: 8

Site Name: ARAD
fort of ashlar construction, embossed stones; in in 3rd quarter of 8th century = smaller inner walls added to existing solid wall to form a modified casemate

Site Name: ASHDOD-YAM
mud-brick wall and glacis

Site Name: B. MIRSIM
public building on acropolis, walls 1.4 m thick plan reconstructed

Site Name: JERUSALEM
7 m thick wall, large stone facing, large rubble fill, superstructure of dressed stone
533 m long, 2 m high, 1 m wide tunnel through limestone rock, brought water from spring outside walls to pools inside

Site Name: LACHISH
30 × 70 m 'palace' rebuilt
double wall = 6 m wide brick lower wall founded on one course of stone, 4–6 m stone-and-brick upper wall
towers of large well-dressed stones

Site Name: MOR
casemate wall

Site Name: R. RAHEL
casemate wall, ashlar masonry

Table 8 (continued)

CENTURY: 7

Site Name: ARAD
last fortress built at Arad, on lines of earlier forts.

Site Name: AREINI
stone retaining wall at base of tell supporting a glacis
stone defensive wall atop glacis on upper edge of tell

Site Name: HASHAVYAHU
gate complex built of dressed stone

Site Name: JEMMEH
public building, mud-brick barrel vaults (building technique described as 'Mesopotamian')

Site Name: R. RAHEL
3.5 m wall, salients and recesses, dressed stones, 2-pair pier gate, stones from local quarry
double-walled, 1.6 m thick exterior wall, 1.1 m thick interior wall, 70 × 50 m inner fort, 18 × 36 m ashlar construction building with ornamental window-balustrades, capitals

Site Name: RABUD
wall rebuild (not counted in data)

Site Name: SHARUHEN
5 m thick, single-layer stone foundation, brick superstructure
230 m² building, brick foundation in clean sand

Table 9. Encircling Walls—Sites South of Map Reference 1450

A. 12th–10th Centuries

	Centuries BCE								
	12th			11th			10th		
Name of Site	Circ. (M)	Wid. (M)	Area (M2)	Circ. (M)	Wid. (M)	Area (M2)	Circ. (M)	Wid. (M)	Area (M2)
ARAD	0	0.0	0	0	0.0	0	400	0.0	1200
AREINI	0	0.0	0	0	0.0	0	0	0.0	0
ASHDOD	950	0.0	2850	1760	0.0	5280	0	0.0	0
ASHDOD-YAM	0	0.0	0	0	0.0	0	0	0.0	0
AZEKAH	0	0.0	0	0	0.0	0	0	0.0	0
B. MIRSIM	0	0.0	0	0	0.0	0	630	0.5	1575
B. SHEMESH	0	0.0	0	0	0.0	0	350	0.5	875
B. ZUR	0	0.0	0	0	0.0	0	0	0.0	0
BEERSHEBA	0	0.0	0	0	0.0	0	300	0.0	1200
EN GEDI	0	0.0	0	0	0.0	0	0	0.0	0
FUL	0	0.0	0	550	0.0	1650	0	0.0	0
GEZER	0	0.0	0	0	0.0	0	0	0.0	0
GIBEON	1000	0.2	2200	0	0.0	0	950	0.0	2850
GILOH	400	0.8	1520	0	0.0	0	0	0.0	0
HASHAVYAHU	0	0.0	0	0	0.0	0	0	0.0	0
HESI	0	0.0	0	0	0.0	0	0	0.0	0

Table 9 (continued)

	Centuries BCE								
	12th			11th			10th		
Name of Site	Circ. (M)	Wid. (M)	Area (M2)	Circ. (M)	Wid. (M)	Area (M2)	Circ. (M)	Wid. (M)	Area (M2)
JEMMEH	0	0.0	0	0	0.0	0	0	0.0	0
JERUSALEM	0	0.0	0	0	0.0	0	1000	0.0	3000
JUDEIDEH	0	0.0	0	0	0.0	0	0	0.0	0
LACHISH	0	0.0	0	0	0.0	0	0	0.0	0
MALHATA	0	0.0	0	0	0.0	0	435	4.0	1740
MASOS	0	0.0	0	0	0.0	0	0	0.0	0
MOR	0	0.0	0	0	0.0	0	0	0.0	0
NAGILAH	0	0.0	0	0	0.0	0	0	0.0	0
NASBEH	0	0.0	0	0	0.0	0	0	0.0	0
R. RAHEL	0	0.0	0	0	0.0	0	0	0.0	0
RABUD	0	0.0	0	0	0.0	0	0	0.0	0
SAFI	0	0.0	0	0	0.0	0	0	0.0	0
SERA'	0	0.0	0	0	0.0	0	0	0.0	0
SHARUHEN	0	0.0	0	0	0.0	0	0	0.0	0
SIPPOR	0	0.0	0	0	0.0	0	0	0.0	0
Totals	2350		6570	2310		6930	4065		12440

Table 9 (continued)
B. 9th–7th Centuries

Centuries BCE

Name of Site	9th Circ. (M)	9th Wid. (M)	9th Area (M2)	8th Circ. (M)	8th Wid. (M)	8th Area (M2)	7th Circ. (M)	7th Wid. (M)	7th Area (M2)
B. MIRSIM	0	0.0	0	0	0.0	0	0	.0	0
B. SHEMESH	0	0.0	0	0	0.0	0	0	.0	0
B. ZUR	0	0.0	0	0	0.0	0	0	.0	0
BEERSHEBA	300	0.0	900	0	0.0	0	0	.0	0
EN GEDI	0	0.0	0	0	0.0	0	0	.0	0
FUL	0	0.0	0	0	0.0	0	0	.0	0
GEZER	0	0.0	0	0	0.0	0	0	.0	0
GIBEON	0	0.0	0	0	0.0	0	0	.0	0
GILOH	0	0.0	0	0	0.0	0	0	.0	0
HASHAVYAHU	0	0.0	2880	0	0.0	0	0	.0	0
HESI	720	0.0	0	0	0.0	0	0	.0	0
JEMMEH	0	0.0	0	0	0.0	0	0	.0	0
JERUSALEM	0	0.0	0	2600	0.0	18200	0	.0	0
JUDEIDEH	0	0.0	0	0	0.0	0	0	.0	0
LACHISH	0	0.0	0	2200	0.0	13200	0	.0	0
MALHATA	435	0.0	1305	0	0.0	0	0	.0	0
MASOS	0	0.0	0	0	0.0	0	0	.0	0
MOR	0	0.0	0	270	0.0	810	0	.0	0

Table 9 (continued)

	Centuries BCE								
	9th			8th			7th		
Name of Site	Circ. (M)	Wid. (M)	Area (M2)	Circ. (M)	Wid. (M)	Area (M2)	Circ. (M)	Wid. (M)	Area (M2)
NAGILAH	0	0.0	0	0	0.0	0	0	.0	0
NASBEH	660	0.0	2640	0	0.0	0	0	.0	0
R. RAHEL	0	0.0	0	710	0.0	2130	710	.5	2485
RABUD	900	0.0	3600	0	0.0	0	0	.0	0
SAFI	0	0.0	0	0	0.0	0	0	.0	0
SERA'	0	0.0	0	0	0.0	0	0	.0	0
SHARUHEN	0	0.0	0	0	0.0	0	850	.0	4250
SIPPOR	0	0.0	0	0	0.0	0	0	.0	0
Totals	3865		14275	6780		37840	2460		9435

Table 10. Public Buildings—Sites South of Map Reference 1450
(all measurements in square meters)

Site Name	12th	11th	10th	9th	8th	7th	6th
Forts							
ABU TABAQ	0	0	0	0	807	0	0
BAGHL	0	0	0	0	204	0	0
DABA'	0	0	0	757	0	0	0
MAQARI	0	0	0	0	338	0	0
SAMRAH	0	0	0	0	1244	0	0
TIBNEH	0	0	0	0	204	0	0
TWEIN	0	0	0	0	405	0	0
Subtotals	0	0	0	757	3202	0	0
Settlements							
ARAD	0	0	225	0	450	225	0
AREINI	0	0	0	0	0	0	0
ASHDOD	0	0	0	0	0	0	0
ASHDOD-YAM	0	0	0	0	0	0	0
AZEKAH	0	0	0	0	400	0	0
B. MIRSIM	0	0	0	0	400	0	0
B. SHEMESH	0	0	0	0	0	0	0
B. ZUR	0	0	0	0	0	0	0
BEERSHEBA	0	0	0	0	0	0	0
EN GEDI	0	0	0	0	0	0	0
FUL	0	618	250	250	0	0	0

Table 10 (continued)

Site Name	12th	11th	10th	9th	8th	7th	6th
Settlements (cont.)							
GEZER	0	0	0	0	0	0	0
GIBEON	0	0	0	0	0	0	0
GILOH	0	0	0	0	0	0	0
HASHAVYAHU	0	0	0	0	0	1235	0
HESI	0	0	0	0	0	0	0
JEMMEH	0	0	0	0	0	830	0
JERUSALEM	0	0	0	0	0	0	0
JUDEIDEH	0	0	0	0	0	0	0
LACHISH	0	0	900	1600	0	0	0
MALHATA	0	0	0	0	0	0	0
MASOS	0	0	0	0	0	0	0
MOR	0	0	0	0	0	0	0
NAGILAH	0	0	0	0	0	0	0
NASBEH	0	0	0	0	0	0	0
R. RAHEL	0	0	0	0	0	1944	0
RABUD	0	0	0	0	0	0	0
SAFI	0	0	0	0	0	0	0
SERA'	0	0	0	0	0	0	0
SHARUHEN	0	0	0	0	0	230	0
SIPPOR	0	0	0	0	0	0	0
Subtotals	0	618	1375	1850	1250	4464	0
Totals	0	618	1375	2607	4452	4464	0

Table 11. Encircling Walls and Public Buildings—Combined Area
(all measurements in square meters)

Site Name	12th	11th	10th	9th	8th	7th	6th
Forts							
ABU TABAQ	0	0	0	0	807	0	0
BAGHL	0	0	0	0	204	0	0
DABA'	0	0	0	757	0	0	0
MAQARI	0	0	0	0	338	0	0
SAMRAH	0	0	0	0	1244	0	0
TIBNEH	0	0	0	0	204	0	0
TWEIN	0	0	0	0	405	0	0
Subtotals	0	0	0	757	3202	0	0
Settlements							
ARAD	0	0	1425	1600	450	225	0
AREINI	0	5280	0	1350	0	2700	0
ASHDOD	2850	0	0	0	3500	0	0
ASHDOD-YAM	0	0	0	0	400	0	0
AZEKAH	0	0	0	0	400	0	0
B. MIRSIM	0	0	1575	0	0	0	0
B. SHEMESH	0	0	875	0	0	0	0
B. ZUR	0	0	0	0	0	0	0
BEERSHEBA	0	0	1200	900	0	0	0
EN GEDI	0	0	0	0	0	0	0
FUL	0	2268	250	250	0	0	0

Table 11 (continued)

Site Name	12th	11th	10th	9th	8th	7th	6th
Settlements (cont.)							
GEZER	0	0	0	0	0	0	0
GIBEON	2200	0	2850	0	0	0	0
GILOH	1520	0	0	0	0	0	0
HASHAVYAHU	0	0	0	0	0	1235	0
HESI	0	0	0	2880	0	0	0
JEMMEH	0	0	0	0	0	830	0
JERUSALEM	0	0	3000	0	18200	0	0
JUDEIDEH	0	0	0	0	0	0	0
LACHISH	0	0	900	1600	13200	0	0
MALHATA	0	0	17400	1305	0	0	0
MASOS	0	0	0	0	0	0	0
MOR	0	0	0	0	810	0	0
NAGILAH	0	0	0	0	0	0	0
NASBEH	0	0	0	2640	0	0	0
R. RAHEL	0	0	0	0	2130	4429	0
RABUD	0	0	0	3600	0	0	0
SAFI	0	0	0	0	0	0	0
SERA'	0	0	0	0	0	0	0
SHARUHEN	0	0	0	0	0	4480	0
SIPPOR	0	0	0	0	0	0	0
Subtotals	6570	7548	13815	16125	39090	13899	0
Totals	6570	7548	13815	16882	42292	13899	0

Table 12. Luxury Items by Period
Excavated Sites South of Map Reference 1450

Period: Iron I

Site Name: B. MIRSIM
—inscribed sherd fragment
—few seals
—2 bronze plow-tips
—8 pieces unidentified bronze
—scaraboid
—very few pieces iron (no count)

Site Name: B. SHEMESH
—2 ivory buttons
—bronze punch
—2 bronze arrowheads
—bronze spatula
—faience amulet
—3 stone weights
—iron sickle blade
—bronze spear head
—3 animal figurines
—human figurine

Site Name: B. ZUR
—scarab
—scaraboid
—steatite seal
—iron pin

Site Name: NASBEH
—39 bronze pins

Period: Iron II

Site Name: B. MIRSIM
—7 inscribed plaques
—inscribed knife-handle
—many pieces of iron (c. 12 shown in plates, 'many more' not shown)
—12 stone cosmetic pallettes
—few pieces bronze (3 shown in plates; no count)

Table 12 (continued)

Site Name: B. SHEMESH
—3 bronze punches
—2 bronze arrowheads
—2 bronze needles
—2 stone pendants
—3 stone weights
—2 bronze fibulae
—bronze weight
—iron spearhead
—iron javelin head
—iron axehead
—iron adze
—iron chisel
—bronze javelin head
—bronze chisel
—2 bronze plow points
—5 animal figurines
—10 human figurines
—clay chariot wheel (toy or cult object)

Site Name: B. ZUR
—bronze ear-ring
—2 iron arrowheads

Site Name: BEERSHEBA
—9 pieces cedar wood imported from Lebanon in stratified context; 27 more in unstratified context dated to this period also since no wood found in stratified context earlier than 9th century

Site Name: GIBEON
—40 clay stoppers and a clay funnel that fit the handle-stamped jars well

Site Name: NASBEH
—60 bronze fibulae

Site Name: SIPPOR
—200 terracotta figurines
—20 stone statuettes
—10 solid terracottas
—2 solid plaques
—8 hand-made solid figurines (the rest are hollow)

Table 13. Luxury Items by Century
Excavated Sites South of Map Reference 1450

Century: 12

Site Name: GEZER
—Ceramic figurine, half-round, female holding breasts, local

Century: 11

Site Name: B. SHEMESH
—metal, mostly bronze, some iron, used for weapons and jewelry not agriculture (no count)
—two ivory buttons

Site Name: B. ZUR
—scarab
—scaraboid
—steatite seal

Site Name: GEZER
—bronze arrowhead, sharpened and grooved by tooling, perfect condition

Century: 10

Site Name: B. SHEMESH
—bronze anklet
—marble cosmetic mixing bowl

Site Name: FUL
—iron plow-tip

Site Name: GEZER
—weight, goethite,
—(incense?) altar 9 cm high, poor work

Site Name: LACHISH
—scaraboid of Shishak, Egyptian make
—iron knife (tomb)
—iron trident (tomb)

Site Name: NASBEH
—bronze fibula

Table 13 (continued)

Century: 9

Site Name: GEZER
—weight, broken, sandstone

Site Name: LACHISH
—4 scarabs, well made
—5 scaraboids, probably local copies
—9 silver ear-rings
—bronze ring

Site Name: NASBEH
—bronze bowl
—bronze fibula

Century: 8

Site Name: ARAD
—4 ostraca

Site Name: B. MIRSIM
—2 inscribed sherds
—pieces of c. 12 fertility figurines

Site Name: LACHISH
—inscription on jar *bt lmlk*
—first five letters of alphabet in order and a picture of a lion scratched
on the rise of a limestone step east of the palace
—17 scarabs, very poor local make
—20 scaraboids (local, simple)
—9 pillar-base figures
—2 clay models of furniture
—16 faience amulets, Egyptian copies
—iron blade (tomb)
—10 scales iron armor
—7 scales bronze armor
—2 bronze fibulae
—4 iron plow-points
—3 iron sickles
—20 silver ear-rings
—3 bronze rings

Table 13 (continued)

Site Name: R. RAHEL
—sherd incised with *l*
—11 fragments of locally manufactured imitations of Cypriote statuary

Century: 7

Site Name: ARAD
—9 ostraca

Site Name: B. MIRSIM
—3 inscribed sherds
—3 limestone weights found in 'West Tower' adjoining city gate
—pieces of c. 27 fertility figurines

Site Name: EN GEDI
—seal, 1 × 1 cm, square and flat
—3 bronze bracelets

Site Name: FUL
—2 iron nails

Site Name: GEZER
—bronze fibula
—basalt hammer

Site Name: GIBEON
—Assyrian scene seal

Site Name: HASHAVYAHU
—7 Hebrew ostraca
—weight
—'large quantities' of Greek pottery

Site Name: JERUSALEM
—2 ostraca inked by a professional scribe (Avigad 1984: 41-42)
—9 iron arrowheads
—bronze arrowhead
—10 fragments of furniture made of imported box-wood

Site Name: LACHISH
—21 ostraca 'letters'
—6 inscribed weights
—10 pillar base figures
—3 clay models of furniture
—40 bronze 'bangles' (anklets or bracelets)
—39 silver ear-rings
—3 bronze rings

Table 13 (continued)

Site Name: NASBEH
—120 Astarte figurines
—bronze bowl
—4 iron plow-points
—7 cosmetic mortars
—7 bone pendants

Site Name: R. RAHEL
—7 terracotta figurines
—clay seal
—2 painted sherds found in 'what is presumed to be the palace of one of the kings of Judah'
—two Assyrian beakers

Century: 6

Site Name: ARAD
—6 ostraca

Site Name: B. SHEMESH
—3 bronze rings
—2 bronze arrowheads
—bronze bird-head handle
—Hebrew seal
—Syro-Hittite seal
—bronze and limestone pendant

Site Name: LACHISH
—remains of an inscription, badly damaged

Table 14. Luxury Items—Aggregate Counts by Type, Class, Century and Period

	Centuries BCE							Sub-Totals	Periods		Grand Totals
									12–10	9–7	
	12	11	10	9	8	7	6		IR1	IR2	
I. Artifact Types											
Bronze		1	2	3	12	51	7	76	57	151	208
Iron			3		18	15		36	8	52	60
Silver				9	20	39		68	0	68	68
Imported			1			12		13	1	21	22
Terracotta figurines	1				34	167		202	5	428	433
Stone statuettes			1					1	1	20	21
Inscriptions					5	9	1	15	1	23	24
Ostraca					4	41	6	51	0	59	59
Seals and Scarabs		3	1	9	37	2	2	54	12	52	64
Cosmetic pallettes			1			7		8	1	7	8
Weights			1	1		51		53	1	60	61
Jewelry			2	11	41	92	4	150	45	214	259
Totals	1	4	12	33	171	486	20	727	132	1155	1287
II. Artifact Classes											
Jewelry		0	3	11	41	99	4	158	46	221	267
Metals		1	5	12	50	105	7	180	65	271	336
Statuary	1	0	1	0	34	167	0	203	6	448	454
Writing		3	1	9	46	52	9	120	13	134	147
Totals	1	4	10	32	171	423	20	661	130	1074	1204

Table 15. Handle-stamped Jars—
Sites South of Map Reference 1450

Name on Stamp	Century BCE	Location of Handles							Totals
		B. Shemesh	Gibeon	Judeideh	Lachish	Nasbeh	R. Rahel	Safi	
Hebron	8	11	1	2	186	8	8		216
	7	1	11	3	12	5	22		54
Ziph	8		1	2	10		4		17
	7		8	2	9	9	31		59
Sokoh	8		1	2	28		2	2	35
	7		9	5	12	4	5		35
Mmst	8		2		1		0		3
	7	1	6	6	7	10	25		55
unknown	8	4	7	5	40	7		4	67
	7	2	34	10	5	43	48		142
rosette	8								
	7						12		12
Totals	8	15	12	11	265	15	14	6	338
	7	4	68	26	45	71	143		357
Grand Totals		19	80	37	310	86	157	6	695

198

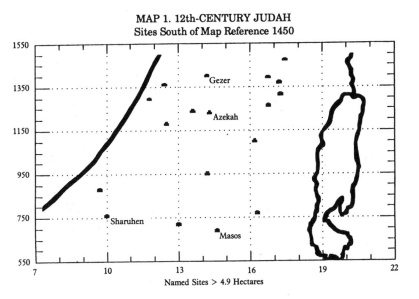

MAP 1. 12th-CENTURY JUDAH
Sites South of Map Reference 1450

Named Sites > 4.9 Hectares

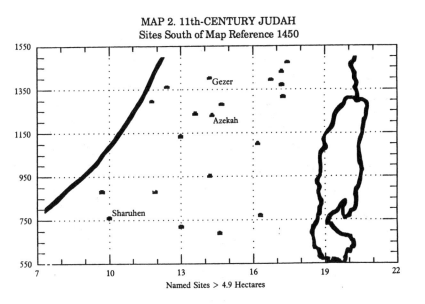

MAP 2. 11th-CENTURY JUDAH
Sites South of Map Reference 1450

Named Sites > 4.9 Hectares

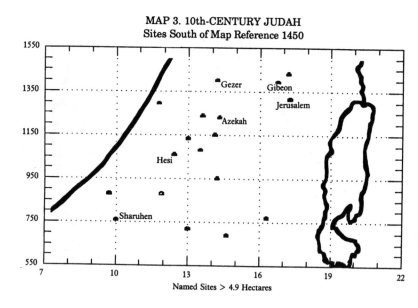

MAP 3. 10th-CENTURY JUDAH
Sites South of Map Reference 1450

Named Sites > 4.9 Hectares

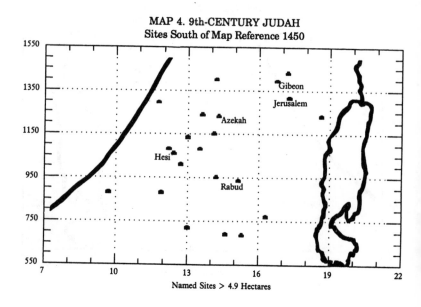

MAP 4. 9th-CENTURY JUDAH
Sites South of Map Reference 1450

Named Sites > 4.9 Hectares

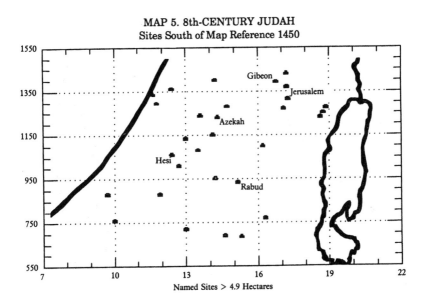

MAP 5. 8th-CENTURY JUDAH
Sites South of Map Reference 1450

Gibeon

Jerusalem

Azekah

Hesi

Rabud

Named Sites > 4.9 Hectares

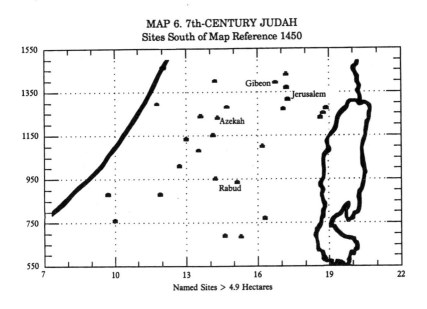

MAP 6. 7th-CENTURY JUDAH
Sites South of Map Reference 1450

Gibeon

Jerusalem

Azekah

Rabud

Named Sites > 4.9 Hectares

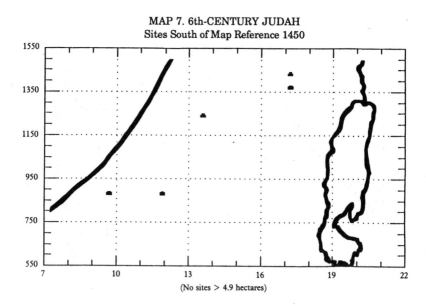

MAP 7. 6th-CENTURY JUDAH
Sites South of Map Reference 1450

(No sites > 4.9 hectares)

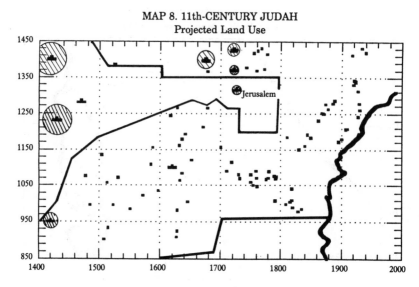

MAP 8. 11th-CENTURY JUDAH
Projected Land Use

In Maps 8–12 hatched area = arable land required to provide for estimated population of sites

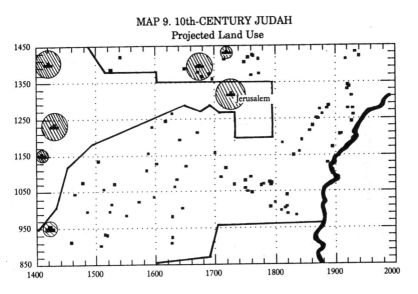

MAP 9. 10th-CENTURY JUDAH
Projected Land Use

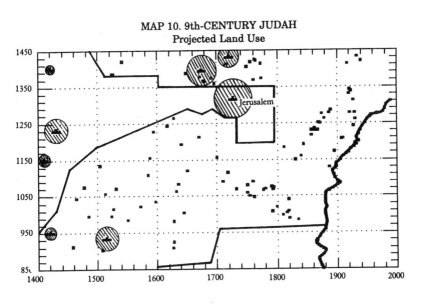

MAP 10. 9th-CENTURY JUDAH
Projected Land Use

MAP 11. 7th-CENTURY JUDAH
Projected Land Use

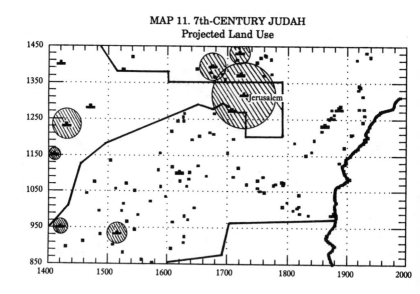

MAP 12. 6th-CENTURY JUDAH
Projected Land Use

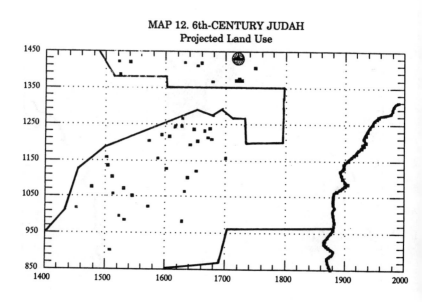

MAP 13. 12th-CENTURY JUDAH—PUBLIC WORKS,
COMBINED AREA
Plot of Land Reference Points vs Area (z-axis)

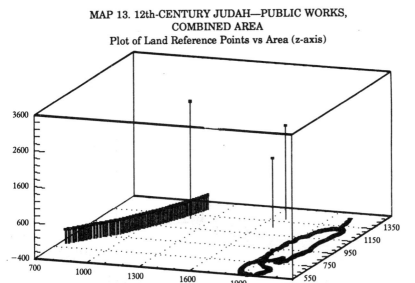

In Maps 13–17, horizontal axes are map reference points; vertical axis is
combined public works area in square meters.

MAP 14. 11th-CENTURY JUDAH—PUBLIC WORKS,
COMBINED AREA
Plot of Map Reference Points vs Area (z-axis)

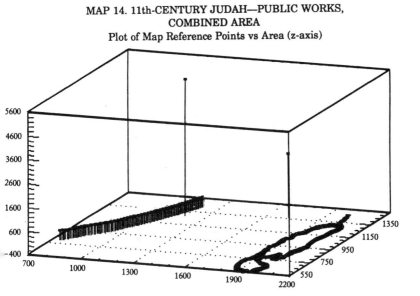

MAP 15. 10th-CENTURY JUDAH—PUBLIC WORKS,
COMBINED AREA
Plot of Map Reference Points vs Area (z-axis)

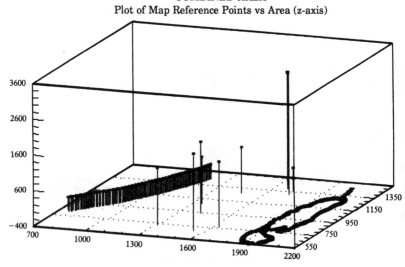

MAP 16. 8th-CENTURY JUDAH—PUBLIC WORKS,
COMBINED AREA
Plot of Map Referencce Points vs Area (z-axis)

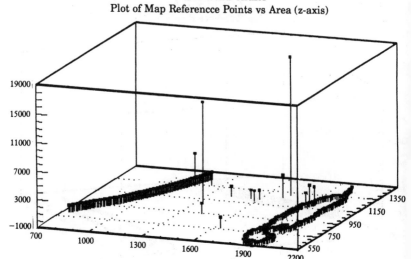

MAP 17. 7th-CENTURY JUDAH—PUBLIC WORKS,
COMBINED AREA
Plot of Map Reference Points vs Area (z-axis)

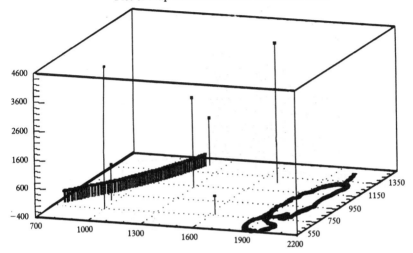

MAP 18. 11th-CENTURY JUDAH—LUXURY ITEMS, AGGREGATE
Plot of Map Reference Points vs Number of Items (z-axis)

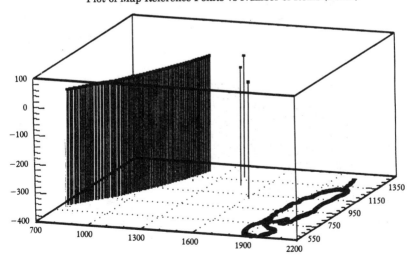

MAP 19. 10th-CENTURY JUDAH—LUXURY ITEMS, AGGREGATE
Plot of Map Reference Points vs Number of Items (z-axis)

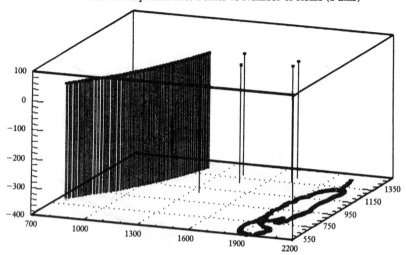

MAP 20. 9th-CENTURY JUDAH—LUXURY ITEMS, AGGREGATE
Plot of Map Reference Points vs Number of Items (z-axis)

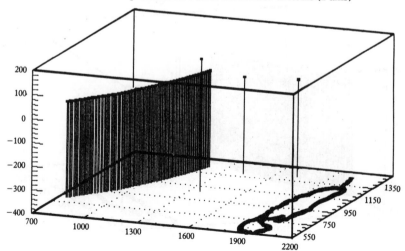

MAP 21. 8th-CENTURY JUDAH—LUXURY ITEMS, AGGREGATE
Plot of Map Reference Points vs Number of Items (z-axis)

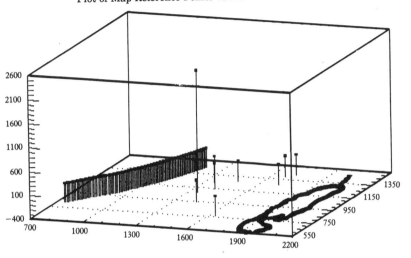

MAP 22. 7th-CENTURY JUDAH—LUXURY ITEMS, AGGREGATE
Plot of Map Reference Points vs Number of Items (z-axis)

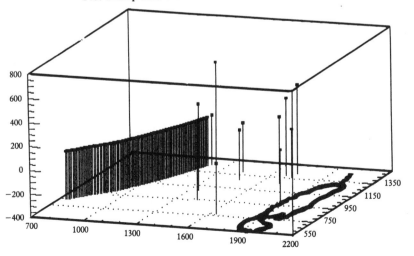

CHART 1. AVERAGE SITE SIZE (HECTARES)

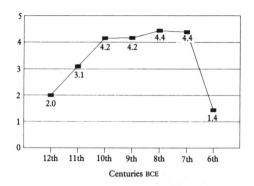

CHART 2. NUMBER OF SURVEYED SITES IN JUDAH
(Judaea, Samaria and Golan Survey)

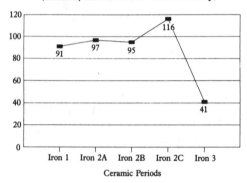

CHART 3. AREA IN EXCAVATED SITES (HECTARES)

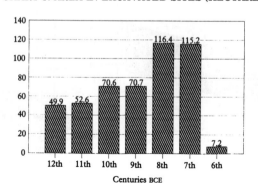

CHART 4. PERCENTAGE AREA

by Site Category

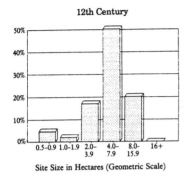

12th Century

Site Size in Hectares (Geometric Scale)

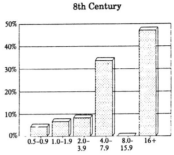

8th Century

Site Size in Hectares (Geometric Scale)

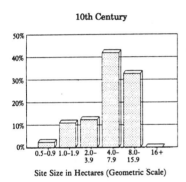

10th Century

Site Size in Hectares (Geometric Scale)

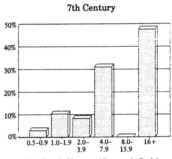

7th Century

Site Size in Hectares (Geometric Scale)

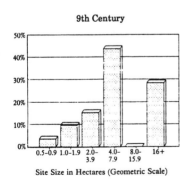

9th Century

Site Size in Hectares (Geometric Scale)

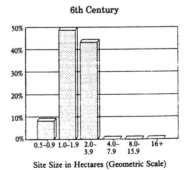

6th Century

Site Size in Hectares (Geometric Scale)

CHART 5. AREA VS RANK

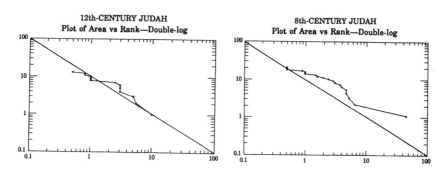

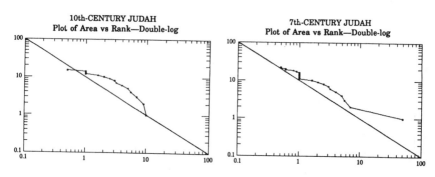

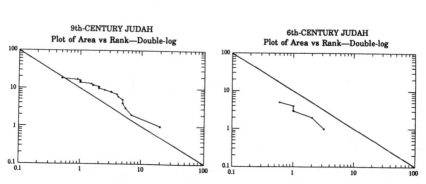

CHART 6. PUBLIC WORKS
No. of Sites, Walls and Buildings

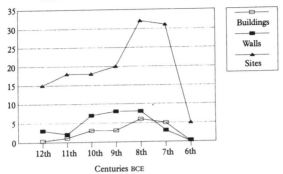

CHART 7. AREA OF WALLS
(Circumference × Width; Square Meters)

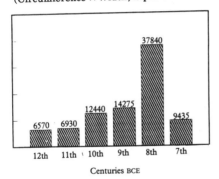

CHART 8. PUBLIC WORKS
Public Buildings Area; Square Meters

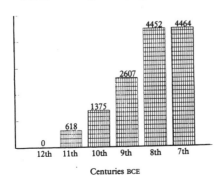

CHART 9. PUBLIC WORKS
Combined Area; Square Meters

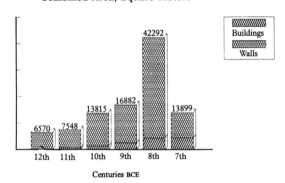

CHART 10. LUXURY ITEMS
By Class and Period

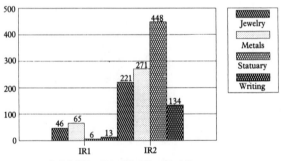

CHART 11. LUXURY ITEMS
By Class and Century

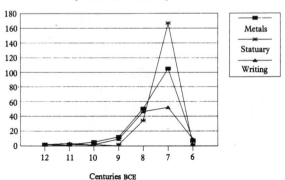

215

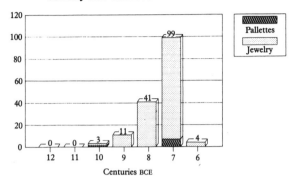

CHART 12. LUXURY ITEMS
Jewelry and Cosmetic Pallettes

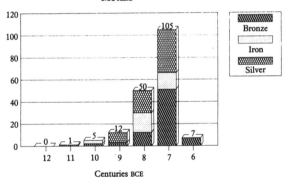

CHART 13. LUXURY ITEMS
Metals

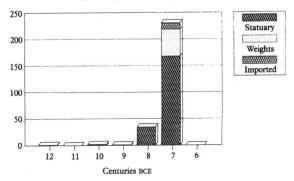

CHART 14. LUXURY ITEMS
Statuary, Weights and Imported

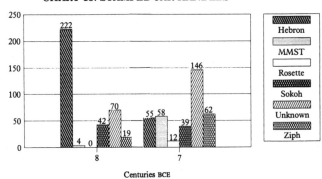

CHART 15. STAMPED JAR HANDLES

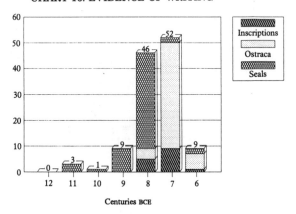

CHART 16. EVIDENCE OF WRITING

BIBLIOGRAPHY OF SITES

Excavated Sites South of Map Reference 1450

GENERAL AND SURVEYS

Avi-Yonah, M., and E. Stern, eds., *Encyclopedia of Archaeological Excavations in the Holy Land* (Eng. edn). Englewood Cliffs, 1975.

Finkelstein, I., 'The Iron Age "Fortresses" of the Negev Highlands', *Tel Aviv* 11 (1984) 189-208.

Gophna, R., 'Sites from the Iron Age between Beer-Sheba and Tell el-Far'a', *Bulletin of the Israel Exploration Society* 28 (1964) 236-46 (Hebrew).

Gophna, R., 'Archeological Survey of the Central Coast Plain, 1977', *Tel Aviv* 5 (1978) 136-47.

Kochavi, M., ed., *Judaea, Samaria and the Golan Archaeological Survey 1967-1968*. Jerusalem, 1972.

Meshel, Z. and R. Cohen, 'Refed and Hatira: Two Iron Age Fortresses in the Northern Negev', *Tel Aviv* 7 (1980) 70-81.

Naveh, J., 'Khirbat al-Muqanna'-Ekron, an Archaeological Survey', *Israel Exploration Journal* 8 (1958) 87-100.

Salzmann, M., 'Selected Bibliography: Publications on Archeological Excavations and Surveys in Israel 1948–1958', *Atiqot* 2 (1959) 165-83.

Salzmann, M., 'Selected Bibliography: Publications on Archeological Excavations and Surveys in Israel 1959–1960', *Atiqot* 3 (1961) 188-198.

Salzmann, M., 'Selected Bibliography: Publications on Archeological Excavations and Surveys in Israel 1961–1963', *Atiqot* 4 (1965), Supplement.

Salzmann, M., 'Selected Bibliography: Publications on Archeological Excavations and Surveys in Israel 1964–1967', *Atiqot* 8 (1969), Supplement.

EXCAVATION REPORTS

Abu Tabaq, Kh.

Cross, F.M., and G.E. Wright, 'El-Buqei'a', *Journal of Biblical Literature* 75 (1956) 223-26.

Cross, F.M., and J.T. Milik, 'El-Buqei'a', *Bulletin of the American Schools of Oriental Research* 142 (1956) 5-17.

Arad

Aharoni, Y., and R. Amiran, *Archeology* 17 (1964) 43-53.

Aharoni, Y., *Israel Exploration Journal* 16 (1966) 1-7.

Amiran, R., *Israel Exploration Journal* 22 (1972) 86-88.

Aharoni, Y., and R. Amiran, *Israel Exploration Journal* 14 (1964) 131-47.

Aharoni, Y., *Biblical Archeologist* 31 (1968) 1-32.

Aharoni, Y., *Bulletin of the American Schools of Oriental Research* 197 (1970) 16-42.

Areinit
Yeivin, S., *First Preliminary Report on the Excavations at Tel Gat* (1956-58), Jerusalem, 1951.
Yeivin, S., *Revue Biblique* 69 (1962) 395-97.
Yeivin, S., *Revue Biblique* 67 (1960) 391-94.
Yeivin, S., *Israel Exploration Journal* 10 (1960) 193-203.
Yeivin, S., *Journal of Near Eastern Studies* 23 (1968) 37-49.

Ashdod
Dothan, M., and D.N. Freedman, 'Ashdod I: The First Season of Excavations, 1962', *Atiqot* 7 (1967).
Dothan, M., 'Ashdod II-III: The Second and Third Seasons of Excavations, 1963, 1965, Soundings in 1967', *Atiqot* 9-10 (1971).
Dothan, M. *Archeology* 20 (1967) 178-86.
Dothan, M., and Y. Porath, *Atiqot* 15 (1982).

Ashdod-Yam
Kaplan, J., *Israel Exploration Journal* 19 (1969) 137-49.

Ashkelon
Garstang, J., *Palestine Exploration Fund Quarterly Statement* (1921) 12-16.
Garstang, J., 'The Philistine Problem', *Palestine Exploration Fund Quarterly Statement* (1921) 162-63.
Garstang, J., 'The Excavation of Askalon, 1920-21', *Palestine Exploration Fund Quarterly Statement* (1921) 73-75.
Garstang, J., 'The Fund's Excavation of Askalon', *Palestine Exploration Fund Quarterly Statement* (1922) 112-19.
Mazar, B., *Encyclopedia Miqra'it*, I, 769-77 (Hebrew).
Phythian-Adams, W.J., 'Report on the Stratification of Askalon', *Palestine Exploration Fund Quarterly Statement* (1923) 60-84.
Tsaferis, V., *Israel Exploration Journal* 17 (1967) 125-26.

Azor
Dothan, M., *Israel Exploration Journal* 8 (1958) 272-74.
Dothan, M., *Israel Exploration Journal* 11 (1961) 171-75.
Perrot, J., *Atiqot* 3 (1961) 1-83.

Beersheba, T.
Aharoni, Y., 'Notes and News', *Israel Exploration Journal* 23 (1973) 254.
Aharoni, Y., 'Notes and News', *Israel Exploration Journal* 25 (1975) 170.
Aharoni, Y., 'Notes and News', *Israel Exploration Journal* 27 (1977) 168-69.
Aharoni, Y., 'The Beersheba Excavations, I-III'. Tel Aviv: Tel Aviv Institute of Archaeology, (1970-72).
Aharoni, Y., *Tel Aviv* 1 (1974) 34-44.
Aharoni, Y., *Tel Aviv* 2 (1975) 146-67.
Homsky, M., and S. Moshkovitz, 'The Distribution of Different Wood Species of the Iron Age II at Tel Beer-Sheba', *Tel Aviv* 3 (1976) 42-48.

Beit Mirsim, T.
Albright, W.F., *Annual of the American Schools of Oriental Research* 12 (1932).

Albright, W.F., *Annual of the American Schools of Oriental Research* 13 (1933) 55-128.
Albright, W.F., *Annual of the American Schools of Oriental Research* 17 (1938).
Albright, W.F., *Annual of the American Schools of Oriental Research* 21-22 (1943).

Beth Shemesh
Mackenzie, D., *Palestine Exploration Fund Annual Report* 1 (1911) 41-94.
Mackenzie, D., *Palestine Exploration Fund Annual Report* 2 (1912-1913) 1-39.
Grant, E., *Beth Shemesh*. Haverford, PA, 1929.
Grant, E., *Ain Shems Excavations, pts. I-II*. Haverford, PA, 1931-1932.
Grant, E., *Rumeilah, being Ain Shems Excavations, pt. III*. Haverford, PA, 1934.
Grant, E., and G.E. Wright, *Ain Shems Excavations, pt. IV. The Text*. Haverford, PA, 1938-1939.

Beth Zur
Sellers, O.R., *Annual of the American Schools of Oriental Research* 38 (1968).
Sellers, O.R., *The Citadel of Beth-Zur*. Philadelphia, 1933.

Bethlehem
Abel, F.M., 'Bethlehem', *Revue Biblique* 32 (1923) 264-72.
Abel, F.M., 'Bethlehem', *Revue Biblique* 35 (1926) 284-88.
Sejourn , P.M., 'Bethlehem', *Revue Biblique* 4 (1895) 439-44.
Cheneau, P., 'Bethlehem', *Revue Biblique* 32 (1923) 602-607.
Amiran, R., 'Bethlehem', *BJPES* 13 (1947) 136-39.

En Gedi
Mazar, B., *Atiqot* 5 (1966) 1-100.
Mazar, B., and I. Dunayevsky, *Israel Exploration Journal* 14 (1964) 121-30.

Ful, T.
Lapp, P.W., *Biblical Archeologist* 28 (1965) 2-10.
Lapp, P.W., *Festschrift für Kurt Galling*. Tübingen, 1970, 179-97.
Sinclair, L., *Annual of the American Schools of Oriental Research* (1960) 34-35.
Albright, W.F., *Annual of the American Schools of Oriental Research* 4 (1924).

Gezer
Macalister, R.A.S., *The Excavation of Gezer 1902–1905 and 1907–1909*, vols. I-III. London, 1912.
Dever, W.G., H.D. Lance and G.E. Wright, *Gezer*, vol. I. *Preliminary Report of the 1964–1966 Seasons*. Jerusalem, 1970.
Dever, W.G., *et al.*, *Gezer*, vol. II. *Reports of 1967–1970 Seasons in Fields I and II*. Jerusalem, 1975.
Finkelstein, I., 'The Date of Gezer's Outer Wall', *Tel Aviv* 8 (1981) 136-45.

Gibeon
Dajani, A.K., 'An Iron Age Tomb at Al-Jib', *Annual of the Department of Antiquities in Jordan* 2 (1953) 66-74.

Pritchard, J.B., *Hebrew Stamps and Inscriptions from Gibeon*. Princeton, 1959.
Pritchard, J.B., *Winery, Defenses and Soundings at Gibeon*. Princeton, 1961.
Pritchard, J.B., *The Water System at Gibeon*. Princeton, 1961.
Pritchard, J.B., *Gibeon: Where the Sun Stood Still*. Princeton, 1962.

Giloh
Mazar, A., *Israel Exploration Journal* 31 (1981) 1-36.

Hebron
Mader, A.E., *Mambre. Die Ergebnisse der Ausgrabungen im heiligen Bezirk, Râmet el-Halîl in Südpalästina*. Freiburg im Breisgau, 1957.

Hesi, T.
Bliss, F.J., *A Mound of Many Cities*. London, 1894.
Petrie, W.M.F., *Tell el Hesy (Lachish)*. London, 1891.
Worrell, J.E., and L.E. Toombs, *Israel Exploration Journal* 24 (1974) 139-41.
Worrell, J.E., and L.E. Toombs, *Israel Exploration Journal* 21 (1971) 177-78, 233-34.
Toombs, L.E., *et al.*, *Palestine Exploration Quarterly* (1974) 19-31.

Horvat Haluqim
Cohen, R., *Atiqot* 11 (1976) 34-50.

Jemmeh, T.
Petrie, W.M.F., *Gerar*. London, 1928.
Mazar, B., 'Yurza: The Identification of Tell Jemmeh', *Palestine Exploration Quarterly* (1952) 48-51.
Aharoni, Y., *Israel Exploration Journal* 6 (1956) 26-31.
Beek, G.W. van, 'Tell Gamma', *Israel Exploration Journal* 27 (1977) 172-73.
Beek, G.W. van, 'Tell Gamma', *Israel Exploration Journal* 20 (1970) 230.
Beek, G.W. van, 'Tell Gamma', *Israel Exploration Journal* 22 (1972) 245-46.
Beek, G.W. van, 'Tell Gamma', *Israel Exploration Journal* 24 (1974) 138-39, 274-75.

Jerusalem
Kenyon, K.M., *Digging Up Jerusalem*. London, 1974.
Kenyon, K.M., *Jerusalem*. London, 1974.
Yadin, Y., ed., *Jerusalem Revealed*. Jerusalem, 1975.
Avigad, N., *Discovering Jerusalem*. Oxford, 1984.
Shiloh, Y., *Qedem* 19 (1984).

Lachish
Tufnell, O., *et al.*, *Lachish, vol. III. The Iron Age*. London, 1953.
Ussishkin, D., *Israel Exploration Journal* 24 (1974) 272-73.
Ussishkin, D., *Tel Aviv* 4 (1977) 28-60.
Ussishkin, D., *Tel Aviv* 5 (1978) 1-98.

Malhata, T.
Kochavi, M., *Israel Exploration Journal* 17 (1967) 272-73.

Masos, T.
Aharoni, Y., A. Kempinski and V. Fritz, *Tel Aviv* 1 (1974) 64-74.
Aharoni, Y., A. Kempinski and V. Fritz, *Tel Aviv* 2 (1975) 97-124.
Aharoni, Y. *Zeitschrift des Deutschen Palästina-Vereins* 91 (1975) 109-34.
Kempinski, A., *Israel Exploration Journal* 26 (1976) 52-53.
Kempinski, A., and V. Fritz, *Tel Aviv* 4 (1977) 136-58.

Mor, T.
Dothan, M., *Israel Exploration Journal* 9 (1959) 271-72.
Dothan, M., *Israel Exploration Journal* 10 (1966) 123-35.
Dothan, M., *Israel Exploration Journal* 23 (1973) 1-17.
Dothan, M., *EAEHL* III (1975) 889-90.

Nagilah
Amiran, R., and A. Eitan, *EAEHL* III (1975) 894-98.

Nasbeh, T.
McCown, C.C., *Tell en-Nasbeh*, vol. I. Berkeley, 1947.
Wampler, J.C., *Tell en-Nasbeh*, vol. II: *The Pottery*. Berkeley, 1947.

Rabud
Kochavi, M., *Tel Aviv* I (1974) 2-33.

Ramat Rahel
Aharoni, Y., *Series Archeologica* 2 (1962).
Aharoni, Y., *Series Archeologica* 6 (1964).

Safi, T.
Bliss, F.J., and R.A., Macalister, *Excavations in Palestine*. London, 1902.
Rainey, A.F., 'The Identification of Philistine Gath', *Eretz-Israel* 12 (1975) 63-76.

Sera'
Oren, E., *Revue Biblique* 80 (1973) 401-405.
Oren, E., *Israel Exploration Journal* 23 (1973) 251-54.

Sharuhen
Kempinski, A., *Israel Exploration Journal* 24 (1974) 145-52.
Petrie, W.M.F., *Ancient Gaza*, vols. I-IV. London, 1931-34.

Sippor, T.
Negbi, O., *Atiqot* 6 (1967) 1-27.
Biran, A., and O. Negbi, 'Tel Sippor', *Israel Exploration Journal* 16 (1966) 160-73.

SELECTED BIBLIOGRAPHY

Adams, R.M.
1975   *Energy and Structure*. Austin: University of Texas.
1981   *Heartland of Cities*. Chicago: University of Chicago Press.
Aharoni, Y.
1982   *The Archaeology of the Land of Israel*, trans. A.F. Rainey. Philadelphia: Westminster Press.
Albright, W.F.
1956   *Archaeology of Palestine*. Harmondsworth, Middlesex: Penguin Books.
1966   *Archaeology, History, and Early Biblical Tradition*. Baton Rouge: Louisiana State University Press.
1971   'The Impact of Archaeology on Biblical Research', pp. 1-16 in *New Directions in Biblical Archaeology*, ed. D.N. Freedman and J.C. Greenfield.
Aldrich, F.T.
1979   'Comments on Computer Graphics Applications in Archaeology', pp. 145-48 in *Computer Graphics in Archaeology*, ed. S. Upham.
Alt, A.
1967   'The Monarchy in the Kingdoms of Israel and Judah', pp. 311-35 in *Essays on Old Testament History and Religion*, trans. R.A. Wilson. Garden City: Doubleday.
1967   'The Formation of the Israelite State in Palestine', pp. 223-310 in *Essays in Old Testament History and Religion*, trans. R.A. Wilson. Garden City: Doubleday.
Athens, S.J.
1977   'Theory Building and the Study of Evolutionary Process in Complex Societies', pp. 353-84 in *For Theory Building in Archaeology*, ed. L.R. Binford.
Balandier, G.
1970   *Political Anthropology*, trans. A.M. Sheridan. New York: Pantheon.
Barkay, G.
1983   'The Divine Name Found in Jerusalem'. *Biblical Archaeology Review* 9/2: 14-19.
Barrois, G.A.
1962   'Trade and Commerce'. *Interpreter's Dictionary of the Bible* IV: 677-83. New York: Abingdon.
Barucq, A.
1964   *Le Livre de Proverbes*. Paris: Librairie Lecoffre.
Bayard, D.T.
1969   'Science, Theory, and Reality in the "New Archeology". *American Antiquity* 34: 376-84.

Beale, T.W.
    1978   'Bevelled Rim Bowls and their Implications for Change and Economic Organization in the Later Fourth Millennium B.C'. *Journal of Near Eastern Studies* 37: 289-313.

Beals, R.L.
    1951   'Urbanism, Urbanization and Acculturation'. *American Anthropologist* 53: 1-10.

Becker, H.
    1950   'Sacred and Secular Societies'. *Social Forces* 28: 361-76.
    1950   *Through Values to Social Interpretation.* Durham: Duke University Press.

Beebe, H.K.
    1968   'Ancient Palestinian Dwellings'. *Biblical Archaeologist* 31: 38-57.

Bennett, J.W.
    1972   'Anticipation, Adaptation, and the Concept of Culture in Anthropology'. *Science 192*: 847-53.
    1976   *The Ecological Transition: Cultural Anthropology and Human Adaptation.* New York: Pergamon Press.

Berry, B.J.L.
    1961   'City Size Distributions and Economic Development'. *Economic Development and Cultural Change* 9: 573-88.

Binford, L.R.
    1962   'Archaeology as Anthropology'. *American Antiquity* 28: 217-225
    1964   'A Consideration of Archaeological Research Design'. *American Antiquity* 29: 425-41.
    1965   'Archaeological Systematics and the Study of Culture Process'. *American Antiquity* 31: 203-10.
    1972   *An Archaeological Perspective.* New York: Seminar Press.
    1977   'General Introduction', pp. 1-10 in *For Theory Building in Archaeology*, ed. L.R. Binford.

Binford, L.R., ed.
    1977   *For Theory Building in Archaeology.* New York: Academic Press.

Binford, L.R. and S.R., eds.
    1968   *New Perspectives in Archeology.* Chicago: Aldine Publishing Company.

Bonte, P.
    1979   'Pastoral Production, Territorial Organization and Kinship in Segmentary Lineage Societies', pp. 203-234 in *Social and Ecological Systems*, ed. P.C. Burnham and R.F. Ellen.

Bright, J.
    1972   *A History of Israel.* 2nd edn. Philadelphia: Westminster.

Brinker, R.
    1946   *The Influence of Sanctuaries in Early Israel.* Manchester: Manchester University Press.

Brown, J.A.
    1981   'The Search for Rank in Prehistoric Burials', pp. 25-37 in *The Archaeology of Death*, ed. R. Chapman, I. Kinnes, and K. Randsborg.

Brunner, H.
    1957   *Altägyptische Erziehung.* Wiesbaden: Harrassowitz.

Burnham, P.C. and R.F. Ellen
    1979   *Social and Ecological Systems*. London, New York: Academic
            Press.
Butzer, K.W.
    1976   *Early Hydraulic Civilization in Egypt*. Chicago: Chicago University
            Press.
    1982   *Archaeology as Human Ecology: Method and Theory for a Contex-
            tual Approach*. Cambridge: Cambridge University Press.
Carneiro, R.L.
    1970   'A Theory of the Origin of the State'. *Science* 169: 733-38.
Cassels, R.
    1972   'Locational Analysis of Prehistoric Settlement in New Guinea'.
            Mankind 8: 212-22.
Castellino, G.R.
    1957   'Les Origines de la civilisation selon les textes bibliques et les textes
            cunéiformes'. *Vetus Testamentum Supplements* 4: 116-37.
Chamberlayne, J.H.
    1963   'Kinship Relations among the Early Hebrews'. *Numen* 10: 153-64.
Chapman, R.
    1982   'Autonomy, Ranking, and Resources in Iberian Prehistory',
            pp. 46-51 in *Ranking, Resource and Exchange*, ed. C. Renfrew and
            S. Shennan.
Chapman, R., I. Kinnes and K. Randsborg
    1981   *The Archeology of Death*. Cambridge: Cambridge University
            Press.
Childe, V.G.
    1950   'The Urban Revolution'. *Town Planning Review* 21: 3-17.
    1951   *Social Evolution*. New York: H. Schuman.
    1957   'Civilizations, Cities and Towns'. *Antiquity* 31: 36-38.
Chisolm, M.
    1970   *Rural Settlement and Land Use: An Essay in Location*. Chicago:
            Aldine.
Claessen, H.J.M. and P. Skalnik, eds.
    1978   *The Early State*. The Hague: Mouton.
Clark, G.A.
    1978   'Review of "Spatial analysis in archaeology" (Hodder and Orton)'.
            American Antiquity 43 (1): 132-35.
    1979   'Spatial Association at Liencres, an Early Holocene Open Site on
            the Santander Coast, North-Central Spain', pp. 121-43 in *Computer
            Graphics in Archaeology*, ed. S. Upham.
Clarke, D.L.
    1978   *Analytical Archaeology*. 2nd edn. New York: Columbia University
            Press.
Clarke, D.L., ed.
    1972   *Models in Archaeology*. London: Methuen.
    1977   *Spatial Archaeology*. London and New York: Academic Press.
Clements, R.E.
    1962   'Temple and Land: A Significant Aspect of Israel's Worship'.
            Transactions of the Glasgow University Oriental Society 19: 16-28.
Cohen, R.
    1979   'The Israelite Fortresses in the Negev Highlands'. *Qadmoniot* 12:
            38-50.

Cohen, R., and E.R. Service
  1978   *Origins of the State: The Anthropology of Political Evolution.*
          Philadelphia. Institute for the Study of Human Issues.
Conover, W.J.
  1971   *Practical Non-Parametric Statistics.* New York: John Wiley and
          Sons.
Coulborn, R.
  1959   *The Origin of Civilized Societies.* Princeton: Princeton University
          Press.
Crenshaw, J.L.
  1985   'Education in Israel'. *Journal of Biblical Literature* 104: 601-15.
Cornfeld, G.
  1976   *Archaeology of the Bible: Book by Book.* New York: Harper & Row.
Cross, F.M.
  1967   'The Origin and Early Evolution of the Alphabet'. *E.L. Sukenik*
          Memorial Volume, Eretz-Israel 8: 8-24.
Cross, F.M., W.E. Lemke, and P.D. Miller, Jr, eds.
  1976   Magnalia Dei: *The Mighty Acts of God. Essays on the Bible and*
          Archaeology in Memory of G. Ernest Wright. Garden City, NY:
          Doubleday.
Cross, F.M., and G.E. Wright, eds.
  1956   'The Boundary and Province Lists of the Kingdom of Judah'. *Jour-*
          nal of Biblical Literature 75: 202-26.
Crumley, C.L.
  1976   'Toward a Locational Definition of State Systems of Settlement'.
          American Anthropologist 78: 59-73.
Crüsemann, F.
  1978   *Der Widerstand gegen das Königtum.* Wissenschaftliche Mono-
          graphien zum Alten und Neuen Testament, 49. Neukirchen-
          Vluyn: Neukirchener Verlag.
  1979   'Alttestamentliche Exegese und Archäologie: Erwägungen an-
          gesichts des gegenwärtigen Methodenstreits in der Archäologie
          Palästinas'. *Zeitschrift für die alttestamentliche Wissenschaft*
          91/2: 177-93.
Dacey, M.F.
  1973   'Statistical Tests of Spatial Association in the Location of Tool
          Types'. *American Antiquity* 38 (3): 320-28.
Daniel, G.E.
  1971   'From Worsaae to Childe: the Models of Prehistory'. *Proceedings of*
          the Prehistoric Society 37 (2): 140-53.
Davis, K.
  1960   'The Origin and Growth of Urbanism in the World'. *American*
          Journal of Oriental Studies 66: 140-53.
Degen, R.
  1978   'Ein aramäisches Alphabet vom Tell Halaf'. *Neue Ephemeris für*
          semitische Epigraphik 3: 1-9.
Demsky, A.
  1971   'Education in the Biblical Period'. *Encyclopedia Judaica* VI: 382-
          98.
Demsky, A., and K. Kochavi
  1978   'An Alphabet from the Days of the Judges'. *Biblical Archaeology*
          Review IV (3): 23-30.

226   *Scribes and Schools in Monarchic Judah*

Dever, W.G.
1970   'Iron Age Epigraphic Material from the Area of Khirbet el-Kom'. *Hebrew Union College Annual* 61: 139-204.
1974   *Archeology and Biblical Studies: Retrospects and Prospects.* Chicago: Seabury-Western Theological Seminary.
Diakonoff, I.M.
1965   'Main Features of the Economy in the Monarchies of Ancient Western Asia', pp. 13-32 in the *Third International Conference of Economic History.* The Hague: Mouton.
1975   'The Rural Community in the Ancient Near East'. *Journal of the Economic and Social History of the Orient* 18: 121-33.
Diringer, D.
1949   'The Royal Jar-Stamps of Ancient Judah'. *Biblical Archaeologist* 12: 70-86.
Doran, J.E.
1970   'Systems Theory, Computer Simulations and Archaeology'. *World Archaeology* 1: 289-98.
Doran, J.E., and F.R. Hodson
1975   *Mathematics and Computers in Archaeology.* Cambridge, MA: Harvard University Press.
Dornemann, R.H.
1983   *The Archaeology of the Transjordan in the Bronze and Iron Ages.* Milwaukee: Milwaukee Public Museum.
Driver, S.R.
1913   *Notes on the Hebrew Text and Topography of the Books of Samuel.* 2nd edn. Oxford: Clarendon Press.
Dumond, D.E.
1975   'The Limitation of Human Population: A Natural History'. *Science* 187: 713-21.
Durkheim, E.
1933   *Emile Durkheim on the Division of Labor in Society.* Trans. G. Simpson. New York: Macmillan Company.
Dürr, L.
1932   *Das Erziehungswesen im Alten Testament und im antiken Orient.* Leipzig: J.C. Hinrichs.
Earle, T.K., and J.E. Ericson
1977   *Exchange Systems in Prehistory.* New York: Academic Press.
1978   *Economy and Social Organization of a Complex Chiefdom.* Ann Arbor: University of Michigan Press.
Effland, R.W.
1979   'Statistical Distribution Cartography and Computer Graphics', pp. 17-30 in *Computer Graphics in Archeology*, ed. S. Upham.
Evans, G.
1958   '"Coming" and "Going" at the City Gate—A Discussion of Prof. Speiser's Paper'. *Bulletin of the American Schools of Oriental Research* 150: 28-33.
1962   '"Gates" and "Streets": Urban Institutions in Old Testament Times'. *Journal of Religious History* 2: 1-12.
1966   'Rehoboam's Advisors at Shechem and Political Institutions in Israel and Sumer'. *Journal of Near Eastern Studies* 25: 273-79.
Falkenstein, A.
1952   'Der Sohn des Tafelhauses'. *Die Welt des Orients* 1: 172-86.

1953   'Die babylonische Schule'. *Saeculum* IV/3: 125-37.
Feder K.L.
1979   'Geographic Patterning of Tool Types as Elicited by Trend Surface Analysis', pp. 17-30 in *Computer Graphics in Archaeology*, ed. S. Upham.
Fichtner, J.
1933   *Die altorientalische Weisheit in ihren israelitisch-jüdischen Ausprägung*. Giessen: A. Töpelmann.
Fish, T.
1944   'The Place of the Small State in the Political and Cultural History of Ancient Mesopotamia'. *Bulletin of the John Rylands Library* 27: 83-98.
Fisher, L.R.
1963   'The Temple Quarter'. *Journal of Semitic Studies* 8: 34-41.
Flanagan, J.W.
1981   'Chiefs in Israel'. *Journal for the Study of the Old Testament* 20: 47-73.
Flannery, K.V.
1967   'Culture History vs. Cultural Process: a Debate in American Anthropology'. *Scientific American* 217: 119-21.
1972   'The Cultural Evolution of Civilization'. *Annual Review of Ecology and Systematics* 3: 399-426.
Frankfort, H.
1950   'Town Planning in Ancient Mesopotamia'. *Town Planning Review* 21: 99-115.
1951   *The Birth of Civilization in the Near East*. Bloomington: Indiana University Press.
Frick, F.S.
1977   *The City in Ancient Israel*. Missoula: Scholars Press.
1979   'Religion and Sociopolitical Structure in Early Israel', pp. 233-53 in *Society of Biblical Literature 1979 Seminar Papers*, ed. P.J. Achtemeier. Missoula: Scholars Press.
1986   *The Formation of the State in Ancient Israel*. Sheffield: Almond Press.
Fried, M.H.
1967   *The Evolution of Political Society*. New York: Random House.
Friedman, J.
1974   'Marxism, Structuralism and Vulgar Materialism'. *Man* 9: 444-69.
Fritz, J. and F. Plog
1970   'The Nature of Archaeological Explanation'. *American Antiquity* 35: 405-12.
Gadd, C.J.
1956   *Teachers and Students in the Oldest Schools*. London: School of Oriental and African Studies.
Garstang, J.
1934   *The Heritage of Solomon: An Historical Introduction to the Sociology of Ancient Palestine*. London: Williams and Norgate.
Gelb, I.J.
1961   'The Early History of the West Semitic People'. *Journal of Cuneiform Studies* 15: 27-47.
1963   *A Study of Writing*. Chicago: University of Chicago Press.

1965   'The Ancient Mesopotamian Ration System'. *Journal of Near East-*
        ern Studies 24: 230-43.
1969   'On the Alleged Temple and State Economies in Ancient Mesopo-
        tamia'. *Studi in onore di Edoardo Volterra*. Rome: Giuffrè Editore.
        6: 137-54.
Geus, C.H.J. de
1975   'The Importance of Archaeological Research into Agricultural
        Terraces'. *Palestine Exploration Quarterly* 107: 65-74.
Gibson, J.C.L.
1971   *Textbook of Syrian Semitic Inscriptions. I: Hebrew and Moabite*
        Inscriptions. Oxford: Clarendon Press.
Gist, N.P. and S.F. Fara
1964   *Urban Society*. 5th edn. New York: Thomas Y. Crowell Company.
Golka, F.W.
1983   'Die israelitische Weisheitsschule oder "des Kaisers neue
        Kleider"'. *Vetus Testamentum* 33: 257-70.
Gordis, R.
1935   'Sectional Rivalry in the Kingdom of Judah'. *Jewish Quarterly*
        Review 25: 237-59.
1950   'Democratic Origins in Ancient Israel—the Biblical *'edah'*,
        pp. 369-88 in the *Alexander Marx Jubilee Volume*, ed. S. Lieber-
        man. New York: Jewish Theological Seminary.
Gottwald, N.K.
1964   *All the Kingdoms of the Earth. Israelite Prophecy and Interna-*
        tional Relations in the Ancient Near East. New York: Harper and
        Row.
1975   'Domain Assumptions and Societal Models in the Study of Pre-
        monarchic Israel'. *Vetus Testamentum Supplements* (Edinburgh
        Congress Volume), pp. 1-12. Leiden: E.J. Brill.
1979   *The Tribes of Yahweh*. Maryknoll: Orbis Books.
Gray, J.
1952   'Tell el Far'a by Nablus: a "Mother" in ancient Israel'. *Palestine*
        Excavation Quarterly 84: 110-13.
1963   *I and II Kings*. Philadelphia: Westminster.
1965   *The Legacy of Canaan*. 2nd edn. Leiden: E.J. Brill.
Green, D.
1974   'Random Model Testing of Archaeological Site Locations in Allen
        and South Cottonwood Canyons, Southwestern Utah', *Kiva* 39: 289-
        99.
Gressmann, H.
1925   *Israels Spruchweisheit im Zusammenhang der Weltliteratur*.
        Berlin: K. Curtius.
Haggett, P.
1965   *Locational Analysis in Human Geography*. London: E. Arnold.
Hallo, W.W.
1962   'New Viewpoints on Cuneiform Literature'. *Israel Exploration*
        Journal 12: 13-26.
Hamilton, R.W.
1962   'Waterworks'. *Interpreter's Dictionary of the Bible* IV: 811-16.
Hamond, F.
1978   'The Study of Archaeological Processes', pp. 1-10 in *Simulation*
        Studies in Archaeology, ed. I. Hodder.

Harris, M.
  1979   *Cultural Materialism: The Struggle for a Science of Culture*. New York. Random House.
Hauser, P.M. and L.F. Schnore, eds.
  1965   *The Study of Urbanization*. New York. Wiley.
Heaton, E.W.
  1968   *The Hebrew Kingdoms*. London: Oxford University Press.
Henry, K.H.
  1954   'Land Tenure in the Old Testament'. *Palestine Excavation Quarterly* 86: 5-15.
Hermisson, H.-J.
  1968   *Studien zur israelitischen Spruchweisheit*. Neukirchen-Vluyn: Neukirchener Verlag.
Hertzberg, H.W.
  1964   *I and II Samuel*. Trans. J.S. Bowden. Philadelphia: Westminster Press.
Herzog, Z.
          'Enclosed Settlements in the Nagav and the Wilderness of Beer-Sheba', *Bulletin of the American Schools of Oriental Research* 250: 41-59.
Hodder, I.
  1975   'Regression Analysis of some Trade and Marketing Patterns'. *World Archaeology* 6: 172-89.
  1977   'Trends and Surfaces in Archaeology', pp. 149-53 in *Computer Applications in Archaeology*, ed. S. Laflin.
  1978   *Simulation Studies in Archaeology*. Cambridge: Cambridge University Press.
  1978   *The Spatial Organization of Culture*. Pittsburgh: University of Pittsburgh Press.
  1982   'Theoretical Archaeology: A Reactionary View', pp. 1-16 in *Symbolic and Structural Archaeology*, ed. I. Hodder.
  1982   *Symbolic and Structural Archaeology*. Cambridge: Cambridge University Press.
Hodder, I. and C. Orton
  1976   *Spatial Analysis in Archaeology*. Cambridge: Cambridge University Press.
Hodson, F.R., D.G. Kendall, and P. Tăutu, eds.
  1971   *Mathematics in the Archaeological and Historical Sciences*. Edinburgh: Edinburgh University Press.
Hodson, F.R.
  1969   'Searching for Structure within Multivariate Archaeological Data'. *World Archaeology* 1: 90-105.
Hole, F., K. Flannery and J. Neely
  1969   *Prehistory and Human Ecology of the Deh Luran Plain*. Ann Arbor: University of Michigan Press.
Hopkins, D.
  1985   *The Highlands of Canaan: Agricultural Life in the Early Iron Age*. Decatur, GA: Almond.
Horwitz, W.J.
  1974   'Some Possible Results of Rudimentary Scribal Training'. *Ugarit-Forschungen* 6: 75-83.
  1979   'The Ugaritic Scribe'. *Ugarit-Forschungen* 11: 389-94.

Jawad, A.J.
1965   *The Advent of the Era of Townships in Northern Mesopotamia.*
        Leiden: E.J. Brill.
Jean, C.F., and J. Hoftizer
1965   *Dictionnaire des inscriptions sémitiques de l'ouest.* Leiden: E.J.
        Brill.
Johnson, A.R.
1967   *Sacral Kingship in Ancient Israel.* 2nd edn. Cardiff: University of
        Wales Press.
Johnson, G.A.
1975   'Locational Analysis and the Investigations of Uruk Local
        Exchange Systems', pp. 285-339 in *Ancient Civilization and Trade*,
        ed. J.A. Sabloff and C.C. Lamberg-Karlovsky.
1976   'Early State Organization in Southwestern Iran: Preliminary Field
        Report', pp. 190-223 in *Proceedings of the IVth Annual Symposium
        on Archeological Research in Iran, 1975.* Tehran: Muzeh-e Iran-e
        Bastan.
1977   'Aspects of Regional Analysis in Archeology'. *Annual Review of
        Anthropology* 6: 497-508.
Johnstone, J., R. Effland, and G. Clark
1977   'The Arizona State University Nearest Neighbor Program: Docu-
        mentation and Discussion', pp. 45-54 in *Computer Applications in
        Archaeology*, ed. S. Laflin.
Kenyon, K.M.
1960   *Archaeology in the Holy Land.* New York: Praeger.
Klapony-Keckel, U.
1974   'Schulen und Schulwesen in der ägyptischen Spätzeit'. *Studien
        zur altägyptischen Kultur* I: 227-46.
Klostermann, A.
1908   'Schulwesen im alten Israel', pp. 193-232 in *Festschrift Theodor
        Zahn.* Leipzig: A. Deichert.
Kochavi, M.
1977   'The Canaanite Palace at Aphek and its Inscriptions'. *Qadmoniot*
        10: 62-68.
Kochavi, M., ed.
1972   *Judaea, Samaria and the Golan, Archaeological Survey, 1967–
        1968.* Jerusalem: Carta.
Kohl, P.L.
1981   'Materialist Approaches in Prehistory'. *Annual Review of Anthro-
        pology* 10: 89-118.
Kraeling, C.H., and R.M. Adams, eds.
1960   *The City Invincible: A Symposium on Urbanization and Cultural
        Development in the Ancient Near East.* Chicago: University of
        Chicago Press.
Kramer, S.N.
1956   'Die sumerische Schule'. *Wissenschaftliche Zeitschrift der
        Martin-Luther Universität Halle-Wittenberg* 5: 695-700.
Krecher, J.
1969   'Schreiberschulung in Ugarit: die Tradition von Listen und
        sumerischen Texten'. *Ugarit-Forschungen* 1: 131-58.

Laflin, S., ed.
1977   *Computer Applications in Archaeology*. Birmingham: University of Birmingham Press.

Lang, B.
1979   'Schule und Unterricht im alten Israel', pp. 186-201 in *La Sagesse dans l'Ancien Testament*, ed. M. Gilbert. Gembloux et Louvain: Duculot.

Lapp, N.L.
1976   'Casemate Walls in Palestine and the Late Iron II Casemate at Tell-el Fûl (Gibeah)'. *Bulletin of the American Schools of Oriental Research* 223: 25-42.

Le Blanc, S.
1971   'An Addition to Naroll's Suggested Formula'. *American Antiquity* 36: 210-11.

Leemans, W.F.
1950   *The Old Testament Merchant: His Business and his Social Position*. Leiden: E.J. Brill.

Lemaire, A.
1981   *Les Écoles et la formation de la Bible dans l'ancien Israël*. Göttingen: Vandenhoeck und Ruprecht.
1984   'Sagesse et écoles'. *Vetus Testamentum* 34: 270-81.

Lowie, R.H.
1927   *The Origins of the State*. New York: Harcourt, Brace and Company.

Macalister, R.A.S.
1905   'The Craftsmen's Guild of the Tribe of Judah'. *Palestine Exploration Fund, Quarterly Statement*: 243-53.

Malamat, A.
1963   'Kingship and Council in Israel and Sumer: A Parallel'. *Journal of Near Eastern Studies* 22: 247-53.
1970   'Organs of Statecraft in the Israelite Monarchy'. *Biblical Archaeologist Reader* 3: 163-98.

Malecki, E.J.
1975   'Examining Change in Rank-Size Systems of Cities'. *Professional Geographer* 27: 43-47.

Mann, P.H.
1965   *An Approach to Urban Sociology*. New York: Humanities Press.

Marfoe, L.
1979   'The Integrative Transformation: Patterns of Sociopolitical Transformation in Southern Syria'. *Bulletin of the American Schools of Oriental Research* 234: 1-42.

Marmorstein, E.
1953   'The Origins of Agricultural Feudalism in the Holy Land'. *Palestine Excavation Quarterly* 85: 111-17.

Mazar, B.
1946   'The Phoenician Inscriptions from Byblos and the Development of the Phoenician-Hebrew Script'. *Leshonenu* 14: 161-81.

McCown, C.C.
1963   'City'. *Interpreter's Dictionary of the Bible* I: 632-38.

McKane, W.
1965   *Prophets and Wise Men*. London: SCM.

Mendelsohn, I.
1940   'Guilds in Ancient Palestine'. *Bulletin of the American Schools of Oriental Research* 80: 17-21.
1941   'The Canaanite Term for "Free Proletarian"'. *Bulletin of the American Schools of Oriental Research* 83: 36-39.
Mendenhall, G.E.
1962   'The Hebrew Conquest of Palestine'. *Biblical Archaeologist* 25: 66-87.
1976   'Social Organization in Early Israel', pp. 132-51 in *Magnalia Dei*, ed. F.M. Cross, *et al.*
Mettinger, T.N.D.
1971   *Solomonic State Officials*. Lund: Gleerup.
Meyers, C.
1976   'Kadesh-Barnea: Judah's Last Outpost'. *Biblical Archaeologist* 39: 148-51.
Moore, C.B.
1975   *Reconstructing Complex Societies: An Archeological Colloquium*. Bulletin of the American Schools of Oriental Research, Supplement 20.
Morgan, C.G.
1973   'Archeology and Explanation'. *World Archaeology* 4: 259-76.
Mueller, J., ed.
1975   *Sampling in Archaeology*. Tucson: The University of Arizona Press.
Naroll, R.
1962   'Floor Area and Settlement Population'. *American Antiquity* 27: 589.
Needham, R.H.
1975   'Polythetic Classification: Convergence and Consequences'. *Man* 10: 349-69.
Neufeld, E.
1960   'The Emergence of a Royal Urban Society in Ancient Israel'. *Hebrew Union College Annual* 31: 31-53.
Nissen, H.J.
1983   *Grundzüge einer Geschichte der Frühzeit des Vorderen Orients*. Darmstadt: Wissenschaftliche Buchgesellschaft.
Norcliffe, G.B.
1977   *Inferential Statistics for Geographers. An Introduction*. London: Hutchinson.
Noth, M.
1956   'David and Israel in 2 Sam 7', pp. 122-30 in *Mélanges bibliques rédigées en l'honneur d'André Robert*. Paris: Bloud & Gay.
1958   *The History of Israel*. 2nd edn. London: A. and C. Black.
1966   *The Old Testament World*. Trans. V.I. Gruhn. Philadelphia: Fortress Press.
Olivier, J.P.J.
1975   'Schools and Wisdom Literature'. *Journal of Northwest Semitic Languages* 4: 49-60.
Otto, E.
1956   'Bildung und Ausbildung im alten Ägypten'. *Zeitschrift für ägyptische Sprache und Altertumskunde* 81: 41-48.

Parrot, A.
1958   *Samaria, the Capital of the Kingdom of Israel*, trans. S.H. Hooke.
        London: SCM.
Parsons, J.R.
1972   'Archaeological Settlement Patterns'. *Annual Review of Anthro-
        pology* 1: 127-50.
Paul, S., and W.G. Dever
1973   *Biblical Archaeology*. Jerusalem: Keter Publishing House.
Pedersen, J.
1947   *Israel, its Life and Culture*. Trans. A. Moller and A.I. Fausboll.
        London: Oxford University Press.
Peebles, C.S., and S.M. Kus
1977   'Some Archaeological Correlates of Ranked Societies'. *American
        Antiquity* 42: 421-48.
Piggott, S.
1955   'The Role of the City in Ancient Civilizations', pp. 5-17 in *The
        Metropolis in Modern Life*, ed. R.M. Fisher. Garden City: Double-
        day.
Plog, F.
1975   'Systems Theory in Archeological Research'. *Annual Review of
        Anthropology* 4: 207-24.
Price, B.J.
1978   'Secondary State Formation: An Explanatory Model', pp. 161-86 in
        Origins of the State, ed. R. Cohen and E.R. Service.
Rad, G. von
1972   *Wisdom in Israel*. Nashville: Abingdon Press.
Rahtjen, B.
1961   'A Note Concerning the Gezer Tablet', *Palestine Excavation Quar-
        terly* 93: 70-72.
Rainey, A.F.
1969   'The Scribe at Ugarit, his position and influence'. *Proceedings of
        the Israel Academy of Sciences and Humanities* 3/4: 126-47.
Redfield, R.
1953   *The Primitive World and its Transformations*. Ithaca: Cornell
        University Press.
Redman, C.L.
1978   'Mesopotamian Urban Ecology: The Systemic Context of the Emer-
        gence of Urbanism', pp. 329-48 in *Social Archeology*, ed. C.L.
        Redman *et al.*
Redman, C.L., *et al.*, eds.
1978   *Social Archeology*. New York: Academic Press.
Redman, C. and P.J. Watson.
1970   'Systematic, Intensive Surface Collection'. *American Antiquity* 35:
        279-91.
Renfrew, C.
1973   *The Explanation of Culture Change*. Pittsburgh: University of
        Pittsburgh Press.
1975   'Beyond a Subsistence Economy, the Evolution of Social Organisa-
        tion in Prehistoric Europe', pp. 64-85 in *Reconstructing Complex
        Societies*, ed. C.B. Moore. Cambridge, MA: American Schools of
        Oriental Research.

1977   'Alternative Models for Exchange and Spatial Distribution', pp. 71-90 in *Exchange Systems in Prehistory*, ed. T.K. Earle and J.E. Ericson.

1984   *Approaches to Social Archaeology*. Cambridge, MA: Harvard University Press.

Renfrew, C., and K.L. Cooke, eds.
1979   *Transformations: Mathematical Approaches to Culture Change*. New York: Academic Press.

Renfrew, C., and S. Shennan
1982   *Ranking, Resource, and Exchange*. Cambridge: Cambridge University Press.

Reviv, A.
1969   'Two Comments on Judges 8:4-17', *Tarbiz* 38: 309-17.

Reynolds, R.G.D.
1976   'Linear Settlement Systems on the Upper Grijalva River: The Application of a Markovian Model', pp. 80-93 in *The Early Mesoamerican Village*, ed. K.V. Flannery. New York: Academic Press.

Richter, W.
1966   *Recht und Ethos. Versuch einer Ordnung des weisheitlichen Mahnspruches* München: Kösel.

Riessler, P.
1909   'Schulunterricht im Alten Testament'. *Theologische Quartalschrift* 91: 606-607.

Rowlett, R. and S. Pollnac
1970   'Multivariate Analysis of Marnian La Tène Cultural Groups', pp. 46-58 in *Mathematics in the Archaeological and Historical Sciences*, ed. F.R. Hodson, D.G. Kendall and P. Tăutu.

Rowton, M.B.
1969   'The Role of Watercourses in the Growth of Mesopotamian Civilization'. *Lišān Mithurti: Festschrift für Wolfram Freiherr von Soden*, ed. W. Röllig. Neukirchen-Vluyn: Neukirchener Verlag.

1976   'Dimorphic Structure and Topology'. *Oriens Antiquus* 15: 17-31.

Sabloff, J.A., and C.C. Lamberg-Karlovsky, eds.
1975   *Ancient Civilization and Trade*. Albuquerque: University of New Mexico Press.

Sabloff, J.A., ed.
1979   *Ancient Civilization: The Near East and Mesoamerica*. Menlo Park, CA: Benjamin/Cummings.

Sanders, J.A., ed.
1970   *Near Eastern Archeology in the Twentieth Century: Essays in Honor of Nelson Glueck*. Garden City, NY: Doubleday.

Sanders, W.T., and D. Webster
1978   'Unilineality, Multilineality, and the Evolution of Complex Societies', pp. 249-302 in *Social Archeology*, ed. C.L. Redman *et al.*

Schiffer, M.B.
1972   'Archaeological Context and System Context'. *American Antiquity* 37: 156-65.

Schmandt-Besserat, D.
1977   *An Archaic Recording System and the Origin of Writing*. Los Angeles: Undena Publications.

Schmid, H.H.
1966   *Wesen und Geschichte der Weisheit.* Zeitschrift für die alttestamentliche Wissenschaft, Beihefte 101. Berlin: A. Töpelmann.
Service, E.R.
1962   *Primitive Social Organization.* New York: Random House.
1975   *Origins of the State.* New York: Norton.
Shiloh, Y.
1970   'The Four-room House: Its Situation and Function in the Israelite City'. *Israel Exploration Journal* 20: 180-90.
1980   'The Population of Iron age Palestine in the Light of a Sample Analysis of Urban Plans, Areas, and Population Density'. *Bulletin of the American Schools of Oriental Research* 239: 25-35.
Silver, M.
1983   *Prophets and Markets: The Political Economy of Ancient Israel.* Boston: Kluwer–Nijhoff.
Simons, J.J.
1952   *Jerusalem in the Old Testament.* Leiden: E.J. Brill.
Sjöberg, G.
1960   *The Preindustrial City: Past and Present.* Glencoe: Free Press.
Smith, C.
1976   *Regional Analysis.* New York: Academic Press.
Soggin, J.A.
1963   'Der judäische 'Am-ha'aretz und das Königtum im Juda'. *Vetus Testamentum* 13: 187-95.
Stager, L.E.
1976   'Farming in the Judean Desert in the Iron Age'. *Bulletin of the American Schools of Oriental Research* 221: 145-58.
Talmon, S.
1978   'The "Comparative Method" in Biblical Interpretation'. *Vetus Testamentum Supplements* 29: 320-56.
Thomas, D.W., ed.
1967   *Archaeology and Old Testament Study.* Oxford: Clarendon Press.
Trigger, B.
1974   'The Archeology of Government'. *World Archaeology* 6/1: 95-105.
Tufnell, O.
1962   'Seals and Scarabs'. *Interpreter's Dictionary of the Bible* 4: 254-59.
Tuggle, H.D., A.H. Townsend, and T.J. Riley
1972   'Laws, Systems and Research Design: A Discussion of Explanation in Archaeology'. *American Antiquity* 37: 3-12.
Ucko, P., R. Tringham, and G.W. Dimbleby, eds.
1972   *Man, Settlement and Urbanism.* Cambridge, MA: Schenkman.
Upham, S., ed.
1979   *Computer Graphics in Archaeology.* Temple: Arizona State University Press
Vaux, R. de
1961   *Ancient Israel: Its Life and Institutions.* Trans. J. McHugh. New York: McGraw-Hill.
1964   'Le sens de l'expression "peuple de pays" et le rôle politique du peuple en Israël'. *Revue d'Assyriologie et d'Archéologie* 58: 167-72.

1970   'On Right and Wrong Uses of Archaeology', pp. 64-80 in *Near East-*
         ern Archeology in the 20th Century, ed. J.A. Sanders. Garden
         City, NY: Doubleday.
Vita-Finzi, C.
1978   *Archaeological Sites in their Setting*. London: Thames and
         Hudson.
Washburn, D.K.
1974   'Nearest Neighbor Analysis of Pueblo I-III Settlement Patterns
         along the Rio Puerco of the East, New Mexico'. *American Antiq-*
         uity 39: 315-35.
Watson, P.J., S.A. Leblanc, and C.L. Redman
1971   *Explanation in Archaeology: An Explicitly Scientific Approach*.
         New York: Columbia University Press.
Weber, M.
1952   *Ancient Judaism*. Trans. and ed. H.H. Gerth and D. Martindale.
         Glencoe: Free Press.
Webster, D.
1980   'Warfare and the Evolution of the State: A Reconsideration'.
         American Antiquity 40: 464-70.
Weisberg, D.B.
1967   *Guild Structure and Political Allegiance in Early Achaemenid*
         Mesopotamia. New Haven: Yale University Press.
Weiss, H. and T.C. Young
1975   'The Merchants of Susa'. *Iran* 13: 1-17.
Westenholz, A.
1974   'Old Akkadian School Texts, Some Goals of the Sargonic Scribal
         Education'. *Archiv für Orientforschung* 25: 95-110.
Whallon, R.
1971   *A Computer Program for Monothetic Subdivisive Classification in*
         Archaeology. Ann Arbor: University of Michigan Press.
1973   'Spatial Analysis of Occupation Floors. I. Application of Dimen-
         sional Analysis of Variance'. *American Antiquity* 38: 266-78.
1974   'Spatial Analysis of Occupation Floors. II. The Application of
         Nearest Neighbor Analysis'. *American Antiquity* 39: 16-34.
Whybray, R.N.
1965   *Wisdom in Proverbs*. London: SCM.
1974   *The Intellectual Tradition in the Old Tesament*. Berlin: W. de
         Gruyter.
Wiessner, P.
1974   'A Functional Estimator of Population from Floor Area'. *Ameri-*
         can Antiquity 39: 343-49.
Williams, R.J.
1962   'Writing and Writing Materials'. *Intepreter's Dictionary of the*
         Bible 4: 909-21.
1972   'Scribal Training in Ancient Egypt'. *Journal of the American Ori-*
         ental Society 92: 214-21.
1975   'A People Come out of Egypt: An Egyptologist Looks at the Old Tes-
         tament'. *Vetus Testamentum Supplements* 28: 238-52. Leiden: E.J.
         Brill.
Wolf, C.U.
1947   'Traces of Primitive Democracy in Ancient Israel'. *Journal of*
         Near Eastern Studies 6: 98-108.

Wright, G.E.
1962   *Biblical Archaeology*. Philadelphia: Westminster.
1967   'The Provinces of Solomon (I Kings 4:7-19)'. *Eretz-Israel* 8: 58-68.
1970   'The Phenomenon of American Archeology in the Near East',
        pp. 3-40 in *Near Eastern Archaeology in the 20th Century*, ed. J.
        Sanders. Garden City, NY: Doubleday.
Wright, G.E., ed.
1965   *The Bible and the Ancient Near East. Essays in Honor of W.F.
        Albright*. Garden City, NY: Doubleday.
Wright, H.T.
1977   'Recent Research on the Origin of the State'. *Annual Review of
        Anthropology* 6: 379-97.
1978   'Toward an Explanation of the Origin of the State', pp. 49-64 in *Ori-
        gins of the State*, ed. R. Cohen and E.R. Service.
Wright, H.T., and G.A. Johnson
1975   'Population, Exchange, and Early State Formation in Southwest-
        ern Iran'. *American Anthropologist* 77: 267-89.
Wylie, M.A.
1982   'Epistemological Issues Raised by a Structuralist Archaeology',
        pp. 39-46 in *Symbolic and Structural Archaeology*, ed. I. Hodder.
Yadin, Y.
1957   'Some Aspects of the Material Culture of Northern Israel during
        the Canaanite and Israelite Periods in the Light of the Excavations
        at Hazor'. *Antiquity and Survival* 2: 165-86.
1958   'Solomon's City Wall and Gate at Gezer'. *Israel Exploration Jour-
        nal* 8: 80-86.
1963   *The Art of Warfare in Biblical Lands in the Light of Archaeological
        Study*. Trans. M. Pearlman. New York: McGraw-Hill.
Yeivin, S.
1959   'Topographic and Ethnic Notes'. *Atiqot* 2: 155-58.
1960   *A Decade of Archaeology in Israel: 1948–1958*. Istanbul: Neder-
        lands Historisch-Archaeologisch Instituut in het Nabaje Oosten.
Zagrell, A.
1982   (Personal Communication).
Zipf, G.
        Human Behavior and the Principle of Least Effort. Cambridge,
        MA: Addison–Wesley.

INDEXES

INDEX OF BIBLICAL REFERENCES

INDEX OF AUTHORS